THE CANADIAN HONOURS SYSTEM

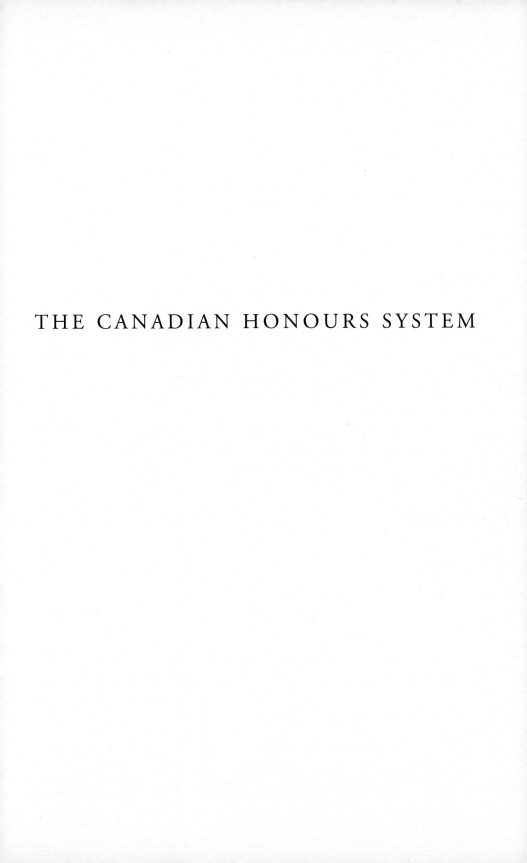

The brave and intelligent expect to leave to their posterity the splendour of their public services, embodied in rank and honour. A country that prohibits such a legacy destroys one of the chief sources of its greatness, and blasts the vital principals of public virtue.

Gallantry: Its Public Recognition and Reward in Peace and War
Sir Arnold Wilson, MP
Captain J.H.F. McEwan, MP

THE CANADIAN HONOURS SYSTEM

Desiderantes Meliorem Patriam

Christopher McCreery

Foreword by General A.J.G.D. de Chastelain,
O.C., C.M.M., C.D., C.H.

DUNDURN PRESS
TORONTO

Copy-Editor: Lloyd Davis
Design: Jennifer Scott
Printer: University of Toronto Press

National Library of Canada Cataloguing in Publication Data

McCreery, Christopher
   The Canadian honours system / Christopher McCreery.

Includes bibliographical references.
ISBN-10: 1-55002-554-6
ISBN-13: 978-1-55002-554-5

   1. Decorations of honor--Canada--History. 2. Decorations of honor--Canada. I. Title.

CR6257.M32 2005   929.8'171   C2005-900941-1

1 2 3 4 5   09 08 07 06 05

| Conseil des Arts du Canada | Canada Council for the Arts | Canadä | ONTARIO ARTS COUNCIL CONSEIL DES ARTS DE L'ONTARIO |

We acknowledge the support of the **Canada Council for the Arts** and the **Ontario Arts Council** for our publishing program. We also acknowledge the financial support of the **Government of Canada** through the **Book Publishing Industry Development Program** and **The Association for the Export of Canadian Books**, and the **Government of Ontario** through the **Ontario Book Publishers Tax Credit** program, and the **Ontario Media Development Corporation's Ontario Book Initiative.**

Care has been taken to trace the ownership of copyright material used in this book. The author and the publisher welcome any information enabling them to rectify any references or credits in subsequent editions.
J. Kirk Howard, President

The author and publisher gratefully acknowledge the support of J. D. Ferguson Historical Foundation in providing a grant to aid in the production of this book.

Printed and bound in Canada.
Printed on recycled paper.
www.dundurn.com

Dundurn Press
8 Market Street, Suite 200
Toronto, Ontario, Canada
M5E 1M6

Gazelle Book Services Limited
White Cross Mills
Hightown, Lancaster, England
LA1 4X5

Dundurn Press
2250 Military Road
Tonawanda, NY
U.S.A. 14150

To my friends

Joyce Bryant and Bruce Beatty.

Her Majesty Queen Elizabeth II
Queen of Canada

Sovereign of the Order of Canada
Sovereign of the Order of Military Merit
Sovereign of the Order of Merit of the Police Forces

TABLE OF CONTENTS

ACKNOWLEDGEMENTS

This is the second major project that I have embarked upon. Indeed, work commenced within days of my completing *The Order of Canada: Its Origins, History and Development,* and went on while I wrote my doctoral thesis. In many ways the three projects were codependent, each being of equal importance in my estimation. So little has been written on the history of honours in Canada, and I hope this work in some small way fills that gap.

A number of people read over this work while it was still a rough manuscript. In particular, Captain Carl Gauthier of the Department of National Defence played a central role in honing the text and ensuring that every detail was accurate and explained. Major Lou Grimshaw was also most helpful in reading through the final text to ensure any last-minute glitches were removed.

At the Chancellery I owe thanks to Bruce Patterson, Saguenay Herald, who assisted me on more than a few occasions, especially with questions relating to heraldry. Similarly, Marie-Paule Thorne also showed a constant interest in my work. Stephen Hart from Rideau Ltd. was invaluable in providing me with statistics and information about the production of Canadian orders. Peter McDermid of the Royal Canadian Mounted Police aided in obtaining photos of the various RCMP medals. At Library and Archives Canada, Debbie Brentnell and Jean Matheson aided with the myriad of photographic requests with great patience and understanding. Major Claude Villeneuve greatly improved those sections re-lated to New France.

General John de Chastelain, who kindly agreed to write the foreword for this book, was also most helpful in editing the text and adding a number of interesting anecdotes. One should be so fortunate as to have such a distinguished foreword author, let alone expert reviewer.

Credit is due my friend Major John Tamplin, who for the past half a century has provided collectors with a wealth of articles, information and enthusiasm about Canadian and Commonwealth medals.

Much credit is owed to Bruce Beatty, who provided me with an unparalleled knowledge of unwritten information about the development of each award in the Canadian honours system.

Encouragement came from my parents, Paul and Sharon, and a number of friends, although two people, Joyce Bryant and Peter Galloway, seemed to possess an endless supply of enthusiasm, and this was freely given.

All of "my" secretaries in the department of History at Queen's University, Judy Vanhooser, and Yvonne Place went well beyond what even I expected. They treated me with the kindness of a friend and the respect of a professor — even though I was but a graduate student.

A large cadre of friends supported me in this project, although they were never entirely sure what precise endeavour I was working on at any particular time — most specifically, Sean Morency, Lindsay Maynard, Richard Goette, Captain Bob Martin, Peter Milliken, John R. Matheson, George Henderson, Sarah Noble, Elaine Wu, Savita Custead, Erum Hasan, Bud Fields, Glen McIntyre and Ian McKay. My employer, Senator Michael Kirby, was most understanding and always willing to allow me time to deal with issues related to publishing.

Lastly, yet possibly most importantly, I am indebted to Nancy Cameron. For more than thirty years my mother's secretary, "Aunt" Nancy gave me my first set of medals. From a numismatic hobby to a passion of study, it all began with a British War Medal and Victory Medal, my Grade 8 graduation gift from Nancy.

Christopher McCreery
The Senate
Ottawa

FOREWORD

Anation's custom of conferring honours on its citizens — to reward or to recognize service or merit — has existed for hundreds, if not thousands, of years. Regarded by some as unnecessary and by others as an important symbol of nationhood, a national honours system says much about the nation itself, including its approach to egalitarianism and merit and its belief in the importance of recognizing performance, professionalism, excellence and courage.

Canada did not adopt its own honours system until 1972, one hundred and five years after Confederation, and it might be said that doing so was but one of a series of steps — including the 1917 battle of Vimy Ridge, the 1931 Statute of Westminster, the delayed 1939 declaration of war, the 1965 Maple Leaf flag, and the 1982 repatriation of the Constitution — that changed Canada's colonial and Dominion status to one of independent nationhood.

Very little has been written about Canada's honours system to date — unsurprising, perhaps, given its short period of existence. Christopher McCreery's detailed and carefully researched book is a welcome addition to the very few existing publications on the subject — including his own book on the Order of Canada. In *The Canadian Honours System*, McCreery traces the development of the Canadian model, from the early dependence on French and subsequently British honours to today's comprehensive system of orders, decorations and medals. He links the controversy surrounding the on-again, off-again Canadian acceptance of British titles, through the prime ministerial tenures of Sir John A. Macdonald (in favour), Sir Robert Borden (not in favour), R.B. Bennett (in favour) and Mackenzie King (not in favour — although he was the most decorated Canadian prime minister in history), to the recent refusal by Prime Minister Jean Chrétien to allow a Canadian with dual citizenship to accept a British peerage.

Not only does McCreery give detailed accounts of the history and development of each of the distinctive orders, decorations and medals that are now part of Canada's honours system, including the precedence of each and the procedures for wearing and caring for their insignia, but he also recounts the history of the proposals that were not approved and the reasons why. He also points out the dangers of introducing too many honours too quickly, and he notes that in France the many different honours for individual departments of government that were created over the years eventually had to be cancelled and replaced by a single National Order of Merit — a lesson for Canada, perhaps, where in addition to national honours, each province now has its own provincial order and where some have started to introduce medals of service.

This book is an important and comprehensive account that should be of interest to all Canadians, as well as a valuable addition to Canadian historical literature. On a subject that is still developing, it will surely need updating from time to time. But for now, the fact that it is both authoritatively and entertainingly written should ensure that it has a wide readership.

General John de Chastelain, O.C., C.M.M., C.D., C.H.
Ottawa

CHAPTER 1

Honours, Awards and Decorations around the World: The Ubiquitous National Institution

Like flags and coats of arms, every country possesses an honours system. At the centre of these systems there is usually a national honour. Britain has the Order of the Garter and Order of the Thistle, France the *Légion d'Honneur*, Japan the Order of the Rising Sun, Canada the Order of Canada, and the list goes on. Indeed, there are only two countries that do not currently posses a national honour: Switzerland and Ireland. All other states and regimes have found a use for honours, and in many ways they are a necessity of nationhood.

The concept of honour is as old as humanity itself. Yet honours — that is, the official bestowal of recognition — are in comparison a relatively recent phenomenon. The concepts of honour and honours are directly linked, although there are important differences. Honour is the notion of adhering to what is right — high respect and good reputation through persistent good deeds. One can lead an honourable life and never receive official recognition in the form of an honour. Honours are official marks of recognition, whether they be conferred by proclamations, titles, grants of arms or insignia. It is equally possible for a person to have received an honour and yet be void of honour. These variables are defined by every civilization in accordance with those social values the particular civilization prizes.

Canada's honours system is derived primarily from two of Canada's founding peoples, the French and British. However, not even these two countries can claim to have invented honours. Throughout modern history a plethora of systems and awards has been designed and used as essential apparatuses of both states and regimes. At times, systems have been displaced by both evolution and revolution — yet always a revised system, roughly patterned on its predecessor, has emerged. All modern honours systems have certain common elements, and the most central of these is the presentation of an insignia — a badge or medal. This tradition can be traced back to 290 BC and the gold button given by Alexander to a high priest for bravery demonstrated in battle. Honour has also been accorded through the bestowal of land and titles, and in ancient Greece a complex system of crowns was devised to reward public and military service. The practice of embossing medallic insignia on breastplates (phaleristics) was initiated by the ancient Romans and has in some ways carried forward to the present day. In India's Pudukkottai state there was an ancient tradition of the raja presenting gifts and honours to loyal subjects. This ritual served not only as a mechanism for recognition, but was also a source of political power. As well, few are unfamiliar with the stories of King Arthur and his Knights of the Round Table. Moving through history, the ideals of chivalry and honours gradually replaced the act of granting land with bestowing knighthoods and insignia.

The purpose of honours is to reward service or valorous acts and to accord recognition to those who, according to the state, are deemed to merit such. At various times honours have also been — and in some countries continue to be — a central tool of patronage. All types of honours are intended to foster a feeling of loyalty and a personal connection to the state or regime.

Our modern national honours system can be divided into three main categories.

ORDERS

These are societies of honour that are instituted by the state, usually to recognize lifelong exemplary service of the highest calibre. Orders are usually divided into several different levels to allow for recognition of those who have rendered service at both the national/international level and at the local or regional level. In Canada we have five national orders: the Order of Canada, the Order of Military Merit, the Order of Merit of the Police Forces, the Royal Victorian Order and the Most Venerable Order of St. John of Jerusalem.

Orders can be "field specific" — the Order of Military Merit, for example, is restricted to those who are members of the Canadian Forces and who have rendered meritorious service over an extended period of time. Similarly, the Royal Victorian Order is primarily awarded to those who have served the Queen or Royal Family in a particularly distinguished manner. The Order of Canada, by contrast, is open to all Canadians in any field or endeavour.

DECORATIONS

This section can be further divided into two subsections: Bravery/ Valour/Gallantry and Meritorious Service.

Bravery/Valour/Gallantry

Awarded for a specific act of bravery, valour or gallantry, bravery awards are bestowed upon those who perform an exemplary act — such as lifesaving — in a time of peace, while valour and gallantry decorations are for valour and devotion to duty in the presence of the enemy. Provisions have been made in the Canadian honours system to allow for valour decorations, such as the Victoria Cross, to be awarded for gallant acts performed while in non-warlike situations (provided they involve a hostile armed force).

Meritorious Service

These are awarded for a specific act of meritorious service, not necessarily over an extended period of time.

MEDALS

There are four types of medals: service medals, commemorative medals, long service medals and other awards.

Service Medals

These are awarded for service in a particular mission or operation. While primarily limited to members of the armed forces, in the Canadian context police officers and civilian personnel are also often included.

Commemorative Medals

Commemorative medals are awarded on the occasion of a special event, such as a coronation or jubilee. These are awarded to members of the military as well as civilians.

Long Service Medals

These are awarded for long service and honourable conduct over a set period of time. The Canadian Forces Decoration is awarded for twelve years of honourable service, while the Police Exemplary Service Medal and Royal Canadian Mounted Police Long Service Medal are awarded for twenty years of honourable service.

Other Awards

Most specifically the Queen's Medal for Champion Shot, awarded for winning an annual marksmanship competition. In the provinces this includes Volunteer and Citizenship Medals.

These three main types of honours emulate directly the British system of honours, which, although ancient, only began to develop in this form in the mid–nineteenth century. Since the fourteenth century England had used its Order of the Garter and Order of the Bath to reward loyal nobles, but in the nineteenth century the Order of the Bath was expanded, while others, such as the Order of St. Michael and St. George, the Order of the Star of India and the Order of the Indian Empire, were created. These were not restricted to nobles, and their membership came to include nontitled members of the military and civil service.

Waterloo Medal obverse

Waterloo Medal reverse

The Battle of Waterloo yielded the first standard-issue medal intended for wear. Created in 1816 at the direction of the Duke of Wellington, in many ways the circular medal — measuring 36 mm in diameter with a ring suspender hung from a ribbon — would serve as the basis for the design of future war medals. There was the additional aspect that the medal was impressed with the recipient's name and issued to officers and men alike.

In 1830 the British Army and Royal Navy each instituted long service medals. The Army Long Service and Good Conduct Medal was awarded for twenty-one years (later reduced to eighteen) in the ranks. The Royal Navy Long Service and Good Conduct Medal was originally awarded for twenty-one years' service as a rating in the Royal Navy (it was later reduced to fifteen). These were the first long service awards, and both continue to be awarded to members of the British Army and Royal Navy.

At various times, officers of the Canadian Army were awarded the Volunteer Decoration (VD) and the Efficiency Decoration (ED). Reserve Naval officers were eligible for the Royal

Navy Long Service Medal obverse

Navy Long Service Medal reverse

Canadian Navy Volunteer Reserve Decoration (VD) or the Royal Canadian Navy Reserve Decoration (VRD), depending on which part of the navy they served in. The Royal Canadian Air Force also had its own set of long service medals: the RCAF Long Service and Good Conduct Medal (for noncommissioned officers) and the Air Efficiency Award (for officers) were awarded to members of the RCAF in the late 1930s and through the 1940s. Until the creation of the Canadian Forces Decoration in 1949, Canadians regularly received these medals and decorations for service in the Canadian Army, Royal Canadian Navy and Royal Canadian Air Force. Indeed, the Canadian Forces Decoration is based upon these awards.

In 1847 the British Military General Service Medal was established, and in the following year the Naval General Service Medal was created to recognize service rendered in specific wars and actions between 1793 and 1840. These were the first "modern" medals to be struck, in the sense that they were intended for wear and awarded to all ranks. These early awards have served as the basis for modern service medals throughout the Commonwealth: their standard design, bearing the Sovereign on the obverse and an allegory on the reverse, is a tradition that continues — most recently with the institution of the South-West Asia Service Medal, which depicts Queen Elizabeth on the obverse and an allegorical figure and Latin phrase on the reverse.

The first standardized bravery decoration was the Distinguished Conduct Medal, created in 1854. Two years later, the Victoria Cross was created; it was novel in that it was issued to all ranks, from private to field marshal. During the First World War a broad range of branch specific

*Naval General Service Medal
obverse*

*Naval General Service Medal
reverse*

awards — for the navy, army and air force — was also established.

Canada is not alone in taking much of its honours structure from Britain. In an evolutionary sense it was a logical and practical step, as Canada had used the British imperial honours system for more than a century. Countries from Australia to Zimbabwe all find the general bases of their honours systems in the British tradition, at least in terms of structure. Australia, Fiji and certain other Commonwealth countries also derive the structures of their national orders from the Canadian experience, all using the three levels and nonpartisan selection criteria that Canada pioneered.

Though influenced by the British tradition, the Canadian honours system is not merely a British honours system covered with maple leaves and fleurs-de-lys. There are significant differences between the Canadian and British honours systems, and between the Canadian honours system and those used in many other countries. The Canadian system is nonpartisan — that is, the prime minister and members of the governing party are neither directly nor indirectly involved in the selection of recipients of Canadian honours. In many countries, such decisions are made by the head of government (the prime minister), and thus honours invariably become a political tool awarded as patronage. However, Canadian honours, specifically the Order of Canada, are evenly awarded to people in all parts of the Canadian population and not just to those involved in politics and business. In many countries it is only members of the political and social elite who are found with neck badges and medals; not so in Canada, which is also one of the few countries that does not engage in automatic diplomatic awards.

In terms of honours there are a variety of different types and criteria. The focus of this study is honours that are officially sanctioned and created by the Crown at the federal level in Canada, although I have also included a section on the various provincial orders. Honours in Canada emanate from the Queen, who is the country's head of state — worldwide, most national honours and awards are created by an instrument approved by the head of state.

This book is the first comprehensive work on the modern Canadian honours system to examine not only the criteria and design of each award, but also the origins and history of each. Much of the information contained herein has never before been published. Unlike previous works on the subject, this book is not intended solely for the collector of Canadian medals, but also for those who have an interest in the history and development of our honours system. It serves as an explanatory guide to every aspect of the system.

The structure of this book is based loosely on Abbott and Tamplin's *British Gallantry Awards* and Michael Maton's *The National Honours and Awards of Australia*. Recognition should also be accorded to Ross Irwin, Edward Denby and John Blatherwick, all of whom have worked to remedy the dearth of information about Canadian honours, decorations and medals over the past forty years through a variety of familiar publications.

The first three chapters briefly set out a history of honours in Canada at the national level. The following twenty-eight examine each order, decoration and medal individually, outlining the origins and history of each along with the criteria, design, designer and other relevant information. The chapters are roughly arranged in order of creation and precedence, but not exactly. Thus the bravery decorations are discussed before the military valour decorations, because the MVDs are directly related to the bravery decorations that preceded them.

Those wishing to examine a more detailed overview of honours in Canada should consult *The Order of Canada: Its Origins, Development and History*, which examines the development of the Canadian honours system from 1867 to the present.

In various entries, the postnominals (the initials a person may list after his or her name to denote the orders and decorations he or she has been awarded) have been listed. These postnominals are era-specific; thus, Dr. Wilder Penfield, who was awarded the Order of Merit in 1953 and later

the Order of Canada in 1967, is listed as "Dr. Wilder Penfield, O.M., C.C., C.M.G.," while Lester Pearson, who was awarded the Order of Canada in 1968 and the Order of Merit in 1972, is listed as "Lester B. Pearson, C.C., C.H." These sorts of anomalies reflect the changing status of British honours within the Canadian honours system.

CHAPTER 2

Honours in Canada to 1867:
A Supplement of Europe

The modern Canadian honours system can find some of its origins in those of two of Canada's founding peoples: the French and British. Canada's Native peoples did not have a formal honours system in the sense of an institution. Rather, the concept of *honour* was more prized than any particular insignia or possession. Service to the community and bravery was recognized in Native communities, not by gold or silver medals, but through respect accorded to the individual — often through the adoption of a chieftainship. When Europeans arrived, this system was complemented through the awarding of Chief's Medals, which French and British officials both made use of to secure the loyalty of a particular Native group. This process was not unidirectional; the Native people quickly learned how to extract better terms and conditions for themselves when accepting such medals from Europeans.

THE HONOURS OF ROYAL FRANCE IN CANADA

Prior to the French Revolution, the Kingdom of France possessed a comprehensive honours system, primarily graded by the hierarchy of French society at the time. The king of France would elevate French subjects to the nobility as dukes, marquises, counts and barons. On one occasion a Canadian, Charles Le Moyne, Seigneur of Longueuil, was made Baron de Longueuil in recognition of his peace negotiations with the Iroquois on behalf of the French Crown. Le Moyne would later go on to serve as governor of Montreal. This now-ancient French title still exists, although the family no longer lives in Canada.

In New France, honours were awarded by the governor on behalf of the king. Prior to an honour being bestowed, the governor general of New France had to receive permission from the French Sovereign. The advice of the governor general was usually followed, although there were occasions when the king of France would bestow an honour without the prior knowledge of the governor. This was, after all, his prerogative as king.

Looking for a way to motivate and reward all the officers of his armies for outstanding and long service, King Louis XIV established the *Ordre Royal et Militaire de Saint-Louis* in April 1693. For the subjects of New France, this was the most familiar honour. It gained the immediate favour of all, and was seen as a very prestigious honour, since the deserving officer would wear the same insignia as a marshal of France or, even better, the king himself. It was the first military reward in modern history to be open to officers in the army or navy, regardless of social status. However, it was awarded only to Catholic officers.

Order of St. Louis obverse

The order consisted of three classes: Knight (with no limit on overall membership), Commander (with a maximum of twenty-four living members) and Grand Cross (a maximum of eight living members). Following the French Revolution, the order was abolished by convention in 1792, although it continued to be used by the government-in-exile, and was revived during the Empire before finally being discontinued by King Louis Philippe in 1830. Nearly three hundred people associated with Canada were appointed to the order; these included French- and Canadian-born officers living in New France, as well as Canadian-born officers serving in France during or after the fall of New France.

The first officer to receive the order was the governor of Montreal, Louis-Hector de Callière, in 1694. Louis de Buade, Comte de Frontenac and governor of New France, was the second, in 1697. The best-known Canadian subject to receive the Order of St. Louis was François Coulon de Villers. Born in Verchères, New France, in 1712, Coulon de Villers went on to serve with great distinction in the French colonial army. In the battle for Fort Necessity on 4 July 1757, Coulon de Villers became the only man ever to defeat George Washington in battle. The governor of New France, Pierre de Rigaud,

Order of St. Louis reverse

Marquis de Vaudreuil-Cavagnal, was the only Canadian to receive the Grand Cross.

With the fall of New France in 1759, one would expect the flow of honours from France to have come to a halt. However, such was not the case; up until the French Revolution, the Crown continued to bestow the Order of St. Louis upon residence of the old colony in recognition of military services rendered prior to 1759. These awards were usually given to veterans whose families had petitioned for belated recognition.

THE STRUCTURE OF THE BRITISH HONOURS SYSTEM IN CANADA

A map of this complex system must first begin with the peerage of the United Kingdom, composed of various levels of nobility: dukes, marquesses, earls, viscounts and barons. Over the span of Canadian history, twelve peerages and one title have been bestowed upon Canadians. Among these, five are considered to be Canadian peerages — that is, awarded after consultation with the Canadian government. The first of these went to Sir George Stephen, who became a baron on 26 June 1891. Stephen, like two other Canadian peers, was president of the Canadian Pacific Railway, and it is not unlikely that he owed his appointment to the "help" he gave the ruling Conservatives in the 1891 election campaign. This connection between the CPR and the awarding of titles strengthened opposition to hereditary honours among some in the Liberal Party of the period, who connected the procedure to the operations of patronage and party financing in the Canadian political system.

The second Canadian (and sole Canadian woman) appointed to the peerage, Lady Susan Macdonald, became Baroness Macdonald of Earnscliffe on 14 August 1891. She was not entitled to sit in the House of Lords and, albeit in the absence of extensive documentation, it seems safe to conclude that she was honoured mainly in memory of her late husband, Prime Minister Sir John Alexander Macdonald.

The next appointment to the peerage, Sir Donald Smith, was another former president of the CPR; he was appointed in his capacity as Canadian High Commissioner to London, becoming the first Baron Strathcona and Mount Royal on June 26, 1900. He continued as Canadian High Commissioner until his death in 1914. Sir Thomas Shaughnessy, the principal catalyst for the 1902 Privy Council Report on honours and titles — and like

Strathcona and Stephen, also a president of the CPR — was elevated to the peerage on 19 February 1916.

The last Canadian to be elevated to the peerage after consultation with the Canadian government was Sir Hugh Graham, president of the Montreal *Star*, whose name figured so prominently in the 1917–19 debate on honours. This appointment was by far the most controversial of the lot, for Graham was remembered vividly for his somewhat questionable fundraising activities on behalf of the Conservatives and his violently pro-imperial editorials in the *Star* at the time of the Anglo-Boer War. The appointment, made over Prime Minister Borden's objections and politically ill timed, may well have been the turning point in making the prospect of Canadian peers a politically unpalatable one.

Canadians appointed to the peerage of the United Kingdom for services to Britain (and not considered "Canadian" peerages) include Sir Arthur Lawrence Haliburton, the first Baron Haliburton, who was born in Nova Scotia and rose to become Britain's permanent under-secretary of state for war. William James Pirrie, head of the famous British shipbuilding firm Harland and Wolff, was made a baron in 1906 and later elevated further in 1921 as Viscount Pirrie. Born in Quebec, Pirrie was also the only Canadian to be made a Knight of the Most Illustrious Order of St. Patrick, Ireland's order of knighthood. Sir Max Aitken, a native of New Brunswick, was raised to the peerage as the first Baron Beaverbrook in 1917. Sir Edward Patrick Morris, the premier of Newfoundland, became the island's only native son to be made a peer, the first Baron Morris of St. John's, in 1918. Although Newfoundland was not part of Canada at the time, it seems appropriate that he should be included in this list. Richard Bedford Bennett, the Canadian prime minister who revived the British honours system in Canada during the 1930s, was raised to the peerage as the first Viscount Bennett in 1941. This occurred several years after Bennett moved to Britain. Following the long tradition of Canadian newspapermen being ennobled, Roy Thompson was made first Baron Thompson of Fleet in 1963. Most recently, in 2000, Conrad Black became Lord Black of Crossharbour, and he is the only Canadian to be appointed as a life peer.

Passing now to those who were awarded hereditary knighthoods, we find the baronets. These were founded in England by James I in 1611 and extended to Ireland in 1619; Scotland had its own baronets, founded in 1625 as part of William Alexander's scheme for settling Nova Scotia and preventing it from falling into French hands. Baronetcies were subsequently amalgamated

Baronet of Nova Scotia

Knight Commander of the Order of the Bath, Civil Division

under the title of "baronets of the United Kingdom." In order of precedence in the United Kingdom, baronets rank just below barons and just above Knights of the Order of the Garter. In total, seven baronetcies were awarded upon the recommendation of the Canadian government: three were awarded to politicians and four to businessmen.

It is telling that, less than five days into the first session of the first Parliament of Canada, the issue of honours was the subject of a stormy debate, on the vexed question of Sir John A. Macdonald's having bettered Georges-Étienne Cartier on the field of honours. (Macdonald had received a Knight Commandership of the Order of the Bath, while Cartier was only made a Companion of the Order, an "insult to himself and the nation he represents.") On 23 March 1868, a motion was introduced championing Cartier's claims to a KCB; less than a month later, Macdonald announced to a cheering House that Cartier had been made a baronet — and hence awarded an honour even more substantial than that given Macdonald himself.

Passing over British orders of knighthood with marginal Canadian significance, we arrive at the Most Honourable Order of the Bath, believed to have been established in 1128 and probably one of the oldest orders of knighthood in the world.[2] This order initially had one class, Knight of the Bath, and consisted of the Sovereign, a prince of royal blood, a great master and thirty-five knights; it was subsequently reorganized into two divisions, civil and military — and three ranks, Knight Grand Cross

(GCB), Knight Commander (KCB) and Companion (CB) — in order to provide awards to officers who served in the Napoleonic Wars. One of the first awards made after the 1815 reorganization was that of a KCB conferred upon Lieutenant-General Gordon Drummond of the British Army, who had been born in Quebec City.

A total of eleven awards of the Knight Grand Cross and Knight Commander of the Order of the Bath were bestowed on Canadians between 1867 and 1935. Sir John A. Macdonald became the first in 1867, when he was made a KCB, civil division; he was later elevated to a GCB in 1884, the first colonial politician to receive the highest level. The redoubtable Sam Hughes, minister of Militia and Defence, acquired the other Canadian civil KCB in 1915; his award could not have made the distinction shimmer more brightly in the eyes of opponents of conscription and the Conservative government. Six KCBs went to military men, while one honoured a member of the RCMP. Since Confederation, 166 Canadians have also received the rank of Companion, the most junior grade of the Order of the Bath.

From Confederation until the Nickle Resolution of 1918, it could be said that the British Order of St. Michael and St. George served as the era's "Order of Canada," as it was the premier award available to Canadian politicians, judges, and civil servants. This was partly because of a change in the rules in 1868, which tipped the scales away from the Order of the Bath and towards this order, instituted in 1818 and initially designed to recognize services in Malta and the Ionian Islands. The order initially consisted of the Sovereign, Grand Master, seven Knights Grand Cross, twelve Knight Commanders and twenty-four Knight Companions. In 1832, the lowest class became non-titular and was renamed Companion of the Order of St. Michael and St. George. The order was enlarged in 1868, 1877 and 1902 to allow for a maximum of 110 Grand Crosses (GCMG), 390 Knight Commanders (KCMG) and 1,775 Commanders of the Order of St. Michael and St. George (CMG). For Canadians, the order was intended to honour "high political or official services as distinct from judicial, literary, scientific or artistic eminence."

In this period, fourteen GCMGs (the award was reserved for governors general, prime ministers and chief justices) were awarded to Canadians, including three Canadian prime ministers — Tupper, Laurier and Borden. Many other Canadians keenly sought to become a Knight Commander of the Order of St. Michael and St. George, partly because it was the most accessible honour, within the reach of eminent senior civil servants, senators, cabinet ministers, provincial premiers or even wealthy party supporters, and

Sir Robert Borden's GCMG insignia

perhaps also because of the splendid insignia involved. Seventy-four of them were successful: thirty-six politicians, six-teen serving or retired lieutenant governors — who were, in general, graduates of the party system — while the remainder went to people in a variety of occupations ranging from university administrators to engineers. The Companion of the Order of St. Michael and St. George was awarded to 382 Canadians. Even William Lyon Mackenzie King, no great admirer of the British honours system, was awarded this distinction — although it is telling that, after 1935, he never wore the insignia of the order.

Of a somewhat different nature was the Royal Victorian Order, founded by Queen Victoria in 1896. There is no official limit on the number of awards, but by tradition they are conferred with the Sovereign's greatest degree of care and discretion. Four Canadians have been awarded the two highest titular levels of the award, Knight Grand Cross (GCVO) and Knight Commander (KCVO); the other levels continue to be awarded to Canadians for services to the Crown in Canada, and the order remains an integral part of the Canadian honours system to this day. As was the case with other awards, it was firmly associated in the early twentieth century with railway executives. King Edward VII, known to be somewhat prone to bestow knighthoods upon unsuspecting friends and visitors, was also clearly impressed by the claims of railway men: Lord Mount Stephen was made a GCVO in 1905, and Lord Strathcona in 1908, while Lord Shaughnessy won the only Canadian KCVO in 1907.

Edward VII was also responsible for the creation in 1902 of the Royal Victorian Chain, which afforded the recipient no titular distinction and was not an order of knighthood, but which nonetheless was considered the most exclusive award available from the Crown as well as a special mark of the Sovereign's esteem and affection. In this period, the award was given to three governors general of Canada: Prince Arthur, Duke of Connaught,

Order of the British Empire

in 1906; Lord Lansdowne, also in 1906; and Lord Athlone in 1935.

A more common award was that of the Most Excellent Order of the British Empire, which consists of five classes, plus a medal, and which has military and civil divisions. The highest level is the Knight/Dame Grand Cross (GBE); the second, the Knight/Dame Commander (KBE/DBE); the lower levels include Commander (CBE), Officer (OBE), Member (MBE) and the British Empire Medal (BEM). Because the order was founded in 1917 and the Nickle Resolution came into effect in 1918, the titular levels were available to Canadians for only the periods between 1917–1919 and 1933–1935. Two GBEs and eight KBEs were awarded to Canadians; of these, two were awarded to businessmen, three to civil servants, two for services in medicine and science (including Sir Frederick Banting, the co-discoverer of insulin) and one for philanthropic deeds. The lower levels of the order were to come into prominence in a flood of recognition of Canadians during and immediately following the Second World War.

Left: British Empire Medal obverse
Above: British Empire Medal reverse

Knights of the United Kingdom (also known as Knights Bachelor because of the title's non-hereditary character), comprise the most junior form of knighthood. Recipients are allowed to preface their name with the appellation "Sir," and since 1929 they have received an oval insignia. A knighthood is a title conferred by the Sovereign, and Knights Bachelor are not connected with any order — they are members of "the ancient concept of knighthood and chivalry," and become such when the Sovereign lays the blade of his or her sword upon the right and then the left shoulder of a kneeling subject. All persons who are made a Knight of the Order of the Garter, of the Order of the Thistle, or of the Order of St. Patrick, or a Knight Grand Cross/Commander or Knight Commander of the Orders of the Bath, of St. Michael and St. George, of the Star of India, of the Indian Empire, or of the British Empire or the Royal Victorian Order are first dubbed as Knight Bachelors and then presented with the insignia of the order into which they have been inducted. Most Canadians who were knighted became Knights Bachelor, and 107 received the honour for services rendered in and to Canada. The award was limited, but not always confined, to "the Bench and men of literary or scientific note." Pressure to award a knighthood to the politically connected came from Canada. Provincial and puisne judges and Chief Justices were most frequently given the honour, receiving forty-two in total, while politicians received eighteen and businessmen fifteen.

Finally, one should mention the Most Venerable Order of the Hospital of St. John of Jerusalem, traceable to the crusading knights of the Middle Ages and incorporated by Royal Charter in 1888. The order — which, notwithstanding the Nickle Resolution and the report of the Special Committee on Honours and Titles, continues to be part of the Canadian honours system — is awarded to people who "have performed or are prepared to perform good service for the order." Many Canadians have been appointed to the order.

In addition to these, a myriad of other awards for both civilians and the military also existed in Canadian history. At the top of the list was the Victoria Cross, the highest award for valour in the British Empire. While the Victoria Cross was instituted in 1856, the majority of other British gallantry awards were established during the First World War. For exemplary service — and sometimes bravery — there was the Distinguished Service Order, primarily restricted to officers above the rank of captain. Other military valour awards were divided by service. For the navy, there were the Distinguished Service Cross, Distinguished Service Medal and the Conspicuous Gallantry Medal. The army possessed the Distinguished

Conduct Medal, Military Cross and Military Medal. The air force had the Distinguished Flying Cross, Air Force Cross, Conspicuous Gallantry Medal, Distinguished Flying Medal and Air Force Medal. Beyond these awards were other general civilian bravery awards such as the George Cross, Albert Medal, George Medal and King's Commendation for Brave Conduct. Canadians have received many of these.

Canadians also received the various British campaign medals for service around the world. In 1899, Queen Victoria approved the creation of the Canada General Service Medal, which was awarded to veterans of the 1866 and 1870 Fenian Raids and the first Riel rebellion. There was also the North West Canada Medal (1885), awarded to the veterans of the second Riel rebellion. Veterans of the Anglo-Boer War received the Queen's South Africa Medal with various battle bars, and those serving in the First World War were eligible for the 1914–15 Star, the British War Medal and the Victory Medal for service overseas. The Second World War brought another set of campaign medals; in all, eleven were awarded to Canadians: the 1939–45 Star, the Air Crew Europe Star, the Atlantic Star, the Pacific Star, the Burma Star, the Africa Star, the Italy Star, the France and Germany Star, the Defence Medal, the Canadian Voluntary Service Medal and the British 1939–45 War Medal. (The Dominion of Newfoundland also had the Newfoundland Voluntary Service Medal.) Canadians were eligible for a maximum of five campaign stars and the three Second World War medals. Unique amongst these was the Canadian Voluntary Service Medal, which was the first war or campaign medal instituted by the

First World War trio of medals: 1914–1915 Star,
1914–18 British War Medal, Allied Victory Medal

Canadian government and was awarded to all Canadian service personnel who served eighteen months' voluntary service during the war. Recipients of the CVSM who served overseas for eighteen months or more were also eligible for an "overseas service bar." Bars were subsequently awarded to those who saw service at Hong Kong and in the Dieppe raid.

The Korean War brought another new medal: the Canadian Queen's Korean War Medal, which, despite some similarities, was distinct from the British Queen's Korean War Medal. It was awarded to those members of the Royal Canadian Navy, Canadian Army and Royal Canadian Air Force who were involved in the Korean War. The Canadian issue differs from the British in that it bears the word *Canada* on the obverse and was struck from .800 silver rather than cupro-nickel. Canada was unique amongst the Commonwealth nations in issuing its own Korean War medal; the others used the British version.

Beyond the campaign and war service medals, there were no fewer than fifteen different long service awards, which varied according to which branch of the Canadian armed forces one was serving in. For members of the Royal Canadian Navy (RCN) there was the RCN Long Service and Good Conduct Medal, the Royal Canadian Navy Reserve (RCNR) and Royal Canadian Navy Voluntary Reserve (RCNVR) Long Service and Good Conduct Medals, and the RCNR and RCNVR Officer's Decorations. Depending on rank, army personnel were at various times eligible for the Colonial Auxiliary Forces Long Service Medal, the Colonial Auxiliary Forces Officer's Decoration, the Colonial Permanent Forces Long Service and Good Conduct Medal, the Efficiency Medal and the Efficiency Decoration. Members of the Royal Canadian Air Force (RCAF) were limited to the Efficiency Decoration, the Air Efficiency Award and the RCAF Long Service and Good Conduct Medal. All of these awards were also used by various other countries in the Commonwealth/Empire. In 1934 the Canadian government created the RCMP Long Service Medal, the first exclusively Canadian long service medal.

Other awards that Canadians were eligible for and received were the various Jubilee and Coronation medals, from Queen Victoria's golden jubilee in 1887 to Queen Elizabeth II's 1953 coronation. The Arctic Medal was awarded to Canadians who served in Sir John Rae's expedition in the 1850s and other Arctic expeditions. The Polar Medal was awarded to members of the RCMP crew of the *St. Roch*, which patrolled the western Arctic in the early years of the Second World War.

While this list of British awards bestowed upon Canadians is not exhaustive, it is representative of the veritable forest of honours, decorations and

From left to right: Imperial Service Order, 1914–18 British War Medal, Allied Victory Medal, 1935 King George V Silver Jubilee Medal, 1937 King George VI Coronation Medal, Colonial Auxiliary Forces Long Service Medal

medals awarded to Canadians from pre-Confederation times until 1967. While British honours are today considered Commonwealth honours, until 1967 they were the Canadian honours system, there being no such indigenous institution. Although the system was extensive, it should be remembered that the award of civilian honours came to a virtual end with the 1918 Nickle Resolution, and that military gallantry awards were only awarded during the two world wars and the Korean War. In peacetime there was a noticeable absence of awards for public or for meritorious military service, aside from the Imperial Service Medals (awarded until 1952) for junior public servants, and various long service medals for members of the military.

Indian Chief Medal obverse   *Indian Chief Medal reverse*

CHAPTER 3

Canadian Honours from Confederation to the Centennial, 1867–1967: Methods of Appointment and the "System"

The award of honours in Canada has always been articulated through the Honours List, originally published in the *London Gazette* and later the *Canada Gazette*. During peacetime the list is published twice yearly, once on the Sovereign's birthday and once around Christmas or New Year's Day. For Canadian civilians, these lists were compiled by the governor general and prime minister — although the level of their co-operation varied — and then submitted to the Sovereign for approval. For members of the Canadian military, honours lists were drawn up by senior military officers and reviewed and augmented by the governor general. Until 1918, the British government had the power to nominate Canadians for honours, although this prerogative came to an end with the Nickle Resolution.

BRITISH HONOURS IN CANADA TO 1867

Prior to Confederation, the British government did not feel obligated to consult the colonial governments of British North America before conferring an honour upon a resident of what would later become the Dominion of Canada. The system was quite simple: the governor or governor general would suggest to the colonial secretary that a particular person be recognized; if the colonial secretary approved the nomination, it would be put forward for the approval of the British prime minister and ultimately the Sovereign. Recommendations did not have to originate with the governor or governor general; in theory, they could have originated from any member of the general public, although in practice it was unlikely that the colonial secretary would have acted upon the recommendation of, say, a Mr. McKay of Bytown, Canada West. Similarly, the colonial secretary could suggest that a particular person in a colony be recognized, and of course the governor of the colony in question, as the local authority, would always be consulted.

Residents of Canada were eligible for most British honours — save those that did not apply to Canada, such as the Order of the Star of India or the Order of the Indian Empire. In the pre-Confederation period relatively few honours were bestowed upon Canadians. Those awarded were usually knighthoods bestowed on judges and senior colonial politicians. There were no junior civil service awards or long service medals for the local constable.

At the time of Confederation, the Dominion government approved the striking of the Confederation Medal. Designed by the British engravers J.B. and A.B. Wyon, the medal depicted Queen Victoria on the obverse and an allegorical figure of four females (representing the four founding provinces) with outstretched arms towards a youthful Lady Britannia. Bronze versions of this medal were given to the Fathers of Confederation, while medals struck in silver were given to members of the first Canadian cabinet and to the governor general, Lord Monck. A single gold Confederation Medal was struck and presented to Queen Victoria.

Bronze Confederaton Medal obverse *Bronze Confederation Medal reverse*

The medals served a dual purpose: in one sense they were commemorative medals awarded to people who had played an important role in Confederation; and occasionally they were also used as awards for meritorious service. The final recipient of the medal was Prime Minister William Lyon Mackenzie King, in 1927. The Confederation Medals were 78 mm in diameter and presented in a small case. As table medals, they were not intended for wear. This was the first medal approved by the Canadian government, although it survives more as a numismatic curiosity than a formal award or part of the early Canadian honours system.

William Lyon Mackenzie King, in court uniform, wearing his CMG

AN EMERGING POLICY, 1867–1917

Following Confederation, a general convention emerged whereby the prime minister of Canada submitted his honours lists to the governor general, who vetted them and submitted them to the Sovereign. The governor general — who was then a British official — also nominated Canadians for honours, usually without the knowledge of the Canadian prime minister. Awards for members of the military were submitted by the General Officer in Command of the Canadian militia to the governor general for transmission to London, although there were some instances when the prime minister nominated senior Canadian officers for honours.

This system of informal consultation functioned fairly well until 1901, when controversy arose over the knighting of Thomas Shaughnessy, president of the Canadian Pacific Railway. The governor general, Lord Minto, suggested to the prime minister that Shaughnessy be knighted on account of his services during the 1901 Royal Visit of the Duke and Duchess of Cornwall and York (the future King George V and Queen Mary). Sir Wilfrid Laurier opposed the idea on the grounds that Shaughnessy was unpopular with Canadians and certainly no friend of the prime minister. Minto, however, disregarded Laurier's advice and sent the nomination forward.

Laurier was furious when Shaughnessy was knighted — it did not help that he learned of the appointment from a newspaper and not the governor general. By 1902, Laurier had drafted an official policy on honours in Canada. It set out that all honours, save the Royal Victorian Order, had to be approved by the prime minister before any list could be sent from the governor general to the king. The governor general and the British government took their time in replying to Laurier's policy, and while they agreed that the prime minister should be involved in reviewing the honours lists and submitting names, they maintained that the governor general would retain the right to nominate Canadians. This policy remained in place until the Nickle Resolution.

DISCONTENT AND DISCORD:
THE NICKLE DEBATES, 1917–19

The First World War brought much social and constitutional change to Canada, and this change included the nation's policy towards honours. Prior to the war there had been some opposition to titular honours such as peerages and knighthoods, but aside from the Shaughnessy case it had been fairly muted. Honours were viewed as necessary, even if they were used as tools of patronage from time to time. This prevailing attitude changed during the Great War as a result of several high-profile controversies. In 1914 a private member's bill was introduced in the House of Commons — one which sought to abolish peerages and knighthoods in Canada, but not other honours. This proposal was poorly received and promptly defeated. By 1917, however, the mood had changed.

In particular, two very public scandals over honours induced Parliament to examine the issue. The first involved the 1915 appointment of the Canadian minister of Militia and Defence, Sam Hughes, as a Knight Commander of the Order of the Bath. Hughes had been pilloried in the press over his mishandling of the Canadian Expeditionary Force, most specifically his involvement with the purchase of the Ross rifle. The more serious outrage occurred in 1917 when Sir Hugh Graham, owner of the Montreal *Star* and a staunch imperialist, was elevated to the peerage as Lord Atholstan — against the advice of the Canadian prime minister and governor general. Graham's peerage was so controversial in part because of his highly unpopular right-wing views and because of an increasing suspicion amongst Canadians of peerages and knighthoods. There was the added fact that Graham had done nothing — either in Canada or Britain — to warrant such an appointment.

This was the only time in Canadian history that the British government ignored advice from both a governor general and prime minister. Westminster's disregard of Ottawa's wishes was related to the fact that the British prime minister, David Lloyd George, was selling peerages and knighthoods to raise funds for his party.

Although the general public was unaware of this, all the evidence now points to Graham having bought his peerage. He was a close friend of Lord Northcliffe and Lord Beaverbrook, who had been involved in similar dealings.

In addition to these events, there was an underlying naïveté about honours in Canada. Peerages and knighthoods were thought to be the same thing — both hereditary — and there was similar confusion regarding the other British Orders of Chivalry. For instance, when the creation of the Order of the British Empire was announced in 1917, Canadian newspapers announced that 300 Canadians were going to be knighted with the new order. This was obviously not the case.

In March 1917, following Graham's elevation to the peerage as Lord Atholstan, Sir Robert Borden drafted a new government policy setting out that all honours must be approved by the Canadian prime minister and that no further hereditary honours (peerages or baronetcies) were to be awarded to Canadians. Only a week after this policy was drafted, William Folger Nickle, the Conservative-Unionist MP for Kingston, introduced a resolution

in the House of Commons requesting that the King cease awarding peerages to Canadians. Nickle had no trouble with knighthoods or other honours — only those that had a hereditary quality. Nickle's resolution was in fact very similar to Borden's new policy. After lengthy debate, the House of Commons adopted a resolution placing power over recommendation for all honours in the hands of the Canadian prime minister, while at the same time asking the King to cease awarding hereditary titles to Canadians. This is what came to be known as the Nickle Resolution, even though Nickle himself voted against the version that eventually passed.

William Folger Nickle

Although the Nickle Resolution was adopted, the debate was far from over. Although some military awards were conferred, Borden did not send forward any further recommendations for honours — he thought the issue was still too contentious to test the new protocol.

Throughout late 1918 and most of 1919, the British press was littered with reports about people purchasing honours. Although this was a problem confined to Britain, many people in Canada assumed that the same practice was followed on this side of the Atlantic as well. Fearing that an avalanche of knighthoods was to accompany the newly created Order of the British Empire, Nickle introduced another motion in April 1919. This one called for the king to "hereafter be graciously pleased to refrain from conferring any titles upon your subjects domiciled or living in Canada." Nickle was now going after both peerages and knighthoods, a departure from his original opposition to only hereditary honours. Following another lengthy debate that in many ways mirrored the one in 1918, the House of Commons voted to create a Special Committee on Honours and Titles, which held several meetings and eventually submitted a report to Parliament that called for the king to cease conferring all honours and titular distinctions, save military ranks and vocational and professional titles, upon residents of Canada. It also recommended that action be taken to extinguish the heritable quality of peerages and baronetcies held by Canadians. The committee approved of the continuance of naval and military decorations such as the Victoria Cross, Military Cross and other decorations for valour and devotion to duty. The final part of the report affirmed the committee's desire to see that no resident of Canada be permitted to accept a title of honour or titular distinction from a foreign (non-British) government. Parliament passed a motion of concurrence with the report and it was adopted.

There has, invariably, been some confusion about the Nickle Resolution and the Report of the Special Committee on Honours and Titles. Neither was a statute, and neither had any standing as anything more than a recommendation — as Prime Minister R.B. Bennett would demonstrate, with respect to the Report of the Special Committee, in 1933. The Nickle Resolution served as a policy document on how a prime minister could submit honours lists, and while it requested that no further hereditary honours be bestowed, it did not prevent Canadians from accepting other honours, whether a knighthood or OBE.

PROHIBITION, 1919–1932

The prohibition on Canadians accepting British honours commenced in 1918 and lasted until 1933. Neither Prime Minister Arthur Meighen nor Mackenzie King submitted honours lists, although it was well within their power to do so. Both leaders hesitated on account of the issue's contentiousness, and Mackenzie King in particular had little interest in such devices. The prohibition was not complete, however, as Canadians living in other parts of the British Empire were still eligible to be awarded honours. The best example was Dr. George Washington Badgerow, a world-renowned ear, nose and throat doctor. Badgerow was born and trained in Canada, although he made his home in Britain. In 1926 the British government requested permission from the Canadian government to allow Badgerow to be knighted. Two years later the Canadian government responded that the award could go forward because Badgerow, although born in Canada, was a resident of Britain and was being rewarded for services he performed in Britain. Thus the prohibition was incidental, and Bennett would prove that there was in fact no legislative prohibition at all, but rather a series of prime ministers who had no interest in honours lists.

BENNETT'S HONOURS LIST, 1932–1935

Prime Minister R.B. Bennett broke the moratorium on honours that had existed in Canada between 1919 and 1933. In fact, Bennett adhered perfectly to the Nickle Resolution and had eighteen Canadians awarded knighthoods and 189 appointed to the various non-titular levels of the British Orders of Chivalry. Bennett solicited nominations from the various lieutenant governors and other officials, and then personally selected each candidate. Unlike previous lists, Bennett's were largely nonpartisan and well distributed amongst the provinces and between both sexes — quite a novelty for the period. Among others, Bennett's lists recognized Sir Frederick Banting, the co-discoverer of insulin; Sir Ernest Macmillan, the noted composer and conductor; Sir Thomas Chapais, the esteemed historian; and Sir Arthur Doughty, the Dominion archivist. At the non-titular level, Lucy Maud Montgomery was made a Commander of the Order of the British Empire and Lester Pearson was made an Officer of the Order of the British Empire.

Public reaction to these awards was muted.

Bennett himself was offered a GCMG, although he declined it and offered it to Mackenzie King, who also declined it. Bennett was the last Canadian prime minister to make use of all aspects of the British honours system, with the last knighthood, a KCMG, going to one of Canada's first diplomats, the Honorable Herbert Meredith Marler, Canada's minister plenipotentiary to Japan.

THE SECOND WORLD WAR

When William Lyon Mackenzie King was returned as prime minister in 1935, the brief revival of British honours was ended. Although Vincent Massey tried to interest King in creating a Canadian order, nothing was done. Thus, Canada entered the Second World War with no policy on honours, other than to allow for the bestowal of gallantry and valour awards. Even this policy was unclear as to who would approve the awards, from where nominations would emanate, and how many were to be allotted for

Canadian service personnel. To deal with these problems a special interdepartmental committee, which would later become the Awards Co-ordination Committee, was founded in early 1940. This committee drafted formal honours policies, the first of which set out that Canadians could receive gallantry decorations "in operations against the enemy." This was ratified through Order-in-Council 1430 on 9 May 1940. There were no provisions for awards to the various British orders of chivalry to Canadians.

Throughout the Second World War numerous proposals were devised to create a Canadian order, but none came to fruition, and thus Canada continued to work within the broader British honours system. In 1942 Parliament again tackled the issue of honours and awards. In July of that year, the Special Committee on Honours and Decorations met and ultimately decided that, in addition to allowing Canadians to receive gallantry and valour decorations, Canadians should be eligible for the non-titular levels of the British orders of chivalry (those not conferring knighthood). It also expressed the opinion that the Canadian government should establish a Canadian Order. Essentially, the committee adhered to the Nickle Resolution — which allowed for the award of honours only on the advice of the Canadian government — while at the same time discarding the proposals of the 1919 Special Committee on Honours and Titles, which sought to cease the award of all British Orders of Chivalry to Canadians.

It was not until 1967, with the founding of the Order of Canada, that the Canadian government would act upon the 1942 proposal to create a Canadian honour. In terms of the other proposals, Canadian service personnel and civilians were made eligible for the non-titular levels of the British Orders of Chivalry (the Order of the Bath, the Order of St. Michael and St. George, the Order of the British Empire and the Imperial Service Order), and honours lists containing appointments to these orders were published during the Second World War. The last such list for civilian appointments to the British Orders of Chivalry was issued in 1946.

Canada's policies were only partially effective — particularly in the case of such senior officials as Vincent Massey, General A.G.L. McNaughton and General Crerar, all of whom received honours during this period. To appoint these men to be Companions of the Order of the Bath or Commanders of the Order of the British Empire — honours usually reserved for colonels — would have been a joke, as their counterparts serving in other British dominions were usually knighted. A special solution was therefore found: they were awarded the Order of the Companions of Honour, which King George V had founded in 1917, at the same time as the Order of the British Empire. Today, the order is limited to sixty-five living members, with specific quotas for different parts of the Commonwealth: forty-five for the United Kingdom, seven for Australia, two for New Zealand and eleven for other Commonwealth countries. In 1943, Canada was offered part of this quota, but it declined. To date, eight Canadians have been appointed to the order: in addition to MacNaughton, Crerar and Massey, there were Charles Best, Arnold Smith, John Diefenbaker, Pierre Trudeau and General John de Chastelain.

THE KOREAN WAR

With the beginning of the Korean War, Cabinet was once again faced with making decisions about honours in Canada. It elected merely to institute a policy similar to that used during the Second World War, which allowed for members of the Royal Canadian Navy, Canadian Army and Royal Canadian Air Force to accept British gallantry decorations and the non-titular levels of the British orders of chivalry. However, in contrast to the Second World War, civilians who made an important contribution to the Korean War effort were not to be permitted to receive any of the non-titular levels of the British orders of chivalry.

THE 1956 POLICY: AN INCOMPLETE SOLUTION, 1956–1967

The end of the Korean War saw the flow of British honours — aside from long service awards — cease once again. In 1956, however, Cabinet passed a directive that instated a more liberal policy towards honours and awards. Cabinet Directive 30 allowed Canadian civilians to receive the George Cross and George Medal for "acts of bravery performed at the risk of death or serious injury." Thus, for the most part, the Canadian honours system consisted of bravery awards: the George Cross, the George Medal, and the Queen's Commendation for Brave Conduct. Allowances were also made to permit appointments, for bravery, to the various levels of the Order of the British Empire. Members of the armed forces were still eligible for the various British gallantry awards, although there were no such allowances for meritorious service awards such as the Order of the Bath or Order of the British Empire. The 1956 policy also allowed for Canadians to accept foreign honours under certain circumstances. This was the first time since the Second World War that Canadian civilians were permitted to accept foreign honours.

The post-1967 honours system finds its basis, initially, in the Order of Canada, established by letters patent signed by Queen Elizabeth II on 17 March 1967. Initially, the order consisted of three separate parts: Companion of the Order of Canada, the Medal of Courage of the Order of Canada, and the Medal of Service of the Order of Canada. These three awards served as the cornerstone upon which the post-1967 Canadian honours system has developed. The development of the Order of Canada has embodied much more than the creation of a single institution; it is rather a project that expanded to include the various Canadian Bravery Decorations, the Order of Military Merit and almost every other order, decoration and medal in the Canadian honours system today. Therefore the 1966–67 developments in the Canadian honours system will be dealt with in Chapter Five.

THE CREATION OF CANADIAN HONOURS TODAY

Proposals to create new honours or medals generally come from the Chancellery of Honours or the Department of National Defence, although they occasionally emanate from individuals or organizations.

The Chancellery researches to ensure that the proposed honour or medal is needed and that it conforms to Canadian honours policy. Once it deems that the honour is needed, a proposal is presented to the Honours Policy Committee — a government body chaired by the clerk of the Privy Council and made up of senior public servants (generally deputy ministers) from various federal departments. If the Honours Policy Committee agrees that the honour is needed, the Chancellery is then directed to propose regulations and a draft order-in-council. Design proposals are also drawn up by the Chancellery, usually in collaboration with the Canadian Heraldic Authority.

The Honours Policy Committee then reviews the proposal again and, if approved, it is passed on to the prime minister for approval. If the prime minister approves the new award an order-in-council is processed through the Privy Council Office. On the advice of the prime minister of Canada, through the governor general's office, the letters patent and design paintings are sent to Buckingham Palace for approval by Her Majesty the Queen. It is only when the Queen signs the letters patent that the honour is considered to be officially created.

Once the paintings and letters patent are signed by the Queen, a press release is sent out by the governor general and the regulations for the new award are published in the *Canada Gazette.*

Amendments to the criteria for Canadian orders, decorations and medals do not have to be approved by the Queen, but can be made by the governor general as her representative in Canada.

CHAPTER 4

Failed Proposals:
What Could Have Been

The current Canadian honours system did not spring fully formed from the collective minds of Parliament. Indeed, many proposals have both preceded it and followed it, and they serve as telling indicators of what the Canadian honours system could have become. Some proposals were quite traditional and in some ways boring, while others, primarily those developed during the 1960s, were much more novel, combining tradition with elements that were less than conventional. This chapter focuses upon those proposals from which some diagrams and other information remain. It is by no means a complete catalogue of proposals or designs, but rather an overview of those that have most interested the author.

At various times the Department of National Defence devised proposals that did not leave the design table; nevertheless they are curious relics that demonstrate that there was — from the 1940s through the 1960s — a definite desire to see uniquely Canadian awards established.

THE ORDER OF ST. LAWRENCE (1866)

Proposed by Lord Monck, Canada's first governor general, who envisioned a uniquely Canadian order of chivalry based upon the Order of the Star of India, the Order of St. Lawrence was quashed in 1866 by the Colonial Office, which viewed such a step as giving Canada too much independence. Thus, Canada continued to work within the broader British honours system.

Monck's proposal called for three levels: Knight Grand Cross of the Order of St. Lawrence (GCSL), Knight Commander of the Order of St. Lawrence (KCSL) and Companion of the Order of St. Lawrence (CSL). As with other British Orders of Chivalry, the top two levels would have conferred knighthood, and thus the recipient would have become "Sir Sean Morency, KCSL." It is likely that the order would also have carried an appellation such as eminent, exalted or excellent.

One can not help but wonder if Canada would still have discarded titular honours had a Canadian order of chivalry similar to that proposed by Monck been established shortly after Confederation.

THE ORDER OF ST. LAWRENCE II (1935 AND 1951)

It would not be until 1935 that another proposal for a Canadian order was advanced by a senior government official. This five-level order was devised by Vincent Massey, and he would advance the proposal not only in 1935 but again in 1951.

The five tiers of Massey's order were: Grand Commander of the Order of St. Lawrence (GCSL), Grand Officer of the Order of St. Lawrence (GOSL), Companion of the Order of St. Lawrence (CSL), Officer of the Order of St. Lawrence (OSL) and Member of the Order of St. Lawrence (MSL).

Massey proposed the order in 1935 to the recently installed governor general, Lord Tweedsmuir, who was quite enthusiastic about the prospect of creating a Canadian order, especially in light of the prohibition on British honours. Almost immediately Tweedsmuir broached the topic with Prime Minister Mackenzie King; needless to say, the conversation did not go well, and a few days later Tweedsmuir received a curt note from the prime minister warning him to avoid the topic of honours in Canada.

The issue was again introduced in 1951, while Massey chaired the Royal Commission on the National Development of the Arts, Letters and Sciences. Although the idea was Massey's, this new proposal was put forward at the direction of Prime Minister Louis St. Laurent. The structure that Massey devised was identical to the one he had proposed in 1935, but this time he added a new unique feature: recipients of the Order of St. Lawrence were to be selected by a neutral, nonpartisan committee — not by the prime minister or any elected politician. When the report of the Royal commission was presented, the honours proposal was classified as secret, and it was suppressed after being shown to the leaders of the opposition.

THE ROYAL ORDER OF CANADA (1940)

Massey devised another proposal in 1940. The Royal Order of Canada was to consist of two levels, companion and officer. Membership was to be limited to fifteen companions and fifty officers. The design of the

insignia would depict the Royal Arms of Canada centred upon a nine-pointed star — to symbolize the nine Canadian provinces — with various other symbols placed between the points of the star. Some viewed this design as symbolically rich, while others found it excessively cluttered. Design issues notwithstanding, the push to create a Canadian order was again halted by the federal cabinet.

Prototype of the Royal Order of Canada

THE CANADIAN DECORATION OF HONOUR AND THE CANADIAN AWARD OF HONOUR (1942)

Realizing that Prime Minister King was not going to accept any proposal that called for the creation of a Canadian order, the government body charged with defining Canadian honours policy, the Awards Coordination Committee (ACC), devised the "non-order order." The

Prototype of the Canadian Award and of Honour

proposal called for two awards to be instituted, "upon the assumption that it might be desirable to establish a senior award which would not be an Order of Chivalry." The two awards were the Canadian Award of Honour (CAH) and the Canadian Decoration of Honour (CDH).

Membership at both levels was to be limited along the same lines as Massey's Royal Order of Canada. Statutes for the awards and detailed designs were drawn up. The badge was to be nine-sided, "charged with three maple leaves conjoined on one stem, proper, superimposed on a laurel wreath seeded proper. And underneath the motto ACER GERENDO in raised letters." The award was to be worn around the neck, while the decoration would be on the left breast. Both were to be hung from a ribbon of watered silk in autumnal colours: red, yellow, green, purple and scarlet (not a conventional ribbon design, to say the least). This proposal, like its predecessors, was rejected by Mackenzie King.

THE CANADA MEDAL (1943)

This is the only proposal outlined in this chapter that received approval and was physically manufactured. The Canadian Meritorious Award, or Canada Medal as it would later become known, was originally intended to serve as an award junior to the Royal Order of Canada or the Canadian Award/Decoration of Honour. As both of these projects failed, the Canada Medal was suddenly elevated from a junior service award to the most senior Canadian honour.

The Canada Medal
Left: English obverse Centre: French obverse Right: Reverse

The Canada Medal was created by a royal warrant signed by King George VI on 27 August 1943. The medal was to be awarded to citizens and non-citizens for "specially valuable and meritorious service of a high standard ... special service of a high degree of merit, such as discharge of special duties superior to the person's ordinary work ... highly meritorious performance of ordinary duties where these have entailed work of a specially trying character."

The Canada Medal depicted King George VI on the obverse and the shield of the Royal Arms of Canada, surrounded by maple leaves, on the reverse. The suspender of the medal carried the word *merit*, or *merite*. Recipients were to be entitled to the postnominal initials CM or M du C. In all, fifteen Canada Medals were struck, eight in English and seven in French.

The ribbon consisted of three stripes, equal in width, of red, white and red. To date, one English version (the one once owned by the master of the Royal Canadian Mint as a sample) has come onto the market. All Canada Medals are stamped with *specimen* on the rim. One pair of medals (English and French) is held in the Royal collection, while the remainder are deposited in Canadian museums.

The first honours list containing awards of the Canada Medal was to be issued on 11 November 1943. Such persons as the king, British Prime Minister Winston Churchill, U.S. President Franklin Roosevelt, Soviet Premier Joseph Stalin and a host of Canadian service personnel were to be included. However, while approval for the medal was given, the medals struck and lists drawn up, no awards were ever made. Repeated requests from the ACC and various government departments were met with a refusal to see the medal awarded.

The Canada Medal, which would be the source of sporadic debate in the House of Commons between 1943 and 1966, remained an official Canadian decoration, the first truly indigenous award for merit ever created by the Canadian government, until 1967, when the Order of Canada was created and the government repealed the royal warrant creating the Canada Medal.

Prototype of the Canadian Medal of Honour

THE CANADIAN MEDAL OF HONOUR (1966)

The 1960s were a particularly creative time in terms of honours. Various sections of the Department of National Defence churned out designs, and chief amongst these was a proposal for a Canadian Medal of Honour. The jewel-encrusted breast badge was to bear an effigy of the Queen in the centre, superimposed on a stylized maple leaf on a star. Between each of the arms of the star were to be the various provincial shields and diamonds. All of this might seem quite strange, but it was a proposal clearly modelled on the Order of Glory of the Soviet Union — the USSR's highest award, which was made of gold and platinum and encrusted with a variety of precious stones.

Prototype of the
Order of Military Merit

THE ORDER OF MILITARY MERIT (1966)

Along with the proposal for the Canadian Medal of Honour came a variety of designs for an Order of Military Merit. While all of the designs incorporated such traditional Canadian symbols as the Queen, the crown, maple leaves and the Royal Arms of Canada, they also have a certain Soviet style to them. This order included both neck badges and breast stars — quite an elaborate system. As only the diagrams survive, we cannot be sure as to exactly what structure the new order was to take.

Prototype of the
Order of Canada

THE ORDER OF CANADA (1967)

When Vincent Massey became involved in the 1966–67 plans to develop a Canadian order, he still favoured the designation "Order of St. Lawrence." With time, however, he relented and recognized that Order of Canada was more appropriate.

In the early stages, Massey wanted the order to have the same five-tiered structure as his original Order of St. Lawrence, but this was soon superseded by a three-level proposal. In addition to assisting in the creation of the constitution of the Order of Canada, Massey also developed some designs. These were drawn by his secretary, Joyce Turpin, and depicted a medal very similar in shape and design to that of the Royal Victorian Order, the primary difference being that a maple leaf — and not a Royal cypher — was to be placed in the centre of the insignia. Massey also had Turpin sew up a red-and-white sash for the proposed Order of Canada.

THE ORDER OF MILITARY MERIT (1971)

Shortly after creation of the Order of Canada in 1967, the Government Decorations Committee considered the need for a special order of merit to recognize military personnel. By 1970 it was realized that the Order of Canada was not being presented to a sufficient number of military personnel, and it was decided that a separate Order of Military Merit should be created. Although it was agreed early on that the Order of Military Merit should consist of three levels (Commander, Officer and Member), designs were drawn up by Bruce Beatty for a five-level order, which was to include the designations Grand Commander, Grand Officer, Commander, Officer and Member. There was also to be a Medal of Merit of the Order of Military Merit.

Multi-levelled Order of Military Merit
Left: Grand Commander Right: Grand Officer

While the Government Decorations Committee decided to proceed with a three-level order instead, a failed attempt to reintroduce the five-tiered structure was made in 1973 by General Jacques Dextraze, then chief of defence staff. What little documentary evidence of this proposal survives indicates that the Medal of Merit was to be used in a manner similar to the way the Meritorious Service Medal and Meritorious Service Cross are presented today — for specific acts of meritorious service.

It should also be noted that this version of the Order of Military Merit featured an effigy of Queen Elizabeth II, rather than a maple leaf and crown, in the centre.

THE HONORARY ORDER OF CANADA (1986)

When the Order of Canada was created in 1967, special allowances were made to permit it to be awarded to non–Canadian citizens. These honorary awards were to be made on the advice of the Queen's Privy Council for Canada (the federal cabinet). For various reasons, only one award was made via this method between 1967 and 1998.

In 1985–86 various proposals were introduced to see a wholly separate Canadian order established, with a membership limited to non-Canadians only. The Mulroney government briefly flirted with the idea of engaging in the diplomatic honours exchange game, whereby Canadian high commissioners and ambassadors would be permitted to accept foreign decorations merely for serving in that country, while foreign diplomats and visiting heads of state would be presented with the new Canadian order. Designs and ribbon were drawn up by Bruce Beatty. The ribbon was white-red-white, the opposite of the Order of Canada's ribbon. The insignia was to follow the same idea, and the white enamel on the snowflake was to be replaced by red enamel. At some point, consideration was given to eliminating the honorary division of the Order of Canada and creating an entirely new Order of Merit, for foreigners only. By 1987 the entire proposal was shelved.

A bolt of ribbon was manufactured, and, having found no official use, it is now used on the insignia presented to fellows of the Royal Heraldry Society of Canada. In 1998, new regulations were adopted to allow for non–Canadian citizens to accept the Order of Canada.

CHAPTER 5

The Order of Canada:
The Basis for Canada's Honours System

THE ORIGINS OF THE ORDER OF CANADA

The idea of creating a Canadian Order can be traced back to 1823 and Lord Bathurst, who was then Britain's colonial secretary. His proposal did not progress past the stage of a rough idea, as King George IV was not favourable towards the idea. This first attempt was followed nearly fifty years later, when Lord Monck, Canada's first governor general, made the same suggestion. He envisioned the Order of St. Lawrence, consisting of three levels, similar to Britain's Order of the Star of India: Knight Grand Cross, Knight Commander and Companion. Alas, the colonial office was not willing to allow the new Dominion to create such a potent symbol of national autonomy, and thus Canada continued to work within the existing British imperial honours system. Indeed, the British Order of St. Michael and St. George was altered in its purpose to meet the demands of Canada and other self-governing parts of the British Empire, and thus became in many ways became the premier honour for a Canadian to receive.

The origins of the Order of Canada as we know it today can clearly be traced back to Vincent Massey, whose persistence and ideas played such a central role in the creation of a uniquely Canadian honour. Massey first broached the subject in 1935 with the newly installed governor general, Lord Tweedsmuir, who was very keen on encouraging the creation of Canadian institutions and subsequently brought the subject up with his prime minister, William Lyon Mackenzie King. King was not enthusiastic about the prospect of reintroducing honours in Canada, let alone creating an indigenous award. Canada's longest-serving prime minister had a certain phobia when it came to honours, going as far as to ask the British Central Chancery of the Orders of Knighthood to cancel his appointment as a Companion of the Order of St. Michael and St. George more than thirty years after he was awarded it. This did not prevent him in later life from accepting the Commonwealth's premier non-titular award in 1947, when he was appointed to the Order of Merit and a number of foreign awards.

Massey initially proposed a Canadian order called the Order of St. Lawrence, consisting of two levels, Companion and Officer. It was a concept he would later reintroduce, again without success, during the early stages of the Second World War. Throughout the war a special committee made up of senior civil servants, the Awards Co-ordination Committee (ACC), met regularly to discuss the issue of honours in Canada. While the committee's task was primarily to develop policy with relation to British awards being bestowed upon Canadians, it would often delve into the subject of creating a Canadian order. To this end, between 1941 and 1946 it submitted no fewer than five different proposals to the prime minister. Each was in turn rejected. In 1942 a special parliamentary committee, the Special Committee on Honours and Awards, called for the creation of a Canadian order, a recommendation that was also ignored. It was at this time that the actual name "Order of Canada" originated, as part of Massey's proposal for a Royal Order of Canada — although it was the under-secretary of state, Ephriam Coleman, and Major General Harry Letson who simplified the name to the Order of Canada. This name persisted in proposals until the creation of the Order of Canada in 1967, although other titles, ranging from the Order of the Beaver, to the Order of St. Lawrence, to the Royal Elizabethan Order, were often suggested.

Early Order of Canada insignia with four dots

Despite the failure of its various proposals, the ACC did manage to have the Canada Medal established in 1943. It was a curious award, to say the least, as it was to be awarded to everyone from privates to heads of state. While extensive lists of recipients were composed, however, the medal was never awarded. Prime Minister King wanted nothing to do with honours, especially the Canada Medal; in his mind, the existing British honours system, though flawed, worked well in Canada, and he had no desire to make forays into the honours debate by creating a Canadian system.

Following the end of the Second World War the demand for civilian honours dropped and the topic of creating a Canadian order was once again put aside. Lord Alexander, Canada's governor general from 1946 to 1952, called for the creation of an Order of Canada in 1948, but this too failed, although he did come up with the ribbon design used by the Order of Canada today. The subject was again reintroduced in a secret report of the Royal Commission on the Arts, Letters and Sciences, which was not coincidentally chaired by Vincent Massey. This time, Massey proposed a five-level Order of St. Lawrence, based upon a structure similar to the Order of the British Empire and France's *Légion d'Honneur*. Most significantly, Massey proposed that the honours list for this new order be composed by a nonpartisan committee, quite unlike the practice that had previously been followed in Canada and Britain, where the prime minister had a direct influence over the flow of honours. Although the proposal was given to the leaders of the opposition parties, it failed to gain the approval of the then prime minister Louis St. Laurent, who was in part concerned about sanctioning the creation of an order that bore a name so similar to his own. One can only imagine the reaction of political opponents if St. Laurent were to bestow an order bearing his name to loyal members of the Liberal Party!

Throughout the late 1950s and early 1960s, the Department of National Defence developed a variety of proposals for the creation of an Order of Canada. These were based upon the Massey Commission and Alexander proposals, although none met with success.

The adoption of the Maple Leaf flag and establishment of the Order of Canada were really part of a larger project on the part of the government to endow Canada with the requisite symbols of nationhood. Before Lester Pearson became prime minister in 1963, he had supported the adoption of a new Canadian flag to replace the Red Ensign. His interest in creating a Canadian order was piqued by his parliamentary secretary, John Matheson, who shared his interest in both the flag and the order. Pearson was most concerned with the flag issue, and thus the question of establishing a Canadian order was temporarily sidetracked. More than a year after the adoption of the Maple Leaf flag — with tensions still high — Pearson and Matheson discussed the possible structure of a Canadian order. Pearson hoped to have an order established in time for the Centennial of Confederation in July 1967. This left less than fifteen months in which to gain the approval of Cabinet and the Queen, to have the insignia designed and manufactured, and most importantly, to draw up a list of worthy recipients.

In March 1966, Matheson was dispatched to Vincent Massey's country estate, Batterwood, to discuss the subject. Their deliberations were productive, and upon his return to Ottawa Matheson presented Pearson with a plan for a three-tiered order consisting of Companions, Officers and Associates. Massey still favoured the name the Order of St.

Lawrence, while Pearson and Matheson wanted the new honour to be called the Order of Canada. Over the next six months various changes were made to the proposal, and the yet-unnamed order's constitution was developed.

The proposal for the establishment of the Order of Canada was presented to Cabinet in November 1966 and the reception was frosty. There was opposition to the order being divided into three separate levels: some ministers viewed this as elitist and not reflective of the sort of honours system Canada needed. Some went so far as to question the need for an honours system at all. Pearson yielded and agreed that the Order of Canada would consist of one level only, and Cabinet finally agreed to allow the plan to go forward.

Pearson was concerned that a single-level order would not reward all those who deserved recognition; after all, his primary motive for proposing the order was to see those who contributed at the local level recognized. Two additions were subsequently made: the Medal of Service, which was in essence a junior level of the Order of Canada, and the Medal of Courage, a separate bravery award that, although part of the order, was quite an independent entity. The Medal of Service and Medal of Courage were approved by Cabinet on the basis that they were not really part of the order, but this would prove a mistake: Pearson's assistants, Gordon Robertson, Jack Hodgson and Michael Pitfield, had cleverly described the medals to seem like minor additions, when in fact they were integral to the structure of the order.

The Queen approved the creation of the order on 21 March 1967. On 17 April, Pearson rose in the House of Commons.

> Mr. Speaker, I would like to announce to the House the establishment of a system of honours and awards for Canada. Practically every sovereign country has such a system, which it uses as a means of recognizing merit or gallantry, or distinguished public service. I believe that recognition of this kind can strengthen national pride and the appreciation of national service.
>
> There has been no system of Canadian honours and awards. The Canada Medal was instituted in 1943 as a possible way of filling the gap, but it has never been awarded and is now being replaced. Because Canada has lacked an official system a number of unofficial and semi-official honours and awards have developed over the years.... It is my pleasure to announce that on the recommendation of the

government Her Majesty has approved the issue of letters patent constituting the Order of Canada.... Any person or organization is invited at any time to suggest names of persons whom they consider worthy of receiving any of these awards.... The government believes that these three awards, the Companion of the Order of Canada, the Medal of Courage and the Medal of Service, will help fill a need in our national life and will enable proper recognition to be given by Canada to its own citizens and to others.[1]

Public reaction was favourable, although there were some initial concerns that the order would become a political tool or patronage plum.

The first honours list was published in the *Canada Gazette* and released to the public on 7 July 1967. The list included such notables as Dr. Wilder Penfield, Vincent Massey, Madame Vanier, Major General George Pearkes, M.J. Coldwell, Gaetan Gélinas, Maurice Richard and Marlene Streit. In total, thirty-five companions and fifty-five Medals of Service were appointed that month. A second list of fifteen companions and forty-five Medals of Service was issued in December 1967. The first recipient of the order was Roland Michener, who was invested by the Queen on 6 July 1967 at Government House.

Since 1971 all viceregal spouses have also been appointed as ex-officio Companions of the Order. The governor general and vice-regal consort remain Companions of the Order when they leave office.

Almost immediately after the first appointments were made in 1967, problems arose with the structure of the order. No awards of the Medal of Courage had yet been made, so it did not pose an immediate problem, but the Medal of Service was quite another issue. It was regarded by many as a second prize to the Companion level, and this was not only because more Medals of Service were awarded than Companions, but also because the design of the insignia implied inferiority. The Companion's insignia was quite beautiful in gold and enamel, while the Medal of Service claimed a rather plain and smaller — though not unattractive — insignia. There was the additional problem that the Medal of Service was intended to recognize important national service, yet there was a desperate need for an award to recognize outstanding *local* service of a significant nature. By 1968 the Advisory Council of the Order of Canada had decided that the order should be restructured into three levels: Companion, Officer and Member — the same arrangement that Pearson had proposed to Cabinet in 1966, when it was deemed unacceptable. This time, however, there was little difficulty in securing acceptance. Those who received the Medal of Service were permitted to exchange their SM for an Officer's insignia, and the Medal of Service was abolished.

The restructured Order of Canada came into being in 1972. Since that time there have been few structural changes, aside from enlargements and an alteration in the mechanism through which honorary members are appointed.

———————

Appointments to the Order of Canada are made by the governor general on behalf of the Queen. The governor general receives the honours list from the order's advisory council, which is chaired by the Chief Justice of the Supreme Court of Canada and which includes the secretary to the governor general (who is also secretary general of the Order), the deputy minister of Heritage, the clerk of the Privy Council, the president of the Royal Society of Canada, the president of the Association of Universities and Colleges of Canada, and up to five other members. Nominations are received from the general public, and the entire process is insulated from political influence.

Although the order's 1967 constitution provided for non–Canadian citizens to be appointed as honorary members on the advice of Cabinet, it was not until 1981 that the first and only such appointment was made. Zena Sheardown, along with her husband and other members of the Canadian Embassy's staff in Tehran, sheltered six Americans during the Islamic revolution in Iran in 1979. Mrs. Sheardown's role was particularly central, since four of the six "houseguests" were billeted with her. She was also at the greatest risk, as she was not a Canadian citizen and was therefore not covered by diplomatic immunity. In 1981 she became an honorary Member of the Order of Canada; when she later became a Canadian citizen, her honorary membership was cancelled and she was simultaneously appointed a Member of the Order of Canada, general division.

In 1997, a new process was introduced whereby the advisory council was given control over honorary appointments. Initially, these appointments could only be made at the officer level, but the new regime was extended to the Member and Companion levels in 1998. To date, in addition to Zena Sheardown, there has been one other honorary Member, Lois Lilienstein, four honorary Officers (Charles Dutoit, John Kenneth Galbraith, James Hiller and Tanya Moiseiwitsch) and four honorary Companions (Nelson Mandela, Queen Elizabeth the Queen Mother, Vaclav Havel and Boutros Boutros-Ghali). Unlike many other countries, Canada has not engaged in the diplomatic game of exchanging awards as gifts. Like the award of all Canadian honours, it can be revoked. This has occurred on two occasions — the first when Zena Sheardown became a Canadian citizen and moved from being a honorary Member to a regular Member of the order, which was more of a transfer from one division to another; the second when Alan Eagleson's appointment as an Officer was terminated in 1998.

To date, more than 4,000 Canadians have been appointed to the Order of Canada. It is a national honour that is open to all fields, and one that recognizes contributions from the local stage to the international.

Every recipient of the Order of Canada also receives a certificate bearing their name, the signature of the governor general and secretary general of the order, and the seal of the order.

The insignia of the order remains the property of the Crown; upon the death of the holder, according to the order's constitution, it is to be returned to the Chancellery, donated to a museum or retained by the family. Still, the prohibition on the sale of insignia has never been enforced with any zeal, and from time to time they have come onto the market.

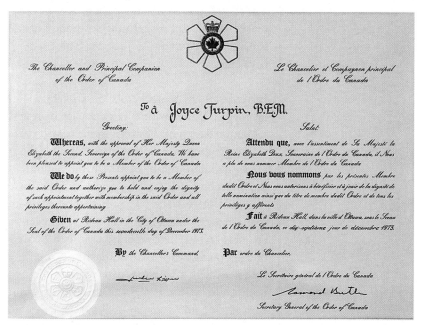

Order of Canada certificate

Sovereign's insignia of the Order of Canada

SOVEREIGN OF THE ORDER OF CANADA

Origins: Every national order has a titular head. In the case of countries with monarchical systems of government, it is generally the Sovereign; in the case of republics, it is the president. As Canada is a constitutional monarchy, it is natural that the Queen serve as the Sovereign of the Order of Canada — it is, after all, from the Crown that all official honours flow.

It has long been a tradition that the Sovereign of an order possess a special insignia to denote his or her position. These insignia are usually encrusted with precious stones and different in some way from those awarded to the general membership of the order. The Order of Canada follows this tradition, and in 1967 it was decided that a special Sovereign's insignia should be commissioned and presented to the Queen. The design was complete in 1968, and was presented to Queen Elizabeth by Governor General Roland Michener on 23 June 1970 at Buckingham Palace.

Insignia: A six-armed cross of 18-karat gold, enamelled white, with a large square diamond set between each of the arms. In the centre, there is a maple leaf surrounded by an annulus, both set with calibre-rubies pavé. On the annulus is the motto in pierced gold. Above the cross, there is a gold St. Edward's Crown with the cap of maintenance enameled red and the ermine enameled white. The arches are set with twenty-one diamonds, with a larger one in the orb. The base is set with a sapphire, two emeralds and two rubies. The reverse is plain, aside from the word *Canada* in gold.

Other: The Sovereign's insignia was manufactured by Garrard and Company, under the supervision of Crown Jeweller William Summers.

Numbers: There has been one Sovereign of the Order of Canada: Her Majesty Queen Elizabeth II.

CHANCELLOR OF THE ORDER OF CANADA

Origins: While every order has a titular head, tradition has also called for there to be a senior official known as either a grand master or a chancellor. Prime Minister Lester Pearson decided that the term "grand master" was a little grandiose for Canada, thus the choice of the title of chancellor. Given that the governor general is the Queen's representative in Canada, it was decided that he or she should also serve as the chancellor of the order and perform most of the ceremonial and administrative duties relating to certain aspects of the order. The Chancellor of the Order of Canada is also styled the "Principal Companion of the Order of Canada."

When a governor general's term expires, he or she ceases to be Chancellor of the Order of Canada but remains a Companion of the Order.

Insignia: The Chancellor's chain was produced by the Royal Canadian Mint. Like the other insignia of the order, it was designed by Bruce Beatty. Marvin Cook and Argo Aarand made the various parts of the chain from gold, and Aarand enamelled them in a small kiln in the basement of his home. The chain is made of twenty-three devices linked together by a double row of small gold links. Twelve of these

Chancellor's Chain of the Order of Canada

Top: Obverse
Below: Reverse

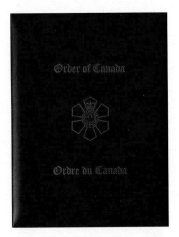

*Case for the Chancellor's Chain
of the Order of Canada*

devices are miniature replicas of the white snowflake; alternating with these are ten devices, each in the form of a red maple leaf on a white background, encircled by the red annulet bearing the motto of the order. The chain is completed by a centre device in the form of the shield from the Arms of Canada ensigned by the Royal crown, each in their proper colours. A Companion's insignia is hung from this device. The insignia of the Order of Canada that hangs from the Chancellor's chain was manufactured by Garrard and Company, the Crown jewellers. The reverse is the same as that of a regular companion's insignia, although a small box that usually contains a three-digit number bears the legend "-C."

The chain — made over a nine-month period, during which Aarand and Cook devoted their lunch hours to the project — was presented to Governor General Roland Michener by E.F. Brown, the acting master of the Royal Canadian Mint, on 22 December 1968.

Other: The Companion's insignia is detachable from the Chancellor's chain, although this is rarely done. The Chancellor's chain is worn primarily on special occasions, such as investitures and sometimes the opening of Parliament. The chain is housed in a large, red leatherette case whose lid is embossed with the insignia of the order in gold. The Chancellor's chain is returned to the government upon retirement.

Numbers: There have been seven Chancellors of the Order of Canada:

Roland Michener, PC, CC, CMM, CD, QC, 1967–1974
Jules Léger, PC, CC, CMM, CD, 1974–1980

Edward Schreyer, PC, CC, CMM, CD,
   1980–1985
Jeanne Sauvé, PC, CC, CMM, CD,
   1985–1990
Ramon Hnatyshyn, PC, CC, CMM, CD,
   QC, 1990–1995
Roméo LeBlanc, PC, CC, CMM, CD,
   1995–1999
Adrienne Clarkson, CC, CMM, COM, CD,
   1999–present

COMPANION OF THE ORDER OF CANADA

Origins: The Companion level of the Order of Canada serves as the highest honour that the Canadian Crown can bestow upon a citizen. It is the oldest, and understandably the most prized, part of the order.

The first recipient of the order was Roland Michener, who was invested by the Queen at Government House on 6 July 1967. The youngest Companion of the Order of Canada was Terry Fox.

Originally, the number of living companions was limited to 150 — not including ex-officio members. In 1995, this was increased to 165. From 1967 until 1995, a maximum of five Companions could be appointed each year, although a provision was made for fifty Companions to be appointed in the Centennial year — there was, after all, a significant backlog of worthy recipients, there having been no civilian honours list since 1946. Since 1995, the annual maximum has been fifteen.

Criteria: Awarded for outstanding achievement and merit of the highest degree, especially service to Canada or to humanity at large.

Companion of the Order of Canada

Top: Obverse
Centre: Reverse
Bottom: Lapel pin

Insignia: A gold stylized snowflake measuring 57 mm wide, covered in white enamel. The obverse bears a single red maple leaf in the centre, surrounded by a red band which contains the words *Desiderantes Meliorem Patriam* in gold. The entire band is surmounted by a St. Edward's Crown — which, on all Companion's insignia, is set with small precious stones. The reverse is also enamelled in white, and the word *Canada* appears in the centre; below it, a small rectangular box contains a three-digit number.

Suspension: A gold ball is mounted to the apex of the uppermost arm of the snowflake, and through this passes a small gold ring, through which passes a 30 mm straight hanger and the ribbon. Hallmarks can sometimes be found on the reverse of this hanger. The Companion's insignia is worn around the neck, although women have the option of wearing it on their left shoulder on a bow.

Ribbon: A white ribbon 38 mm wide, edged on each side with 9 mm of red. Recipients wear a red maple leaf on their undress ribbon.

Bars: None

Postnominals: Recipients are entitled to use the postnominals C.C.

Number of Awards: 417

Other: Insignia issued between 1967 and 1983 were manufactured by Garrard and Company, the Crown jewellers. The Companion's insignia was made of 18-karat gold.
From 1984 until 1996 the Companion's insignia was made by Rideau of St. Laurent, Quebec. The Rideau issues were made of 18-

karat gold until November 1993, when it was decided to change the composition to gold-plated sterling silver (to reduce the cost of the insignia). In 1996, Henry Birks & Sons began making the insignia, the frame of which continues to be gold-plated sterling silver. The manufacturing work on the Birks issues is done by Pressed Metal Products of British Columbia. Rideau has resumed manufacturing the insignia as of November 2004.

In mid-1984 the four small dots located in the circlet that bears the motto of the Order of Canada were replaced with a small quadrangle, because the enamel around the dots tended to flake off. In 2001, the thickness of the suspender was changed from 1.25 mm to 1.75 mm.

MEDAL OF COURAGE OF THE ORDER OF CANADA

Origins: The Medal of Courage was not part of the original Order of Canada proposal submitted to Cabinet in November 1966. It was added a month later, and was announced as part of the Order of Canada when the new honours system was unveiled in April 1967. However, the first Order of Canada honours only contained appointments of Companions and Medals of Service. The Government Decorations Committee — the body charged with administering the Medal of Courage — did not put forward any names, as prime minister Pearson wished for the first recipient of the Medal of Courage to be presented with the medal at a special event and not be lumped in with the other recipients of the Order of Canada.

There was to be no limit on the number of awards made annually.

Medal of Courage of the Order of Canada obverse

*Medal of Courage of the
Order of Canada reverse*

Originally, it was to be known as the Gallantry Medal of the Order of Canada, but the name was changed to Medal of Courage because it translates into French more easily. The government planned to continue using the Victoria Cross, George Cross and Queen's Commendation for Bravery as the principal bravery awards, while the Medal of Courage was to take the place of the George Medal. The criteria for the latter two medals were very similar.

Placing a gallantry award within an order was not unique, and it closely followed the pattern established by the Order of the British Empire, which included the Empire Gallantry Medal — an award that had itself been replaced by the George Cross in 1940. Despite this change, the Order of the British Empire continued to be awarded for gallantry from 1957–1974, and the last Canadian recipient was General Dextraze, who was made a Commander of the Order of the British Empire for his brave conduct during the 1964 United Nations Mission in the Congo.

In March 1968, Pearson decided that Canadians should no longer be eligible for British bravery awards — such as the Victoria Cross, George Cross and Queen's Commendation for Bravery. Suddenly, the Medal of Courage was to be elevated from an intermediate bravery award to one that would recognize all acts of bravery. This idea was almost immediately dismissed as impractical by officials at Government House, and a new proposal emerged to have the Medal of Courage divided into three levels. This too was rejected, and by October 1968 a proposal had emerged for the establishment of three separate bravery awards. It was not until 1972 that the final proposal was adopted. The Medal of Courage was abolished and replaced by the

Cross of Valour, the Star of Courage and the Medal of Bravery.

Criteria: Awarded to a person who performs an act of conspicuous courage in circumstances of great danger.

Insignia: A gold stylized snowflake measuring 34 mm across, the obverse depicting a single maple leaf enclosed within two circles and surmounted by a Royal crown. The reverse bears a single gold disc with the word *Courage* around the top of the disc, with four small dots in the base of the disc.

Suspension: A small, hollow silver ball at the apex of the uppermost arm of the snowflake, through which passes a gold ring.

Ribbon: A 34 mm white ribbon edged with 7 mm of red on each side. Recipients were to wear a gold maple leaf in the centre of their undress ribbon.

Bars: Subsequent awards were to be recognized with a single gold bar, bearing a maple leaf in the centre. No bars were ever manufactured.

Postnominals: Recipients were to be entitled to use the postnominals C.M.

Other: The insignia was made of gold-plated sterling silver, and was manufactured by Garrard and Company. Only twenty-four Medals of Courage were made (twenty men's issue, and four women's issue on bows).

The twenty-four Medals of Courage were delivered to Government House, contained within individual black leatherette cases stamped with "C.M." on the lid. On 23 February 1984, the Royal Canadian Mint melted eighteen of the Medals of Courage, leaving only six in existence. These are held by the Chancellery and other agencies of the Canadian government.

Number of Awards: None

MEDAL OF SERVICE OF THE ORDER OF CANADA

Medal of Service of the Order of Canada obverse

Medal of Service of the Order of Canada reverse

Origins: As with the Medal of Courage, the Medal of Service was not included in the early proposals made to Cabinet for the Order of Canada. As noted, Cabinet turned down Prime Minister Pearson's original proposal for a three-tiered Order of Canada on the grounds that it was elitist. As a partial remedy the Medal of Service was developed to serve as a junior version of the Companion level. It was added to the proposal for the Order of Canada in February 1967, and announced in April 1967 alongside the Companion of the Order of Canada and the Medal of Courage. Although part of the Order of Canada, it was called the Medal of Service so that Cabinet would approve it without suspecting that it was a different level of the same order. A limit of fifty Medals of Service could be awarded each year, with the exception of the Centennial year of 1967, in which provision was made for 100 Medals of Service to be awarded. There was no limit on the overall membership of the Medal of Service of the Order of Canada.

Almost immediately there were problems with the Medal of Service, as it was seen as inferior to the Companion level. In a few cases, people actually refused to accept the Medal of Service as they felt entitled to be appointed as a Companion. There was the added aspect that the plain silver Medal of Service looked quite austere compared with the 18-karat-gold-and-enamel Companion's insignia. In October 1968, at about the same time that a replacement for the Medal of Courage was being considered, the government and the Advisory Council of the Order of Canada tentatively agreed that the Medal of Service should be abolished and replaced by two new levels, Officer and Member. The restructuring of the Order of Canada was completed in 1972, and recipients of the Medal of Service were invited to exchange their SM insignia for that of an Officer of the Order of Canada.

Criteria: Awarded for achievement and merit of a high degree, especially service to Canada or to humanity at large.

Insignia: A silver stylized snowflake measuring 34 mm across, the obverse depicting a single maple leaf enclosed within two circles and surmounted by a Royal crown. The reverse bears a single silver disc with the word *Service* around the top, with four small dots in the base of the disc.

Ribbon: A 34 mm white ribbon edged with 7 mm of red on each side. Recipients were to wear a silver maple leaf in the centre of their undress ribbon.

Suspension: A small, hollow silver ball at the apex of the uppermost arm of the snowflake, through which passes a silver ring.

Bars: No bars could be awarded to the Medal of Service, although one could be elevated to the level of Companion. This occurred in three instances only.

Postnominals: Recipients were entitled to use the postnominals S.M.

Other: The insignia was made of sterling silver and manufactured by Garrard and Company. While 319 Medals of Service were approved by the governor general, only 294 were actually awarded. From 1967 to 1971, Garrard delivered a total of 300 Medals of Service to the Canadian government. On 23 February 1984, the Royal Canadian Mint melted 189 of the exchanged Medals of Service, leaving fewer than 120 in existence. The reverse lower arm of the medal was engraved with the name of the recipient in small block capitals. Medals awarded to men simply had their initials and surname (e.g., V.F. McADAM), while those awarded to women bore both their given name and surname (eg., ELSINORE BURNS). A number of unnamed examples are known to exist.

Number of Awards: 319 appointments, 294 actual awards

OFFICER OF THE ORDER OF CANADA

Origins: This level of the Order of Canada, instituted in March 1972 and made effective for 1 July 1972, is the successor to the Medal of Service. The award serves as recognition for significant lifetime contributions to Canada or to the international community. A maximum of sixty-four persons can be appointed each year. There is no limit on the overall membership.

Criteria: Made for achievement and merit of a high degree, especially service to Canada or to humanity at large.

*Officer of the Order of Canada
obverse*

Insignia: A gold stylized snowflake measuring 46 mm wide, covered in white enamel. The obverse bears a single gold maple leaf in the centre, surrounded by a red band which contains the words *Desiderantes Meliorem Patriam* in gold. The entire band is surmounted by a St. Edward's Crown. The reverse is plain brushed gold (silver gilt) with a raised disc bearing the word *Canada*, with a three- or four-digit number engraved below.

Suspension: A gold ball is mounted to the apex of the uppermost arm of the snowflake, and through this passes a small gold ring, through which passes a 20 mm straight hanger and the ribbon. Hallmarks can sometimes be found on the reverse of this hanger. The Officer's insignia is worn around the neck, although women have the option of wearing it on their left shoulder on a bow.

Ribbon: A white ribbon 38 mm wide, edged on each side with 9 mm of red. Recipients wear a gold maple leaf on their undress ribbon.

Bars: None, although an Officer can be elevated to Companion.

Postnominals: Recipients are entitled to use the postnominals O.C.

Other: Sterling hallmarks and the maker's name are impressed on the lower reverse arm of the insignia. From 1972 until 1983 Garrard and Company manufactured the officer's insignia. In 1983 Rideau of St. Laurent, Quebec, began manufacturing the insignia and continued to do so until 1996. From 1996 to 2004 Birks manufactured the

Top: Officer of the Order of Canada reverse
Bottom: Officer of the Order of Canada lapel pin

insignia. Rideau has resumed manufacturing the insignia as of November 2004.

Number of Awards: 1,655

Member of the Order of Canada obverse

MEMBER OF THE ORDER OF CANADA

Origins: This level was added after the 1972 restructuring of the Order of Canada. In many ways it is the most important and most inclusive level in the order, being that it is awarded for services of a local or very specific nature. Pearson intended the Order of Canada to be awarded to people who had made contributions to Canada not only at the national level, but also at the most local level. When the Advisory Council of the Order of Canada began to review the order's structure in 1968, it was apparent that those who had made significant contributions at the local level or in a specialized field were not eligible to be appointed as Companions of the order, nor did they qualify to be awarded the Medal of Service, as both required contribution of a national or international calibre. Fewer than ten per cent of those who were awarded the Medal of Service had made local contributions. A maximum of 136 persons can be appointed each year. There is no limit on the overall membership.

Criteria: Made for distinguished service in or to a particular locality, group or field of activity.

Insignia: A silver stylized snowflake measuring 38 mm wide, covered in white enamel. The obverse bears a single silver maple leaf in the centre, surrounded by a red band that contains the words *Desiderantes Meliorem Patriam* in silver. The entire band is surmounted by a St. Edward's Crown. The reverse is plain brushed silver with a raised disc bearing the word *Canada*, with a three- or four-digit number engraved below.

Suspension: A silver ball is mounted at the apex of the uppermost arm of the snowflake, and through this passes a silver ring and the ribbon. The member's insignia is worn on the left breast, although women have the option of wearing it on their left shoulder on a bow if they have no other medals.

Ribbon: A white ribbon 38 mm wide, edged on each side with 9 mm of red. Recipients wear a silver maple leaf on their undress ribbon.

Bars: None, although a member can be elevated to Officer or Companion. To date, only one person has been elevated from a member to Companion.

Postnominals: Recipients are entitled to use the postnominals C.M.

Other: Sterling hallmarks and the maker's name are impressed on the lower reverse arm of the insignia. From 1972 until 1982 Garrard and Company manufactured the officer's insignia. In 1982 Rideau of St. Laurent, Quebec, began manufacturing the insignia and continued to do so until 1996. From 1996 to 2004 Birks manufactured the insignia. Rideau has resumed manufacturing the insignia as of November 2004.

Number of Awards: 2,986

Top: Member of the Order of Canada reverse
Bottom: Member of the Order of Canada lapel pin

SUCCESSIVE ENLARGEMENTS AND CHANGES
TO THE ORDER OF CANADA, 1967–2003

	Companion	Officer	Member
1967	50 annual (150 max.)	100 (Medal of Service)	None
1972	5 annual (150 max.)	40	80 (new level)
1983	5 annual (150 max.)	46	92
1994	5 annual (150 max.)	50	100
1995	15 annual (165 max.)	50	100
1997	Change in policy towards honorary appointments		
1998	15 annual (165 max.)	52	106
1999	15 annual (165 max.)	64	136
2000	Membership in the advisory council increased by five		

HALLMARKS ON THE REVERSE OF THE ORDER OF CANADA

Manufacturer	Companion	Officer	Member
Garrard and Company	Occasionally a hallmark on the hanger (G&Co), with British 18k proof marks	G&Co, along with British sterling proof marks for Birmingham	G&Co, along with British sterling proof marks for Birmingham
Rideau *Rideau Issue Order of Canada reverse*	18k is marked on the reverse of the mounting ball at the top of the insignia. Early issues made of sterling silver are un-hallmarked. Those made after 2004 are laser engraved with a silver hallmark on the side on the lower arm. RIDEAU +R STER	RIDEAU + R STER	RIDEAU + R STER
Birks	Unhallmarked	BIRKS STERL	BIRKS STERL

CHAPTER 6

The Order of Military Merit

Special orders are a product of the Middle Ages, when they were developed to recognize defenders of the realm. To be successful in the civil sphere, one was invariably required to be proficient in the art of war; thus the concept of honours in general finds its root in military service. The most famous of these military orders is Britain's Order of the Bath. Thought to have been established in 1128, it is probably the oldest order of knighthood in the world. Over time, however, the Order of the Bath was split into a civil and military division, and Canadians would go on to be recognized with it — most notably Sir John A. Macdonald, who was made a Knight Commander of the Order of the Bath in 1867 and was later elevated to a Knight Grand Cross of the Order of the Bath. The military division of the Order of the Bath includes some of Canada's most prominent military leaders, Sir Arthur Currie, Sir William Otter and Sir Richard Turner were all appointed Knight Commanders prior to or during the First World War.

Other military orders of antiquity include France's Royal Military Order of St. Louis. Founded by Louis XIV on 5 April 1693, it was awarded to those of the Catholic faith who had rendered distinguished services to the Crown and to France. It was the principal honour bestowed on members of the Canadian militia and French army serving in Canada prior to 1759.

It is primarily in these two orders that we find the basis for the structure and ethos of the Order of Military Merit. Both consisted of three levels and were awarded for exceptionally meritorious service; both also have a direct connection to Canadian history. Although scarcely thirty years old, then, the Order of Military Merit can claim a much more ancient heritage. Within these traditional orders, military rank determined which level one could be awarded. Generals were usually appointed at the Knight Grand Cross, while majors were made companions or chevaliers.

It is hard to believe that, for nearly thirty years between the end of the Second World War and the establishment of the Order of Military Merit in 1972, members of what are today the Canadian Forces were not eligible for any honours or awards other than for bravery or long service. This vacuum of honours for meritorious service was one of the main catalysts that prompted the creation of the Order of Canada, and the role of the Canadian Forces in pushing for a uniquely Canadian honours system should not be underestimated.

With the foundation of the Order of Canada in 1967, one would assume that the military's desire for a system of honours and awards had been met. This was, however, not the case. Early proposals for the order, dating back to 1944, had suggested that it include civilian and military divisions, a concept that was derived from two of the main British Orders of Chivalry, the Order of the Bath and the Order of the British Empire. These recommendations were not followed. Also, in 1966, the Department of National Defence had developed proposals for a Forces Meritorious Cross and Forces Meritorious Medal, but these plans were shelved in favour of the Order of Canada, which was viewed as the best solution to the absence of a system of military exemplary service awards. The general feeling within DND was that it would therefore be used to recognize both civil and military achievements, in a fashion similar to France's *Légion d'Honneur*. As it turned out, in its early days the Order of Canada was being conferred almost exclusively as a civilian honour, and those military officers who *were* admitted to the new order were either retired or being recognized for nonmilitary accomplishments.

Within six months of the first investiture ceremony in 1967, changes to the order's structure were being sought. The body that was charged with making improvements — the Working Group on Honours and Awards — briefly considered the possibility of dividing the Order of Canada into military and civil divisions, although this idea was not well received by the order's advisory council.[3] There was consensus that a separate award for the military was needed, because "recognition of distinguished service has important moral implications."[4]

As a result of a submission to Cabinet seeking approval for the award of the Order of the British Empire (three MBEs and two BEMs) to Canadians for service in United Nations missions, Cabinet agreed in principle on 5 May 1966 to an examination of the desirability of establishing Canadian awards for meritorious military service. The government's Decorations Committee considered a related proposal in early December 1969, and a memorandum was sent to Cabinet later that month. Cabinet responded by requesting a more detailed proposal.

The solution emerged in a report of the Decorations Committee issued in January 1970. That report proposed the creation of a new order, consisting of three levels, to recognize "Military Merit."[5] By December 1971 the idea had evolved into the Order of Military Merit, which was to consist of three levels: Commander, Officer and Member. Recipients of the new order were to be selected by a special council, composed of one member appointed by the governor general and five others who are members of the Canadian Armed Forces and are appointed by the chief of defence staff. There are strict limits on the total number of annual awards, capped at one-tenth of one per cent of the Canadian Forces' strength. Of these awards, only 6 per cent can be made at the Commander level, 30 per cent at the Officer level, and the remaining 64 per cent at the Member level. Non-Canadians can be appointed as honorary members of the order, and General Richard Myers of the United States Air Force was the first to be appointed — as an honorary CMM, in February 2005. To date there has also been one termination of an appointment and one resignation from the order.

The motto of the order is *Officium Ante Commodum*. The name of the order can be traced back to the Kingdom of France, where the *Ordre du Mérite Militaire* was awarded to Protestant military officers who had rendered outstanding service to the Crown.[6]

As with the Order of Canada, the Queen is Sovereign of the Order and she wears a special jewelled Sovereign's insignia. The Sovereign's badge was presented to the Queen in July 1973 by Governor General Roland

Prototype of the Order of Military Merit

Michener aboard the Royal yacht *Britannia* while it was anchored off of Kingston, Ontario. The governor general is Chancellor of the Order and usually wears the CMM on a ribbon around his neck or, in the case of ladies, on a bow worn on the left shoulder. A special Chancellor's chain also exists, and it is usually only worn during investiture ceremonies.

The order consists of two divisions: the general division, for members of the Canadian Armed Forces, and the honorary division, which is open to members of allied foreign armed forces.

Recipients of the Order of Military Merit are given a certificate bearing their name, the signature of the governor general and the secretary general of the order, and the seal of the order.

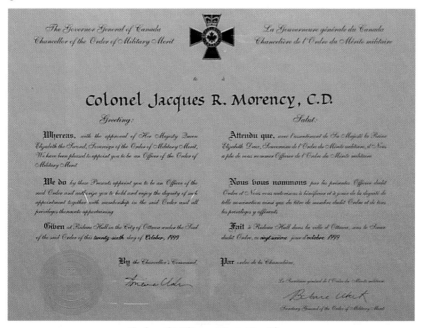

Order of Military Merit Certificate

The insignia of the order was designed by Bruce Beatty. Insignia issued between 1972 and 1984 were manufactured by Spink and Son of London and bear an English silver hallmark. Rideau of St. Laurent, Quebec, made the insignia from 1983 until 1994, and they are currently made by Birks & Sons, although most of the work is done by Pressed Metal Products of British Columbia. All of the Spink and Son issues of the CMM were made of 18-karat gold. The CMM insignia made by Rideau were made of 18-karat gold until November 1993, when sterling silver was specified to cut costs. The Officer's and Member's insignia are also made of sterling silver.

SOVEREIGN OF THE ORDER OF MILITARY MERIT

Origins: As with the Order of Canada and most national honours, the Sovereign is presented with a special insignia.

Insignia: An 18-karat gold four-armed cross, enamelled over scalloped machine work in translucent blue. Between each of the arms, a rectangular diamond is set between two just-off-square diamonds. In the centre of the cross, there is a maple leaf surmounted by an annulus, both of which are set with calibre rubies pavé. On the annulus the words *Merit — Merite — Canada* appear in finely pierced gold. Above the cross there is a gold St. Edward's Crown with seven diamonds set in the ermine, three in each of the fleurs-de-lys and a larger one in the orb. On the arches are twenty-one pearls. The base is set with a sapphire, two emeralds and two rubies. The cap is enamelled red.

Other: The Sovereign's insignia was manufactured by Garrard and Company, under the supervision of Crown Jeweller William Summers. It was housed in a blue leatherette case lined with white satin and blue velvet.

CHANCELLOR OF THE ORDER OF MILITARY MERIT

Origins: As with the Order of Canada and most national honours, the senior official is presented with insignia of office

Insignia: A chain of ten maple leaves alternating with four naval crowns (representing the

Sovereign's insignia of the Order of Military Merit

*Chancellor's Chain of the
Order of Military Merit*

*Case for the Chancellor's Chain
of the Order of Military Merit*

navy), four mural crowns defaced with a maple leaf (representing the army), and four aerial crowns composed of wings (representing the air force). The chain is completed by a centre device in the form of the shield from the Arms of Canada ensigned by the Royal Crown, each in their proper colours. The governor general's Commander's insignia is hung from this device. The entire chain was made of 9-karat gold and bears hallmarks for London, 1972. The chancellor's chain was made by Spink and Son of London. It is housed in a large blue leatherette case whose lid is embossed with the insignia of the order. The interior of the case is lined with white satin and red velvet.

Other: As the governor general only wears the Chancellor's chain on special occasions, such as investitures, the insignia of the Order of Military Merit is detachable so that the governor general can wear his or her Commander's insignia from a ribbon. The chancellor's chain is returned to the government upon retirement. The chain, like the other insignia of the order, was designed by Bruce Beatty.

Numbers: There have been seven Chancellors of the Order of Military Merit.

Roland Michener, 1972–1974
Jules Léger, 1974–1980
Edward Schreyer, 1980–1985
Jeanne Sauvé, 1985–1990
Ramon Hnatyshyn, 1990–1995
Roméo LeBlanc, 1995–1999
Adrienne Clarkson, 1999–present

PRINCIPAL COMMANDER OF THE ORDER OF MILITARY MERIT

Origins: In most national military orders, the chief of the armed forces is usually an ex-officio member. In Canada this means that the chief of the defence staff (CDS) serves as the Principal Commander of the Order of Military Merit. Most chiefs of the defence staff have been either Officers or Commanders of the Order of Military Merit prior to their appointment as CDS; nevertheless, they are presented with a special insignia for wear during investitures and state occasions.

Principal Commander's Chain of the Order of Military Merit

Insignia: A chain of ten maple leaves alternating with four naval crowns (representing the navy), four mural crowns defaced with a maple leaf (representing the army) and four aerial crowns composed of wings (representing the air force). The chain is completed by a centre device in the form of the arms of the Canadian Forces in their proper colours. The Principal Commander's insignia is hung from this device. The entire chain was made of 9-karat gold and bears hallmarks for London, 1972. The Principal Commander's chain of the Order of Military Merit was made by Spink and Son. It is housed in a large blue leatherette case whose lid is embossed with the insignia of the order. The interior of the case is lined with white satin and red velvet.

Other: As the chief of the defence staff only wears the Principal Commander's chain on special occasions, such as investitures and sometimes the opening of Parliament, the insignia of the Order of Military Merit is detachable so that the Commander's insignia can be worn from a ribbon. The chain is returned to the government upon retirement. The chain, like the other insignia of the order, was designed by Bruce Beatty.

Numbers: There have been thirteen Principal Commanders and one acting Principal Commander.

General F.R. Sharp, CMM, DFC, CD, 1972
General J.A. Dextraze, CC, CBE, CMM, DSO, CD, 1972–1977
Admiral R.H. Falls, CMM, CD, 1977–1980
General R.M. Withers, CMM, CD, 1980–1983
General G.C. Theriault, CMM, CD, 1983–1986
General P. Manson, CMM, CD, 1986–1989
General A.J.G.D. de Chastelain, OC, CMM, CD, CH, 1989–1993
Admiral J. Anderson, CMM, CD, 1993–1994
General A.J.G.D. de Chastelain, OC, CMM, CD, CH, 1994–1995
General J. Boyle, CMM, CD, 1995
Vice Admiral L.E. Murray, CMM, CD (acting), 1996–1997
General M. Baril, CMM, CD, 1997–2001
General R.R. Henault, CMM, CD, 2001–2005
General R. Hillier, CMM, CD, 2005–present

COMMANDER OF THE ORDER OF MILITARY MERIT

Criteria: Appointments are made for outstanding meritorious service in duties of great responsibility. This level is awarded to those holding the rank of brigadier general/commodore or above.

Insignia: A blue enamelled cross pattée in gold; in the centre of the insignia is a circlet surmounted by a Royal crown, with a red maple leaf in the centre. The circlet is circumscribed by the words *Merit — Mérite — Canada.* The reverse is plain and bears a three-digit number and silver hallmark.

Suspension: The top of the insignia has a small ball in the centre through which a ring passes, through which a 25 mm hanger passes. The insignia is worn around the neck.

Ribbon: A blue ribbon 38 mm wide, edged on either side by 5 mm of gold. Commanders wear a miniature insignia of the CMM in the centre of the ribbon (denoted by a red maple leaf in the centre of the miniature insignia). Prior to 1983 Commanders simply wore a red maple leaf in the centre of their ribbon.

Bars: There are no provisions for additional awards.

Postnominals: Recipients are entitled to use the postnominal initials C.M.M.

Other: In terms of promotions within the order, only General Maurice Baril has held all three levels (MMM, OMM, CMM) as well as serving as Principal Commander of the order. A recipient who is elevated is only entitled to use one set of postnominals.

Number of Awards: 182 (including one honorary appointment: General Richard Myers, USAF).

Commander of the Order of Military Merit

Commander of the Order of Military Merit lapel pin

*Officer of the
Order of Military Merit*

*Officer of the
Order of Military Merit
lapel pin*

OFFICER OF THE ORDER OF MILITARY MERIT

Criteria: Appointments are made for outstanding meritorious service in duties of responsibility. This level is primarily awarded to officers between the ranks of major and colonel. There have been instances where a chief warrant officer of the Canadian Forces has been awarded the OMM on account of the significance of his responsibilities.

Insignia: A blue enamelled cross pattée in gold, and in the centre of the insignia is a circlet surmounted by a Royal Crown, with a gold maple leaf in centre, the circlet is circumscribed by the words *Merit — Mérite — Canada.* The reverse is plain and bears a silver hallmark.

Suspension: The top of the insignia has a small half-circle, through which a ring passes attaching it to a gold laurelled bar. The OMM is worn on the left breast.

Ribbon: A blue ribbon 38 mm wide, edged on either side by 5 mm of gold. Officers wear a miniature insignia of the OMM in the centre of the ribbon (denoted by a gold maple leaf in the centre of the miniature insignia). Until 1983, Officers wore a gold maple leaf in the centre of their ribbon.

Bars: There are no provisions for additional awards, although one can be elevated within the order.

Postnominals: Recipients are entitled to use the postnominal initials O.M.M.

Other: An issue number is typically engraved on the edge of the lower arm. The silver hallmarks and maker's name vary according to the manufacturer. Those made by Spink and Son are hallmarked on the reverse of the suspension bar, with the number engraved on the edge of the lowermost arm. Those made by Rideau and Birks are marked on the reverse of the cross, with the serial number engraved in the centre of the reverse.

Number of Awards: 900

MEMBER OF THE ORDER OF MILITARY MERIT

Criteria: Appointments are made for exceptional service and performance of duty. Awarded to persons from non-commissioned ranks and junior officers below the rank of major/lieutenant commander.

Insignia: A blue enamelled cross pattée in silver. In the centre of the insignia is a circlet surmounted by a Royal crown, with a silver maple leaf in the middle. The circlet is circumscribed by the words *Merit — Mérite — Canada*. The reverse is plain and bears a silver hallmark.

Suspension: The top of the insignia has a small half-circle through which a ring passes, attaching it to a silver laurelled bar. The insignia is worn on the left breast.

Ribbon: A blue ribbon 38 mm wide, edged on either side by 5 mm of gold. Members wear a miniature insignia of the MMM in the centre of the ribbon (denoted by a silver maple leaf in the centre of the miniature insignia). Prior to

Member of the Order of Military Merit

Member of the Order of Military Merit lapel pin

*Spink Order of Military Merit,
standard blue*

*Spink Order of Military Merit,
Prussian blue*

*Spink Order of Military Merit
reverse*

Spink hallmarks

1983, Members simply wore a silver maple leaf in the centre of their ribbon.

Bars: There are no provisions for additional awards, although one can be elevated within the order.

Postnominals: Recipients are entitled to use the postnominal initials M.M.M.

Other: An issue number is typically engraved on the edge of the lower arm. Those made by Spink and Son are hallmarked on the reverse of the suspension bar, with the number engraved on the edge of the lowermost arm. Those made by Rideau and Birks are hallmarked on the reverse of the cross, with the serial number engraved in the centre of the reverse.

Number of Awards: 2,116

CHAPTER 7

The Order of Merit of the Police Forces

As the Order of Merit of the Police Forces is the most recent addition to the family of Canadian honours, there is little direct history to be recounted about it. It is notable that Canada is one of the few countries to possess a separate order for its police services; in most other nations, outstanding service in the police force is recognized through the award of a civil order, such as the Order of the British Empire in Britain or the Order of National Merit in France.

Prior to the centennial of the Royal Canadian Mounted Police in 1973, there were questions as to whether members of the country's various police forces could be made eligible for the recently established Order of Military Merit. The idea was quickly scrapped, although it was not without logic. In May 1935, Major General Sir James MacBrien, the Commissioner of the RCMP, was made a Knight Commander of the Order of the Bath, military division. Thus there was a precedent for military awards being used to recognize the police.

Following the establishment of the Police Exemplary Service Medal in 1982, the Canadian Association of Police Chiefs, which had lobbied for more than a decade, seemed satisfied with the single award, although by mid-1996 there was hope that a new civil order, aside from the Order of Canada, would be created and opened up to the police. Instead, an order was established solely for the police, as the government did not wish to create a broad new civil order for fear it would affect the public perception of the Order of Canada.

The new order was approved by the Queen in October 2000 and was officially announced by Governor General Adrienne Clarkson on 19 March 2001. In most respects, it is the Order of Military Merit in disguise. Even the insignia is identical to that of the Order of Military Merit, and can only be distinguished by its different ribbon. These facts had the initial effect of causing some dissension within the Department of National Defence, although this seems to have dissipated.

Recipients of the Order of Merit of the Police Forces receive a certificate bearing their name, the signature of the governor general and the secretary general of the order, and the seal of the order.

As with the Order of Canada and Order of Military Merit, the Queen is Sovereign of the order and the governor general acts as Chancellor during his or her term. The commissioner of the RCMP is the Principal Commander of the order during his or her time in office.

Appointees are selected by the Advisory Committee of the Order of Merit of the Police Forces, which consists of the president of the Canadian Association of Chiefs of Police (who acts as chair), the deputy commissioner of the RCMP, one person who is the head of a provincial police force (Ontario or Québec), three municipal or regional chiefs of police, the president of the Canadian Police Association, and the deputy secretary of the Chancellery.

Provision is made for the appointment of one honorary Commander, Officer and Member per year. The constitution of the order also sets out a yearly maximum number of awards: one-tenth of one percent of the average number of persons who were employees of police forces during the particular year. Within this quota are further limits on the types of awards. Elevation within the order is permitted. Investitures are held once a year.

SOVEREIGN OF THE ORDER OF MERIT OF THE POLICE FORCES

Origins: As with the Order of Canada and most national honours, the Sovereign is presented with a special insignia. While a special Sovereign's insignia was made for both the Order of Canada and Order of Military Merit, such an insignia has yet to be made for the Order of Merit of the Police Forces. And since the insignia of the Order of Merit of the Police Forces is identical to that of the Order of Military Merit (aside from the ribbon), it is unlikely that such an insignia will be made. It seems unfortunate that, while both the Chancellor and Principal Commander of the Order of Merit of the Police Forces have been presented with special insignia, the Queen, as Sovereign of the order, has not.

Insignia: None to date.

Numbers: There has been one Sovereign of the Order of Merit of the Police Forces: Queen Elizabeth II.

CHANCELLOR OF THE ORDER OF MERIT OF THE POLICE FORCES

Origins: While every order has a titular head, it has also been a tradition for there to be a senior official know as either a grand master or chancellor. As the governor general is the Queen's representative in Canada, it was decided that he or she should also serve as the chancellor of the order and perform most of the investiture and administrative duties relating to certain aspects of the order. Following the precedent set by the Order of Canada, it was decided that the term chancellor should be used for the second-highest official of the order.

When a governor general retires from the office, he or she ceases to be Chancellor of the Order of Merit of the Police Forces, but remains a Commander of the order.

Insignia: A neck chain composed of fourteen gold natural maple leaves and thirteen silver shields, alternating and joined by gold chain links. Each of the silver shields is defaced with a provincial or territorial flower in gold. The chain is completed by a centre device in the form of the shield from the Arms of Canada ensigned by the Royal crown, each in their proper colours. The Commander's insignia is hung from this device. The Chancellor's chain of the Order of Merit of the Police Forces was made by Pressed Metal Products of British Columbia.

Chancellor's Chain of the Order of Merit of the Police Forces

Other: As the governor general only wears the Chancellor's chain on special occasions, such as investitures, the insignia of the Order of Merit of the Police Forces is detachable so that it can be worn from a ribbon. The Chancellor's chain is returned to the government upon retirement.

Numbers: There has been one chancellor of the Order of Merit of the Police Forces: Adrienne Clarkson, 2000–present

PRINCIPAL COMMANDER OF THE ORDER OF MERIT OF THE POLICE FORCES

Origins: The Order of Merit of the Police Forces is almost entirely based on the Order of Military Merit. Thus, following this pattern, the head of the national police force (the Royal Canadian Mounted Police) is ex-officio the Principal Commander of the Order of Merit of the Police Forces.

Insignia: A neck chain composed of fourteen gold natural maple leaves and thirteen silver shields, alternating and joined by gold chain links. Each of the silver shields is defaced with a provincial or territorial flower in gold. The chain is completed by a centre device from which the Commander's insignia is hung. The Principal Commander's chain of the Order of Military Merit was made by Pressed Metal Products of British Columbia.

Other: As the commissioner of the RCMP only wears the Principal Commander's chain on special occasions, such as investitures and sometimes the opening of Parliament, the insignia of the Order of Merit of the Police Forces is detachable so that it can be worn from a ribbon. The Chancellor's Chain is returned to the government upon retirement.

Numbers: There has been one Principal Commander of the Order of Merit of the Police Forces: Commissioner Giuliano Zaccardelli, COM.

COMMANDER OF THE ORDER OF MERIT OF THE POLICE FORCES

Criteria: The Commander level of the order is awarded for outstanding meritorious service and demonstrated leadership in duties of great responsibility and over an extended period.

Insignia: A blue enamelled cross pattée in gold. In the centre of the insignia is a circlet surmounted by a Royal crown, with a red maple leaf in the centre. The circlet is circumscribed by the words *Merit — Mérite — Canada.* The reverse is plain and bears a three-digit number and silver hallmark.

Suspension: The top of the insignia has a small ball in the centre through which a ring passes, through which a 25 mm hanger passes. The insignia is worn around the neck.

Ribbon: Consists of equal proportions of blue, gold and blue. Commanders wear a miniature insignia of the COM in the centre of the undress ribbon. The maple leaf in the centre of the Order of Merit of the Police Forces insignia — as worn on the ribbon and lapel — bears a natural maple leaf so as to

Top: Commander of the Order of Merit of the Police Forces obverse
Centre: Reverse
Bottom: Lapel pin

differentiate it from the stylized maple leaf used by the Order of Military Merit.

Bars: There are no provisions for additional awards.

Postnominals: Recipients are entitled to use the postnominal initials C.O.M.

Other: Of the maximum number of appointments that may be made to the order each year (one-tenth of one per cent of those on police forces), no more than 6 per cent may be made at the Commander level.

Number of Awards: 10

OFFICER OF THE ORDER OF MERIT OF THE POLICE FORCES

Criteria: Officers are appointed for outstanding meritorious service in duties of responsibility over an extended period.

Insignia: A blue enamelled cross pattée in gold. In the centre of the insignia is a circlet surmounted by a Royal crown, with a gold maple leaf in the centre, circumscribed by the words *Merit — Mérite — Canada*. The reverse is plain and bears a silver hallmark, and an issue number is typically engraved on the edge of the lower arm.

Suspension: The top of the insignia has a small half-circle through which a ring passes, attaching it to a gold laurelled bar. The insignia is worn on the left breast.

Ribbon: Consists of equal proportions of blue,

Officer of the Order of Merit of the Police Forces obverse

gold and blue. Officers wear a miniature insignia of the OOM in the centre of the undress ribbon.

Bars: There are no provisions for additional awards, although one can be elevated within the order.

Postnominals: Recipients are entitled to use the postnominal initials O.O.M.

Other: Of the maximum number of appointments that may be made to the order each year (one-tenth of one per cent of those on police forces), no more than 30 per cent may be made at the Officer level.

Number of Awards: 34

Top: Officer of the Order of Merit of the Police Forces reverse Bottom: Lapel pin

MEMBER OF THE ORDER OF MERIT OF THE POLICE FORCES

Criteria: Members are appointed for exceptional service or performance of duty over an extended period.

Insignia: A blue enamelled cross pattée in silver. In the centre of the insignia is a circlet surmounted by a Royal crown, with a silver maple leaf in the centre, circumscribed by the words *Merit — Mérite — Canada*. The reverse is plain and bears a silver hallmark, and an issue number is typically engraved on the edge of the lower arm.

Suspension: The top of the insignia has a small half-circle through which a ring passes, attaching it to a silver laurelled bar. The insignia is worn on the left breast.

Member of the Order of Merit of the Police Forces obverse

Top: Member of the Order of Merit of the Police Forces reverse
Bottom: Lapel pin

Ribbon: Consists of equal proportions of blue, gold and blue. Members wear a miniature insignia of the MOM in the centre of the undress ribbon.

Bars: There are no provisions for additional awards, although one can be elevated within the order.

Postnominals: Recipients are entitled to use the postnominal initials M.O.M.

Other: The annual limit is set at the maximum number of awards available to be conferred (one-tenth of one per cent of those employed by police forces), *less* the number of Commanders and Officers appointed that year. In other words, once the number of Commanders and Officers is known, the remainder of the available appointments may be made at the Member level.

Number of Awards: 53

CHAPTER 8

The Queen's Personal Honours

While all honours in Canada emanate from the Sovereign, the Queen has little direct control over who receives the bulk of Canadian honours and awards. Although she approves the awarding of the Order of Canada and various bravery decorations, there is no known instance of the Queen personally nominating a person or requesting that a certain award be made or withheld. This falls in line with the constitutional position of the Sovereign as being able to advise her ministers, but not to make actual policy.

Nevertheless, the Queen does possess four separate honours which she can bestow upon Canadians. These are the Order of Merit, the Royal Victorian Chain, the non-titular levels of the Royal Victorian Order and the Royal Victorian Medal. The honours list is generally compiled by the Queen's Canadian secretary and submitted directly to her. This unusual protocol is in place in part because of the highly limited number of awards bestowed, and because of the type of service — personal service to the Queen or the Canadian Crown — being recognized. However, consent from the Canadian government is usually sought when the Queen wishes to bestow the Order of Merit or Royal Victorian Chain upon a Canadian.

The Order of the Companions of Honour has been included in this chapter, in part because of the historic connection between this order and Canada, and the fact that there are instances where the award has been initiated by the Sovereign and not the prime minister (of the United Kingdom or Canada), as is usually the process. Thus the CH falls into a sort of grey area within the Canadian honours system.

The power to grant honours is considered part of the Royal prerogative and the residual powers of the Crown. Over the past five hundred years the power of the Sovereign has gradually been eroded by elected officials, and this also applies to the Sovereign's power to bestow honours. By the end of the nineteenth century the Sovereign had lost control over almost all of the various British orders of chivalry. Queen

Victoria was unable to draw up honours lists, as this task had, through constitutional convention, been delegated to the prime minister and other senior ministers in the British government.

In 1896 Queen Victoria established the Royal Victorian Order, a special order of chivalry over which she as Sovereign possessed complete control. No prime minister or other government official submits names for the Royal Victorian Order; selection is done by a committee within the Royal household, and the proposed honours list is then sent to the Queen. This in part explains why it is so carefully awarded. The order consists of five levels: Knight/Dame Grand Cross, Knight/Dame Commander, Commander, Lieutenant (known until 1984 as Member Fourth Class) and Member. Attached to the order is the Royal Victorian Medal, which is awarded in three grades: gold, silver and bronze.

King Edward VII expanded upon his mother's institution, establishing the Royal Victorian Chain and the Order of Merit in 1902. The Royal Victorian Chain is awarded as "a pre-eminent mark of the Sovereign's esteem and affection," while the Order of Merit is bestowed for "exceptionally meritorious service." These two awards remain amongst the most senior and most exclusive in the Commonwealth. Needless to say, both are sparingly bestowed.

In 1946, King George VI regained complete control over the Order of the Garter and the Order of the Thistle. Because they confer the title "Sir," no Canadian has ever been appointed to these orders. Vincent Massey was to be made a Knight of the Garter in 1959, but the Diefenbaker government refused to allow him to accept the award because it was a knighthood.

The Order of Merit and the Royal Victorian Chain have proven very useful in the Canadian context, where titular honours such as knighthoods and peerages are prohibited. On no fewer than two occasions William Lyon Mackenzie King was offered a knighthood, but in each instance he refused. King had a curious phobia of honours and therefore had no desire for a title. King George VI was well aware of this, yet he desperately wanted to recognize his Canadian prime minister after more than twenty years of exemplary service. Other leaders during the Second World War, such as Winston Churchill and South Africa's Jan Smuts, had been awarded the Order of Merit, and George VI decided that Mackenzie King should join them. After several days of contemplation and introspection, King decided to accept the Order of Merit. Churchill and Smuts would later joke with him that OM stood for "the Old Man Order."

The Royal Victorian Chain proved useful in the case of Vincent Massey, whom the Queen wished to appoint a Knight of the Garter — a move that would have made him the first from an overseas Dominion. Both the St. Laurent and Diefenbaker governments refused to allow the Queen to make the award. In place of the Order of the Garter, then, Massey became only the second person of non-Royal blood to be awarded the Royal Victorian Chain. It was Massey's most treasured honour.

The Royal Victorian Order was awarded to Canadians from its inception until 1946. It was only in 1972, with the restructuring of the Canadian honours system, that awards of the Royal Victorian Order resumed. Appropriately, the first Canadian to receive the Royal Victorian Order after the restructuring was Esmond Butler, secretary to the governor general, who had been instrumental in the creation of the Order of Canada and the Canadian Bravery Awards.

Canadians have also been appointed Knights Grand Cross and Knight Commanders of the Royal Victorian Order, although not for nearly a century: Lord Mount Stephen and Lord Strathcona, two of Canada's great railway builders, were both made GCVOs; Lord Shaughnessy, another railway man, was made a KCVO. (King Edward VII seemed to have a real affection for Canadian railway barons!) Canadians who went on to serve in the British government, such as Sir Edward Peacock and Sir Edwin Leather, were also admitted to the order, as a GCVO and KCVO respectively. During the 1939 Royal visit of King George VI and Queen Elizabeth, Canada's governor general, Lord Tweedsmuir, was made a GCVO on the Royal train as it travelled across Canada — making him the first person to have been knighted in a moving train.

Today, the Order of Merit, the Royal Victorian Chain and the Royal Victorian Order remain part of the broader Canadian honours system. Although no Canadian currently holds the Order of Merit or the Royal Victorian Chain, it remains the Queen's constitutional prerogative to bestow these non-titular honours. Every year, approximately ten Canadians are appointed to the Royal Victorian Order, primarily in recognition of exemplary service to the governor general or a lieutenant governor.

Mackenzie King's
Order of Merit GVIR Issue
Top: Obverse
Bottom: Reverse

Order of Merit Ribbon

THE ORDER OF MERIT

Origins: Founded by King Edward VII on 23 September 1902. It is the most exclusive non-titular order in the Commonwealth, being limited to twenty-four members. It has typically been reserved for those who have rendered "exceptionally meritorious service," and in the Canadian context this has usually meant most outstanding service of international magnitude. Three Canadians have been admitted to the order, and while no Canadian has received it since 1971, it remains a Commonwealth award for which Canadians are eligible.

Insignia: A gold eight-pointed cross of red and blue enamel. Within a wreath set upon a centre of blue enamel, the motto of the order, *For Merit,* appears in gold letters. The reverse also bears a laurel wreath, with the Royal cypher in the centre. The entire insignia is surmounted by a gold Tudor crown, set with seed pearls. The insignia is manufactured by John Pinches of London. Military recipients of the order have a slightly different insignia in that crossed swords are added. To date there have been no awards of the military OM to a Canadian, although a number of governors general received the OM with swords (including the Duke of Connaught and Lord Alexander).

Suspension: A ring passes through the top of the Crown, through which a 20 mm suspension loop passes, through which the ribbon passes.

Ribbon: 50 mm in width, half Garter blue and half Bath red.

Criteria: Any citizen of the Commonwealth who has rendered particularly outstanding service in the military, or exceptionally meritorious service towards the advancement of art, literature and science, qualifies. In the Canadian context it has been used to recognize outstanding service, which in other parts of the Commonwealth would usually be recognized through the bestowal of a knighthood.

Bars: None

Postnominals: Recipients are entitled to use the postnominals O.M.

Other: Recipients are also given a certificate bearing their name, signed by the Queen and embossed with the seal of the order.

Number Awarded to Canadians: 3[7]

The Right Honourable William Lyon Mackenzie King, PC, OM, CMG, 1947
Colonel, Dr. Wilder Penfield, OM, CC, CD, 1953
The Right Honourable Lester B. Pearson, PC, OM, CC, OBE, 1971

THE ORDER OF THE COMPANIONS OF HONOUR

Origins: Founded by King George V on 4 June 1917, the order was originally established to recognize a non-titular alternative to the various British orders of chivalry. Over time it has largely been treated as a junior level of the Order of Merit. Originally limited to only fifty members, it was initially bestowed upon leaders who had performed conspicuous service during the First World War. As it was established simultaneously with the Order of the British Empire, and

Lester B. Pearson's
Order of Merit EIIR Issue
Top: Obverse
Bottom: Reverse

Order of the Companions of Honour obverse

given the Canadian prohibition on honours that came into effect in 1918, there was no opportunity for a Canadian to be appointed to the order in the early years of its existence.

In 1943 the British government decided to expand the order, and Canada, Australia, New Zealand and South Africa were asked as to whether or not they would like a certain number of honours to be allotted for their residents. Australia and New Zealand were keen to be involved, while, not surprisingly, Canada and South Africa respectfully declined the offer. At this time, Canadian officials were in the process of creating the Canadian Award of Honour, the Canadian Decoration of Honour and the Canada Medal. The Canadian government felt that with the impending establishment of these new Canadian awards, there would be no need for Britain to put aside a certain number of CH appointments.

The revised 1943 statutes of the order set out the following quotas: United Kingdom, 45; Australia, 7; New Zealand, 2; other Commonwealth nations, 11 — for a total of 65.

Had Canada accepted the British offer, it would have been allotted seven appointments, while Australia's quota would have been reduced to five. Appointments would have been made by the Sovereign, based on the advice of the prime minister — a procedure that was used in the United Kingdom, Australia and New Zealand (upon the advice of their respective prime ministers). As it is, advice to the Sovereign as to which Canadians should be appointed to the order has come from a variety of officials.

The first CH to be bestowed upon a Canadian was awarded to General Harry Crerar, the general officer commanding the First Canadian Division in 1944. He had been nominated as a Knight Commander of the Order of the British Empire, but the Canadian government would not entertain such an award. The CH was therefore considered because it was not a knighthood, yet it was still a senior order of chivalry. The recommendation to the King came from the Canadian minister of National Defence, after being cleared by Prime Minister Mackenzie King.

Vincent Massey's CH appointment, the second to a Canadian, was initiated by King George VI. Initially, Prime Minister King refused to approve the appointment, but he acquiesced after considering Massey's outstanding record of service. The King presented Massey with his insignia the night before Massey returned to Canada.

General McNaughton was appointed to the order on the advice of the Canadian prime minister. He would be the last Canadian to be appointed to the order for twenty-five years. This dry spell ended when Dr. Charles Best, the co-discoverer of insulin, was appointed. He was followed by Arnold Smith, the first secretary general of the Commonwealth, who was appointed to the order in 1975, at the initiative of the Queen.

John Diefenbaker had refused the order when he was first offered it in 1962 — at which time he was serving as prime minister — but accepted an appointment in 1976. The British prime minister put his name forward, after consulting Prime Minister Trudeau. There is some evidence that Trudeau initiated the appointment, feeling that Diefenbaker deserved recognition and no doubt being aware that, as an active politician (which he would remain until his death), the former prime minister was ineligible for the Order of Canada.

Trudeau himself would be made a CH in 1984, shortly after his final retirement from politics. His appointment was initiated by both the British and Canadian governments.

The most recent Canadian to be appointed to the order is General John de Chastelain, former chief of the defence staff and former Canadian ambassador to the United States. His appointment was in recognition of his work on the Northern Ireland peace process. His award is considered to be a "British" one because his nomination was made by the British prime minister.

The versatility of the Order of the Companions of Honour has been well proven; indeed, it has been the Canadian recipients who have expanded the limits of what type of service the order can recognize. From McNaughton's appointment, which was in many ways in recognition of his gallant conduct, and Massey's service as Canadian High Commissioner to the United Kingdom, to Trudeau and Diefenbaker's service as Canada's head of government, the range of fields that could be recognized is unlimited.

One can easily envision a few Canadians today who already hold the highest level of the Order of Canada, yet are deserving of additional recognition. The CH could easily fill this need. There is no reason why the Canadian prime minister could not follow in the footsteps of prime ministers King and Trudeau and make a few suggestions to the Queen. Neither the 1969 statutes of the order, nor Canadian policy, preclude future awards. Sadly, knowledge of this fact is largely forgotten or ignored.

Criteria: Any citizen of the Commonwealth who have rendered conspicuous service of national importance. Like the Order of Merit, in the Canadian context it has been used to recognize outstanding service, which in other parts of the Commonwealth would usually be recognized through the bestowal of a knighthood.

Insignia: A silver gilt oval badge measuring 75 mm tall and 42 mm wide, surmounted by a Tudor or St. Edward's crown. The circumference of the badge is enamelled in blue and bears the text *In Action Faithful and in Honour Clear.* At the centre of the insignia is a rectangular plaque containing an effigy of a knight on horseback under an oak tree. The reverse of the insignia carries the Royal cypher surmounted by a crown.

It was not until 1988 that the crown on the insignia was changed to a St. Edward's crown, despite the fact that Queen Elizabeth had requested the change in 1953. Thus, aside from General de Chastelain's CH, all the insignia awarded to Canadians bear the Tudor crown.

Suspension: A small ring passes through a mounting loop which is mounted on the reverse of the crown. Through this small ring passes a decorative loop, through which the ribbon passes.

Ribbon: A 40 mm wide ribbon, carmine in colour, with borders of gold thread.

Bars: None

Postnominals: Recipients are entitled to use the postnominals C.H.

Other: Recipients are also given a certificate bearing their name, signed by the Queen and embossed with the seal of the order.

The Order of the Companions of Honour Ribbon

Number Awarded to Canadians: 8[8]

General Harry Crerar, CH, CB, DSO, CD,
  5 July 1945
The Right Honourable Vincent Massey, PC,
  CH, CC, CD, 22 May 1946
**General the Honourable A.G.L.
  McNaughton**, PC, CH, CB, CMG,
  DSO, CD, 13 June 1946
Dr. Charles Best, CH, CC, CBE,
  12 June 1971
Arnold Smith, OC, CH, 29 April 1975
**The Right Honourable John George
  Diefenbaker**, PC, CH, QC, 1 January
  1976
The Right Honourable Pierre Elliot Trudeau,
  PC, CC, CH, QC, 4 July 1984
General A.J.G.D. de Chastelain, OC,
  CMM, CD, CH, 31 December 1998

THE ROYAL VICTORIAN CHAIN

Origins: Like the Order of Merit, the Royal Victorian Chain was established by King Edward VII in 1902. It has been awarded to two Canadians, both former governors general.

Criteria: Awarded by the Queen as a pre-eminent mark of the Sovereign's esteem and affection towards such persons as Her Majesty especially desires to honour.

Insignia: The chain consists of roses, trefoils, thistles and lotuses (two of each, and one extra rose), connected by a double gold chain consisting of seven links. In the centre of the chain is the Royal cypher of King Edward VII, "ERI," enamelled in red and surmounted by the Imperial Crown. From

*The Royal Victorian Chain
obverse*

*The Royal Victorian Chain
reverse*

this hangs a white Maltese cross of eight points, the centre of which contains an oval circumscribed by a blue border, containing the word *Victoria*. The centre of the oval is crimson enamel, in the centre of which is the Royal cypher of Queen Victoria, "VRI." Both the Crown and Queen Victoria's Royal cypher are set in diamonds.

Suspension: A small eyelet connects the insignia of the Maltese cross to the actual chain.

Ribbon: For men, there is no ribbon associated with this honour. For women, the ribbon of the Royal Victorian Order is fashioned into a bow, upon which part of the chain is attached for wear on the left breast.

Bars: None

Postnominals: There are no postnominal initials associated with this award.

Other: More than ninety-five of the awards made have been to foreign monarchs or foreign heads of state. Vincent Massey's award was only the second made to a commoner; Roland Michener's was the third. Recipients of the chain are also given a certificate bearing their name, signed by the Queen and embossed with the seal of the order.

Number of Awards: 2

The Right Honourable Vincent Massey, PC, CH, CC, CD, 1960
The Right Honourable Roland Michener, PC, CC, CMM, CD, 1974 (chain number 52)

The Royal Victorian Order certificate

THE ROYAL VICTORIAN ORDER

Origins: Founded by Queen Victoria in 1896 and consisting of five levels: Knight/Dame Grand Cross, Knight/Dame Commander, Commander, Lieutenant and Member. Canadians are ineligible for the two most senior levels of this order.

Criteria: There is no set criteria for the Royal Victorian Order, other than extraordinary or personal services to the Sovereign or to the Royal family. CVOs are typically awarded to senior officials, such as the secretary to the governor general and organizers of Royal visits. LVOs are typically awarded to long-serving secretaries to lieutenant governors, ladies in waiting, and long-serving aides de camp. MVOs are awarded to equerries, protocol officers and those serving as the Queen's principal aide de camp during her various visits to Canada. The most recent appointments to this order (and the Royal Victorian Medal) were made during the Queen's golden jubilee visit in October 2002.

The Royal Victorian Order is manufactured by Collingwood and Company of London. All awards of the order are accompanied by a certificate bearing the name of the recipient and the signatures of the Queen and embossed with the seal of the order.

COMMANDER OF THE ROYAL VICTORIAN ORDER

Insignia: An eight-point Maltese cross, with a gold frame 50 mm in width, filled with white enamel, in the centre of which is an oval circumscribed by a blue border containing the word *Victoria*. The centre of the oval is crimson enamel, in the centre of which is the Royal cypher of Queen Victoria, "VRI." The reverse is plain and stamped with an inventory number.

Suspension: A small eyelet is mounted at the apex of the uppermost arm of the Maltese cross, through which passes a 20 mm hanger and ribbon. The CVO is worn around the neck.

Ribbon: Blue in colour, 45 mm wide, edged on each side with 3 mm red, 3 mm white and 3 mm red.

Bars: None

Postnominals: Recipients are entitled to the postnominals C.V.O.

Number Awarded: 44

LIEUTENANT OF THE ROYAL VICTORIAN ORDER

Insignia: An eight-point Maltese cross, with a gold frame 44.5 mm in width, filled with white enamel, in the centre of which is an oval circumscribed by a blue border containing the word *Victoria*. The centre of the oval is crimson enamel, in the centre of which is the Royal cypher of Queen Victoria, "VRI." The reverse is plain and stamped with an inventory number.

Suspension: A small eyelet is mounted at the apex of the uppermost arm of the Maltese cross, through which passes a small gold ring and ribbon. The LVO is worn on the left breast.

Commander of the Royal Victorian Order obverse

Commander of the Royal Victorian Order reverse

Lieutenant of the Royal Victorian Order obverse

Lieutenant of the Royal Victorian Order reverse

Member of the Royal Victorian Order obverse

Member of the Royal Victorian Order reverse

Ribbon: Blue in colour, 32 mm wide, edged on each side with 1 mm red, 1 mm white and 1 mm red.

Bars: None

Postnominals: Recipients are entitled to the postnominals L.V.O.

Number Awarded: 70

MEMBER OF THE ROYAL VICTORIAN ORDER

Insignia: An eight-pointed Maltese Cross, with a gold frame 41 mm in width, in frosted silver, the centre of which contains an oval circumscribed by a blue border containing the word *Victoria*. The centre of the oval is of crimson enamel, and in its centre is the Royal cypher of Queen Victoria, "VRI." The reverse is plain and stamped with an inventory number.

Suspension: A small eyelet is mounted at the apex of the uppermost arm of the Maltese cross, through which passes a small silver ring and ribbon. The MVO is worn on the left breast.

Ribbon: Blue in colour, 32 mm wide, edged on each side with 1 mm red, 1 mm white and 1 mm red.

Bars: None

Postnominals: Recipients are entitled to the postnominals M.V.O.

Number Awarded: 44

THE ROYAL VICTORIAN MEDAL (GOLD, SILVER AND BRONZE)

Origins: Established by Queen Victoria in 1896 as a reward for servants of the Royal household who had rendered personal service to the Queen and the Royal family. The medal has three levels: gold, silver and bronze. The medal is part of the Royal Victorian Order, although until 1984 recipients were not entitled to use any postnominals.

Criteria: Available for servants of the Royal household (including Government House), junior civil servants such as drivers and housekeepers, and non-commissioned members of the Canadian Forces, who have rendered personal service to the Queen and the Royal family. Awarded at the discretion of the Sovereign.

Insignia: A 28 mm circular medal, struck in gold (silver gilt), silver and bronze, depending on the level of award. The obverse bears a youthful effigy of Her Majesty the Queen, surrounded by *Elizabeth II Dei Gratia Regina F D*. The reverse of the medal bears an uncrowned Royal cypher surrounded by ribbons and laurels, with *Royal Victorian Medal* upon a curled ribbon in the base. The medals are struck at the Royal Mint in London.

Suspension: A small ring passes through an eyelet attached to the medal.

Ribbon: 32 mm wide blue ribbon, edged on each side with 2 mm red, 2 mm white and 2 mm red.

Bars: Additional awards can be made, and bars

The Royal Victorian Medal obverse

The Royal Victorian Medal reverse

have been awarded to the silver and bronze medals, although no bars have yet been issued for the gold.

Postnominals: Recipients are entitled to the postnominals R.V.M.

Other: One can be awarded the gold, silver and bronze RVM and wear all of them simultaneously.

Number of Awards: 22

CHAPTER 9

The Most Venerable Order of the Hospital of St. John of Jerusalem

Along with the Royal Victorian Order, the Most Venerable Order of the Hospital of St. John of Jerusalem (the Order of St. John) constitutes one of the oldest components of the Canadian honours system. It predates even the Royal Victorian Order, but it was not until 1990 that the Order of St. John was formally incorporated into the Canadian honours system.

The order has played an important role in the early development of the Canadian honours system. Indeed, it was inquiries from officials of the order that helped prompt Prime Minister R.B. Bennett to reinstitute the honours list in the early 1930s.

The Order of St. John "is a working order of charitably minded men and women whose philanthropy is expressed principally through its two foundations, the St. John Eye Hospital in Jerusalem and the St. John Ambulance Association and Brigade."

The original Order of St. John of Jerusalem had been established in England during the twelfth century, after the First Crusade, to maintain a hospital in Jerusalem, but King Henry VIII passed a law dissolving it in 1540. A number of attempts were made to revive the order, primarily in France.

The earliest origins of the order in Canada can be traced back to New France and Acadia. Knights of Malta held a variety of high offices, this included at various times, the governor of Quebec and lieutenant governor of Acadia. The order ceased to operate in Canada following the fall of New France.

In 1831, the Grand Priory of the British Realm of the Most Venerable Order of the Hospital of St. John of Jerusalem was re-established, while the St. John Ambulance Association, with the purpose of offering first-aid training and transportation of the sick and wounded, came into existence in 1877. With this development the order found a new purpose and membership grew steadily. The Ambulance Association also gave rise to the St. John Ambulance Brigade. Queen Victoria granted the order a Royal charter in 1888, and with this the Sovereign became the Sovereign and patron of the order.[9]

The Canadian branch of the order got an informal start in 1883, when the inaugural first-aid course was held in Quebec City. In March 1895, Canada's deputy surgeon general, George Sterling Ryerson, was authorized by the Grand Priory to establish a branch of the St. John Ambulance Association in Canada. Sir George Airy Kirkpatrick, the lieutenant governor of Ontario, became the association's first president and would play an important role in establishing the order in Canada. The order's first Canadian ambulance division was established in London, Ontario, in 1909.

When the Nickle Resolution was adopted in 1918, all honours came to a virtual end in Canada — and, as a 15 September 1919 memorandum written by the Minister of Justice confirms, this included awards of the Order of St. John. The award of the order had served as a reward for devoted volunteers; thus, the organization was denied an important aspect of its operation. During the premiership of William Lyon Mackenzie King, a number of unofficial inquiries were made as to the status of the order and whether or not it could still be awarded to Canadians. Mackenzie King, reluctant to deal with the honours issue, merely cited the Nickle Resolution as a blanket prohibition on all honours, including the Order of St. John.

In October 1930, following his election as prime minister, R.B. Bennett received a letter from the sub-prior of the order, the Earl of Scarborough, who explained the nature of the order's work in Canada and why he thought that the Nickle Resolution was never intended to prevent the award of the order. By November of the same year, after discussing the matter with the order's grand prior, the Duke of Connaught — himself a former governor general of Canada — Bennett decided "it was absurd that you [the Order of St. John] have been treated as you have." In essence, this signalled Bennett's agreement to allow the resumption of awards of the order in Canada. Despite this tacit assent, however, Bennett did not immediately change the government's policy towards the order, as he was planning to revive the annual honours list and not just the Order of St. John. By 21 June 1931, only a day before the order was to celebrate the centenary of its revival in England, Bennett cabled Scarborough: "After careful consideration our Government has concluded that appointments in your ancient Order are not subject to the restrictions of the resolution of the House of Commons, and we will accept responsibility for any Canadian appointments." With that, the way was clear for the Order of St. John to once again be awarded in Canada. The very next day, Scarborough sent a message to Bennett, thanking him for looking into the matter and also informing the prime minister that a number of Canadians were to receive the order as part of the centennial celebrations.

*Queen Elizabeth II in the
robes of the Order of St. John*

More than a year later, on 20 October 1932, Bennett received notice that the Grand Priory wished to appoint him a Knight of Grace. Bennett accepted the honour, one that recognized his role in helping the order in Canada as well as his position as prime minister of Canada. Bennett's involvement in the order was not fleeting; he would go on to represent Canada at a number of conferences. Bennett also saw that the lieutenant governors of each province — if they so wished — became involved in the order.

The resumption of awards of the Order of St. John to Canadians resulted in the establishment of the Commandery of Canada in 1934. By 1946 the Canadian branch was elevated to a full priory, with the governor general serving as the Prior of Canada.

The Order of St. John was reorganized in 1999 and the priories in Canada, Australia, New Zealand, South Africa, Scotland, Wales and the United States were put on an equal footing as the priory in England. The International Secretariat of the Order of St. John came into existence in October 1999 to serve the Grand Council.

At the international level, the Grand Prior is appointed by the Sovereign head of the order after consultation with the Grand Prior's Advisory Council. The Grand Council consists of the various Great Officers: the Lord Prior, the Prelate, the Deputy Lord Prior, the Sub-Prior and a senior representative from each of the eight priories. Priories exist in Australia, Canada, New Zealand, South Africa, England, Scotland and Wales. There are also thirty branches of the order in various Commonwealth countries, and the Republic of Ireland is considered an associate body. The current Lord Prior is Eric Barry, a Canadian.

There are several officers of the order:

Sovereign Head of the Order	HM Queen Elizabeth II
Grand Prior	HRH The Duke of Gloucester, KG, GCVO
Lord Prior of St. John	Eric Barry, CD
Prior of Canada	The Governor General of Canada
Vice-Priors	Each of the Lieutenant Governors and Territorial Commissioners

The Queen is the Sovereign head of the order. In Canada the governor general is invited to serve as prior of the order, and at that time he or she is simultaneously appointed a Knight or Dame of Justice, as is their spouse. Each lieutenant governor and territorial commissioner is invited to become a vice-prior, and those who accept are appointed as Knights/Dames of Grace. Since 1990 the order has been classified as part of the Canadian honours system.[10]

All levels of the Order of St. John are awarded to any citizen who has performed — or is prepared to perform — good service for the order and who undertakes to conform to the rules of the order. There are no set criteria for receipt of each level, but in general one must be promoted through the ranks. Since 1992 there has been no religious requirement for membership in the order.

The order has various branches across Canada, and nominations for admission to or promotion within the order are initiated at the branch level before they pass on to the provincial council. From here they are forwarded to the priory, where they

Roland Michener in the robes of the Order of St. John

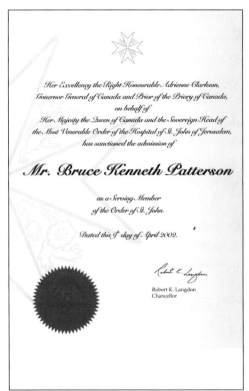

Her Excellency the Right Honourable Adrienne Clarkson, Governor General of Canada and Prior of the Priory of Canada, on behalf of Her Majesty the Queen of Canada and the Sovereign Head of the Most Venerable Order of the Hospital of St. John of Jerusalem, has sanctioned the admission of

Mr. Bruce Kenneth Patterson

as a Serving Member of the Order of St. John.

Dated this 9th day of April 2002.

Robert K. Langdon
Chancellor

are considered by the awards committee. The awards committee then transmits its list to the governor general, who approves the nominations on behalf of the Queen. In addition to the insignia of the order, recipients also receive a certificate bearing their name.

The Order of St. John certificate

BAILIFF OR DAME GRAND CROSS

Insignia: The breast star measures 92 mm across and is a white enamel Maltese cross set in gold-coloured metal. For men there is a sash worn on the left hip, from which is hung a white enamel Maltese cross set in gold with alternating lions and unicorns between each arm. It measures 85 mm across. The insignia for women is slightly smaller, measuring only 59 mm across.

Suspender: The breast star is attached by a straight pin mounted on the back of the star. The sash badges are usually attached by a small ring at the top of the Maltese cross, which is connected to another ring which is clipped onto the sash below the bow.

Bailiff Grand Cross of the Order of St. John

Order of St. John lapel pin

Ribbon: The ribbon is black morae: the men's sash badge is 120 mm in width, and that for women is 58 mm wide.

Bars: None

Postnominals: Recipients are entitled to use the postnominals G.C.St.J., within the order.

Other: A variety of insignia exist, ranging from very high-quality versions set in 18-karat gold or silver gilt to the more recent gold-coloured issues. As with other levels of the order, many recipients choose to purchase older issues of higher quality.

Number of Awards: Generally, only twelve male and seven female members of the order are Bailiff or Grand Dame Crosses, and Canada unusally has one man and one woman at this level.

There have been three Canadian Dame Grand Crosses and three Bailiff Grand Crosses.

The Right Honourable Vincent Massey, PC, CH, CC, GCStJ, CD, appointed 1955
Margaret MacLaren, GCStJ, appointed 1963
Commissioner Leonard Nicholson, OC, MBE, GCStJ, appointed 1971
Kathleen Gilmour, MBE, GCStJ, appointed 1975
Brigadier General Cyrille J. Laurin, OBE, GCStJ, appointed 1980
Mlle. Yvette Loiselle, GCStJ, appointed 1983

KNIGHT OR DAME OF GRACE
OR OF JUSTICE

*Knight/Dame of Justice of the
Order of St. John*

Insignia: The breast star measures 78 mm across and is a white enamel Maltese cross set in silver with embellishments for Knights or Dames of Grace and gold without embellishments for Knights or Dames of Justice. For men there is a neck badge which measures 58 mm across and is a white enamel Maltese cross, set in silver for Knights or Dames of Grace and gold for Knights or Dames of Justice. Women wear their "neck" insignia from a bow.

Suspender: The breast star is attached by a straight pin mounted on the back of the star. For the neck badge, a small eyelet is mounted on the top of the insignia, through which passes a 25 mm suspender bar which is connected to the neck ribbon.

Ribbon: Black morae ribbon 38 mm in width.

Bars: None

Postnominals: Recipients are entitled to use the postnominals K.St.J., or D.St.J., within the order.

Other: A person who is a Knight or Dame of Grace can be reappointed as a Knight or Dame of Justice if he or she can prove to the Genealogist of the Priory that he or she is entitled to bear arms or is a prior of a priory. Most Knights or Dames are promoted from the Commander level; it is very seldom that someone who has not previously been awarded the order will be appointed as a Knight or Dame.

Number of Awards: Approximately 12–16 are awarded each year. There is no accurate count of the total number of Knights/Dames of Justice or Grace appointed in Canada since the order's inception.

*Commander of the
Order of St. John*

COMMANDER

Insignia: A 58 mm wide Maltese cross with a silver frame, enamelled in white, with alternating lions and unicorns between each arm.

Suspender: A small eyelet is mounted on the top of the insignia, through which passes a 25 mm suspender bar which is connected to the neck ribbon.

Ribbon: Black morae ribbon 38 mm in width.

Bars: None

Postnominals: Recipients are entitled to use the postnominals C.St.J. within the order.

Other: Few people are appointed as Commanders without having already having been an Officer or Member of the order.

Number of Awards: Approximately forty are awarded each year. There is no accurate count of the total number of Commanders appointed in Canada since the order's inception.

OFFICER

Insignia: A 45 mm Maltese cross with a silver frame, enamelled in white, with alternating lions and unicorns between each arm.

Suspender: A small eyelet on the insignia is connected to a larger silver ring, through which passes the ribbon.

Ribbon: Black morae ribbon 38 mm in width.

Bars: None

Postnominals: Recipients are entitled to use the postnominals O.St.J., within the order.

Number of Awards: Approximately 100 are awarded each year. There is no accurate count of the total number of Officers appointed in Canada since the order's inception.

Officer of the Order of St. John

SERVING MEMBER

Insignia: There have been a wide variety of insignia used for this level of the order over the past century. Currently the insignia measures 38 mm across and is a plain, bright silver Maltese cross with alternating lions and unicorns between each arm.

Suspender: A small eyelet on the insignia is connected to a larger silver ring, through which passes the ribbon.

Ribbon: Black morae ribbon 38 mm in width.

Bars: None

Postnominals: Recipients are entitled to use the postnominals S.B.St.J. or S.S.St.J. within the order.

Serving Member of the Order of St. John

Serving Member lapel pin

Other: This level was formerly classified as Serving Brother or Serving Sister of the Order of St. John.

Number of Awards: Approximately 300 are awarded each year. There is no accurate count of then total number of Serving Members appointed in Canada since the order's inception.

CHAPTER 10

The Provincial Orders

T he establishment of provincial orders is not an entirely recent event. However, their acceptance and incorporation into the broader Canadian order of precedence is. Details about the history of the provincial orders are scarce, primarily because, as most have only been founded in the past two decades, documents related to their creation remain sealed.

The first province to found an order was Quebec, with the Order of Agricultural Merit of the Province of Quebec, in 1925. The origins of this order can be traced back to 1869, with the passage of the Department of Agriculture and Colonization Act, which charged the Department of Agriculture with the twin goals of ensuring the growth and success of agricultural endeavours and increasing immigration to Quebec.

The act also created a Council of Agriculture, composed of twenty-three Quebec farmers and agricultural experts, which was given the responsibility of organizing agricultural societies in each county and district and holding competitions. These competitions were designed "[t]o encourage, by means of special prizes, the cultivation of certain variety of plants and grain, which it is desirable to extend throughout the province."[11] Initially, the Quebec Agricultural Merit Awards were in the form of large bronze medals, 50 mm in diameter, which depicted the arms of Quebec on the obverse and engraved with the name of the recipient on the reverse.

In 1889 the Agricultural Merit Awards were standardized and given

Quebec Agricultural Medals

four levels: Distinguished Exceptional Merit (gold medal), Distinguished Merit (silver), Great Merit (bronze) and Merit (diploma/certificate).

The gold medal was awarded to the farmer who had "most distinguished himself" during the five years since receiving the silver medal. The silver medal was awarded to a person who had "obtained in the competition 85 out of 100 points allowed for perfect cultivation." The bronze medal was awarded for 75 points "for perfect cultivation," and the diploma was awarded for a score of 65 points.

The diplomas and certificates were regulated by the lieutenant governor-in-council (the provincial cabinet) and changed from time to time. Provisions were also made to allow for persons based outside of Canada to receive awards in recognition of "public service or in scientific missions or by works or publications on agriculture." Quebec's Minister of Agriculture was an ex-officio holder of the gold medal.

This entire system was modernized on 3 April 1925 with the creation of the Order of Agricultural Merit of the Province of Quebec, instituted for the "purpose of encouraging agriculturalists by honours and rewards, and to acknowledge services rendered to agriculture."

The new order was divided into three levels — the Commander of the Order of Agricultural Merit of Quebec (Distinguished Exceptional Merit, formerly the gold medal), Officer of the Order of Agricultural Merit of Quebec (Distinguished Merit, formerly the silver medal), Knight/Chevalier of the Order of Agricultural Merit (Great Merit, formerly the bronze medal) — as well as the Diploma of Merit.

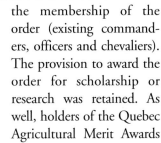

The lieutenant governor-in-council was responsible for setting out the conditions under which competitions for these awards would be held. Judges for competitions were appointed by the minister of Agriculture and were selected from the membership of the order (existing commanders, officers and chevaliers). The provision to award the order for scholarship or research was retained. As well, holders of the Quebec Agricultural Merit Awards

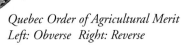

Quebec Order of Agricultural Merit
Left: Obverse Right: Reverse

were transformed into holders of the Quebec Order of Agricultural Merit at the appropriate levels. It would appear that the minister of Agriculture became an ex-officio Commander of the order as well.

This order was based upon *l'Ordre du Mérite Agricole* of France, and it highlights the importance of agriculture to Quebec at this time. Until the 1960s, the award was accompanied with a medal hung from a ribbon, but this was changed in 1964. The order was renamed *l'Ordre national du mérite agricole* in 2001, and its purpose remains to recognize excellence in agriculture. The award insignia is now a circular medal not suited for wear. While it is a prestigious award, it is not associated with *l'Ordre national du Québec* and is not part of the broader Canadian honours system.

The Ministry of Agriculture was not the only provincial body to latch onto the desire to reward exceptional service. Quebec's minister of Education founded an Order of Scholastic Merit on 22 March 1928 through an act of the Quebec National Assembly. The order was divided into three levels: the Order of Scholastic Merit First Class (and the diploma of merit), the Order of Scholastic Merit Second Class (and the diploma of great merit), and the Order of Scholastic Merit Third Class (and the diploma of distinguished merit).

Teachers, school inspectors and principals were all eligible. Those working in the Roman Catholic school system were nominated by a board composed of five members of the Roman Catholic Committee of Education, while those working in the Protestant school system were nominated by a board composed of five members of the Protestant Committee of Education. The Superintendent of Education was an ex-officio member of both selection boards, as well as an ex-officio member of the Order of Scholastic Merit Third Class. Each committee was allowed to define the criteria for award of the Order of Scholastic Merit. It is also interesting to note that each committee was responsible for designing its own insignia. (The minister of Education was not involved in this process.) Thus, the Roman Catholic insignia was different from the Protestant version.

Awards of the Order of Scholastic Merit appear to have ceased during the Quiet Revolution in Quebec during the 1960s.

Prior to the founding of the Canadian honours system in 1967, British Columbia was the only other Canadian province to have a provincial order. The Order of the Dogwood was founded in 1966. It was British Columbia's highest award, and appointments were recommended to the lieutenant governor by a special advisory council. The Order of the Dogwood was awarded to British Columbians who had "served with the greatest distinction and excelled in any field of endeavour benefiting the people of the province of British Columbia or elsewhere." Between 1966 and 1989 the order was awarded a total of thirteen times, and it largely fell out of use by the late 1970s.

None of these provincial orders were ever officially recognized by the federal government and were therefore never "official." Thus, a recipient was not allowed to wear his Order of Agricultural Merit or Order of the Dogwood with Canadian war service medals or other officially sanctioned awards.

MODERN PROVINCIAL HONOURS

In 1938, Prime Minister William Lyon Mackenzie King's deputy minister of Justice warned him that the provinces were quite capable of creating their own awards and having their respective lieutenant governors sanction them. Although such awards would not be "official," there was a fear that, with time, they would become viewed as such. The incorporation of the provincial orders into the Canadian order of precedence — their acceptance as legitimate awards — was in many ways a concession to the provinces and came about in part out of a desire to avoid federal-provincial conflict.

Throughout the 1970s and 1980s, various lieutenant governors lobbied to be appointed ex-officio members of the Order of Canada. Consideration had been given to making each lieutenant governor a Vice Chancellor of the Order of Canada, but the Advisory Council of the Order of Canada did not favour this idea and it was abandoned.

The provincial orders have an interesting relationship with the Order of Canada: on average, 30 per cent of those who receive a provincial honour are already recipients of one of the levels of the Order of Canada.

All of the modern provincial orders — unlike those created at the federal level — have been established by acts of the respective provincial legislatures and existed in law prior to being recognized by the federal government. The Queen is not sovereign of any of the provincial orders, although in some cases she has given approval for the use of the crown on insignia.

The provincial orders are included in the Canadian order of precedence not in the order which they were created, but rather in the order that each province requested that the federal government recognize its order. Although Alberta was the first province to create a provincial order, Quebec was the first — in 1984 — to request that its order be incorporated into the Canadian order of precedence and recognized as an official award.

On 9 May 1991 the federal government passed Order-in-Council 1991-841, which recognized the provincial orders that existed at that time: *l'Ordre national du Québec,* the Saskatchewan Order of Merit, the Order of Ontario, the Order of British Columbia and the Alberta Order of Excellence. Since that time, other provincial orders have been added.

All of the provincial orders consist of one level — except Quebec's, which has three. In general, the orders are similar in that their criteria and the method used to select recipients are based on those used by the Order of Canada, with a strong emphasis on public nominations. The lieutenant governor of each province is the chancellor of his or her respective order — except in Quebec, where there is no chancellor.

Each provincial order is accompanied by a full-size insignia; with the exception of Prince Edward Island, all contain or are based on the respective provincial flowers. Recipients also receive a lapel pin and certificate. Insignia of nearly all the provincial orders are worn around the neck — or on a bow by women, if they prefer. The exception is the insignia of the Chevalier of *l'Ordre national du Québec,* which is worn on the left breast.

In all provinces aside from Quebec, provincial and federal politicians and judges are prohibited from receiving a provincial order while serving in office. The only province to issue a special insignia (or collar chain) to the chancellor of its order is Saskatchewan.

L'ORDRE NATIONAL DU QUEBEC

Origins: *L'Ordre national du Québec* was established by an act of the Quebec National Assembly and given Royal assent on 20 June 1984. The order consists of three levels — Grand Officer, Officer and Knight — and is therefore based on the Order of Canada as well as the more antique Quebec Order of Agricultural Merit. There is no chancellor of the order, although in all but name the prime minister of Quebec acts in this capacity. The *Ordre national du Québec* is the most liber-ally awarded of the provincial orders.

Criteria: The order recognizes those men and women of Quebec who have distinguished

L' Ordre national du Québec,
Grand Officer

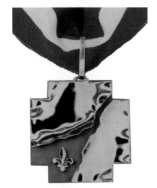

L' Ordre national du Québec,
Officer

L' Ordre national du Québec,
Knight

themselves in science, technology, the arts, social action at home and abroad, or through accomplishments that are admired by all. The level awarded to a recipient is associated with the calibre of his or her contribution.

Appointments are made by the prime minister of Quebec, on the advice of the Conseil de l'Ordre, through an order-in-council. This committee is made up of nine members, all of whom are elected from within the order.

Nominations are made by the general public. The order may also be bestowed posthumously, making it one of the first in the Commonwealth to allow such appointments. There are no annual limits on the number of appointments to each level; however, there are usually three G.O.Q. appointments, ten O.Q. appointments and fifteen C.Q. appointments.

Insignia: The insignia varies according to level, but all three have a feature in common: a stylized Geneva cross bisected by a shape representing the course of the St. Lawrence River, with a fleur-de-lys at the mouth of the river.

The insignia of the **Grand Officer/Grand Officier** is an 18-karat gold Geneva cross measuring 60 mm wide, with a white enamelled fleur-de-lys in the lower left-hand corner of the cross. The insignia of the **Officer/Officier** is a Geneva cross of 18-karat gold and oxidized silver, measuring 40 mm wide, with a silver fleur-de-lys in the lower left-hand corner. And the insignia of a **Knight/Chevalier** is a circular silver medal, 40 mm in diameter, superimposed with a Geneva cross bisected by the St. Lawrence River and with a silver fleur-de-lys at the lower left-hand corner of the cross.

The reverse of all three insignia bears the motto of the order — *Honneur au Peuple du Québec* — as well as a three-digit serial number.

Suspender: For the insignia of the Grand Officer and Officer, a small loop is affixed to the middle of the uppermost part of the cross. Through this passes a 20 mm loop and the ribbon of the order. The insignia of a knight is suspended by a small ball mounted on the top of the medal, through which passes a silver ring and the ribbon of the order. The knight's insignia is worn on the left breast.

L' Ordre national du Québec, reverse of Knight's insignia

Ribbon: The ribbon is 38 mm wide, with a 12 mm central white stripe flanked by stripes of blue.

Bars: None

Other: The order adopted a motto on 3 April 1985: "Honneur au Peuple du Québec"/"Honour to the People of Quebec." The order was designed by Madeleine Dansereau.

Number of Awards: Grand Officer, 62 (3 to foreigners); Officer, 167 (15 to foreigners); Knights, 276 (12 to foreigners)

THE SASKACHEWAN ORDER OF MERIT

Origins: The idea to create the Saskatchewan Order of Merit first emerged in 1980, when the province marked its seventy-fifth anniversary as part of Confederation. At this time a special interdepartmental committee was founded to investigate the possibility of creating a provincial award.

The Saskatchewan Award of Merit was established by an order-in-council in 1985. The award was renamed the Saskatchewan

Saskatchewan Order of Merit

*Saskatchewan
Order of Merit, post-2004 issue.*

*Post 2004 Saskatchewan
Order of Merit ribbon.*

Order of Merit by a subsequent act, which received Royal assent on 10 May 1988. The order consists of one level. Since 1988, the lieutenant governor of the province has served as chancellor, and in 2001 the lieutenant governor was made an ex-officio member. There is no annual maximum number of appointments to the order, although the number is usually less than ten.

In 2000 a provision was added to allow for posthumous awards (to be made within a year of the person's death). In 2001 a further provision was added to allow for honorary appointments, the first of which went to His Royal Highness the Prince of Wales (Prince Charles).

Criteria: Awarded in recognition of individual excellence, outstanding achievement and exceptional contributions to the social, cultural and economic well-being of the province and its residents.

Appointments are made by the lieutenant governor on the advice of the Saskatchewan Order of Merit Advisory Council. The council consists of a person appointed by the president of the executive council (the premier of Saskatchewan), the Chief Justice of Saskatchewan (or the Chief Justice of Queen's Bench), the cabinet secretary (or the clerk of the executive council), the president of one of the province's two major universities (the universities of Saskatchewan and Regina), the provincial archivist, and not more than five members appointed by the president of the executive council.

Insignia: A 45 mm silver-gilt insignia in the shape of a six-pointed star (red lily). In the centre are the provincial shield of arms, surmounted by a Royal crown. The reverse is plain and contains a three-digit serial number. In 2005 the insignia of the order will be changed to include the provincial motto *Multis e Gentibus Vires* ("From Many Peoples, Strength").

Suspender: A small ring is affixed to the uppermost arm of the red lily, through which passes a 21 mm hanger and the ribbon of the order.

Ribbon: Prior to 2005, the ribbon is 38 mm wide, with a 12 mm central gold stripe bordered on either side by 13 mm of green. Beginning in 2005 the central stripe will be green, while the outer stripes will be gold.

Bars: None

Postnominals: S.O.M.

Number of Awards: 122

THE ORDER OF ONTARIO

Origins: On 14 June 1973 the province of Ontario established the Ontario Medal for Good Citizenship to recognize outstanding citizens of the province. From this medal flowed the idea that Ontario should create its own order. Established by an act of the provincial parliament, the Order of Ontario received Royal assent in 1986. The order consists of one level. The lieutenant governor is chancellor of the order and an ex-officio member. There is no annual maximum number of appointments, although the largest number appointed in a single year has been twenty-seven.

Order of Ontario

Criteria: Awarded to recognize the highest level of individual excellence and achievement in any field. Appointments are made by the lieutenant governor on the advice of the Advisory Council of the Order of Ontario, which consists of the Chief Justice of Ontario, the speaker of the legislative assembly (provincial parliament), the secretary of the cabinet, and a maximum of six distinguished members of the Order of Ontario.

Insignia: A stylized, silver-gilt trillium 54 mm wide, enamelled in white, is superimposed on a triangular green-enamel trillium leaf. In the centre is a provincial shield surmounted by a Royal crown. The reverse is plain and contains a three-digit serial number.

Suspender: A small loop is affixed to the uppermost point of the trillium leaf, through which passes a 21 mm loop and the ribbon of the order.

Ribbon: A 38 mm ribbon with outer edges of red and a central white stripe superimposed with stripes of gold, green and gold.

Bars: None

Postnominals: O.Ont.

Number of Awards: 373

THE ORDER OF BRITISH COLUMBIA

Origins: Established by an act of the provincial legislative assembly, the Order of British Columbia received Royal assent on 21 April 1989. The order consists of one level. The lieutenant governor is chancellor of the order and an ex-officio member.

Criteria: Awarded to recognize those who have served with the greatest distinction and excelled in any field, to the benefit of the people of the province or elsewhere.

Appointments are made by the lieutenant governor through a decision of the lieutenant governor-in-council (the provincial cabinet) on the recommendation of the advisory council. The Advisory Council of the Order of British Columbia consists of the lieutenant governor, the Chief Justice of British Columbia, the speaker of the legislative assembly, the president of one of British Columbia's public universities, the president of the Union of B.C. Municipalities, the deputy minister responsible for the Order of British Columbia, and two recipients of the order from the previous year. Nominations are sought from the general public.

Insignia: A silver-gilt insignia 54 mm wide, in the shape of a dogwood flower in white enamel with green leaves in the background. The centre of the flower is defaced with the provincial shield of arms surmounted by a Royal Crown. The reverse of the insignia is plain and contains a three-digit serial number.

Suspender: A small ring is mounted on the top of the insignia, through which passes a 21 mm loop, through which passes the ribbon of the order.

Ribbon: A 38 mm wide ribbon composed of green, white, yellow and dark blue.

Bars: None

Postnominals: O.B.C.

Order of British Columbia

Other: The insignia of the order was designed by Bruce Beatty.

Number of Awards: 217

THE ALBERTA ORDER OF EXCELLENCE

Alberta Order of Excellence

Origins: Founded by an act of the provincial legislature, the order received Royal assent on 16 November 1979, and is the oldest provincial order, although it was not awarded until 1981. The order started off as a badge/table medal not intended for wear, but was later modified for wear around the neck. The order consists of one level. The lieutenant governor is chancellor of the order.

Criteria: Awarded to persons who have rendered service of the greatest distinction and of singular excellence, for or on behalf of the residents of Alberta. The order is awarded by the lieutenant governor on the advice of the Alberta Order of Excellence Council, which is made up of the lieutenant governor and six other Albertans who are chosen by the lieutenant governor-in-council. There is no limit on the number of annual awards; the largest number of appointments in a single year has been six.[12]

Insignia: A silver-gilt cross (51 mm wide) with four arms. Between each arm of the cross is a rose leaf. The arms are enamelled in translucent blue; the centre of the cross contains the arms of the province surrounded by the words *The Alberta Order of Excellence*. The reverse is plain, aside from a maple leaf and a wreath of wheat.

Suspender: A small ring is mounted on the top of the cross, through which passes a loop and the ribbon.

Ribbon: A 38 mm ribbon, composed of blue, white, burgundy and gold.

Bars: None

Postnominals: A.O.E.

Number of Awards: 53

THE ORDER OF PRINCE EDWARD ISLAND

Origins: The Order of Prince Edward Island was founded by an act of the provincial legislature and receive Royal assent on 29 May 1997. The lieutenant governor of the province is chancellor of the order and is also an ex-officio member. The order consists of one level, and a maximum of three awards may be made each year.

Criteria: Awarded in recognition of outstanding individual excellence achievement and outstanding contributions to the social, cultural or economic well-being of Price Edward Island and its residents.

The order is awarded by the lieutenant governor on the advice of the Order of Prince Edward Island Advisory Council. Nominations come from the general public. The council is composed of the chief justice of P.E.I., the president of the University of P.E.I., the clerk of the executive council, and two residents of each county in the province (appointed by the lieutenant governor-in-council).

*Order of
Prince Edward Island*

Insignia: A circular gold medal with the provincial shield in the centre, circumscribed by the words *Merit — Prince Edward Island* on English issues and *Mérite — Île du Prince Édouard* on French issues. The reverse is engraved with a three-digit number starting at 01 for the English issues, 001 for French issues, and C-1 for chancellor's medals.

Suspender: A gold loop 21 mm in length.

Ribbon: A ribbon 38 mm wide, edged with 3 mm of white, with three central stripes of rust red (13 mm), white (6 mm) and green (13 mm).

Bars: None

Postnominals: O.P.E.I.

Number of Awards: 32

THE ORDER OF MANITOBA

Origins: Founded by an act of the provincial legislature and given Royal assent on 14 July 1999. The order replaced the unofficial "Order of the Buffalo Hunt," which was established in 1957. The order consists of one level, and the lieutenant governor of the province is the chancellor of the order and an ex-officio member. A maximum of eight appointments may be made annually (a special provision was made for twenty to be appointed in the year that the order was founded).

Criteria: The order recognizes those who have demonstrated excellent and achievement in any field of endeavour, benefiting in an outstanding

Order of Manitoba

manner the social, cultural or economic well-being of Manitoba and its residents.

Awards are made by the lieutenant governor on the advice of the Advisory Council of the Order of Manitoba, which consists of the Chief Justice of Manitoba, the clerk of the executive council, the president of one of the province's three universities, and not more than four people appointed by the lieutenant governor-in-council (the provincial cabinet) for a term of three years. Any citizen may make a nomination.

Insignia: A stylized crocus (the provincial flower) 58 mm wide, enameled in powder blue with a gold frame. In the centre is the provincial shield of arms surmounted by a Royal Crown. The reverse is plain and contains a three-digit serial number.

Suspender: A gold loop 21 mm in length.

Ribbon: A white ribbon, 38 mm wide, superimposed with broad stripes of powder blue and a thin central stripe of red.

Bars: None

Postnominals: O.M.

Number of Awards: 73

THE ORDER OF NEW BRUNSWICK

Origins: Created by an act of the provincial legislature and given Royal assent on 20 December 2000. The design of the order's insignia was officially unveiled on 19 November 2001. The order consists of one level. The lieutenant

Order of New Brunswick

governor of the province is chancellor of the order and an ex-officio member.

Criteria: The Order of New Brunswick recognizes those who have demonstrated excellence and achievement and have made outstanding contributions to the social, cultural or economic well-being of New Brunswick and its residents.

The order is awarded by the lieutenant governor on the advice of the Advisory Council of the Order of New Brunswick, which consists of a chair (appointed by the provincial cabinet), the Chief Justice of New Brunswick, the clerk of the executive council, the president of one of the province's universities, and three to five members of the community (appointed by the executive council — i.e., the provincial cabinet). A maximum of ten appointments may be made each year. Nominations are sought from the general public.

Insignia: A stylized violet, enameled in deep blue with a silver-gilt frame. In the centre is the provincial shield of arms, surmounted by a Royal crown. The enamel was originally supposed to be a deep purple colour (the purple violet is New Brunswick's provincial flower), although this proved too difficult to manufacture, so it was changed to a deep blue. The reverse of the insignia bears a three-digit number.

Suspender: A gold loop 21 mm in length.

Ribbon: A 38 mm ribbon, edged on either side in red, with a central yellow stripe superimposed with a purple stripe.

Bars: None

Postnominals: O.N.B.

Number of Awards: 18

THE ORDER OF NOVA SCOTIA

Origins: Established by an act of the provincial legislature and given Royal assent on 1 June 2001. The order consists of one level. The lieutenant governor is chancellor of the order and an ex-officio member.

Nova Scotia has a curious history in terms of honours. In 1624, James I created the Baronets of Nova Scotia (a hereditary knighthood), primarily as a tool to raise funds for the colonization of Nova Scotia. With time, the baronetcies came to be awarded for merit. The insignia of the Baronets of Nova Scotia bears some resemblance to that of the Order of Nova Scotia in that the coat of arms used on each order is the same.

The Order of Nova Scotia

Criteria: Awarded to residents of Nova Scotia who have distinguished themselves by an outstanding contribution to the cultural life or to the social or economic well-being of the province, by an outstanding achievement or by excelling in any field of endeavour to the benefit of the people of the province of elsewhere.

Appointments are made by the lieutenant governor on the advice of the Advisory Council of the Order of Nova Scotia, which consists of a chair (appointed by the premier), the Chief Justice of Nova Scotia, the clerk of the executive council, three members appointed by the premier (one of whom is a president of one of the province's universities), a member appointed by the leader of Her Majesty's Loyal Opposition, and a member appointed by the leader of each recognized provincial political party. The order is unusual in that it may be awarded posthumously. A maximum of five appointments may be made a year (a special provision allowed for ten appointments in the year of the order's founding). Nominations are sought from the general public.

At the time that the order was created, all former lieutenant governors of the province were appointed.

Insignia: A 61 mm badge in the shape of a mayflower (the provincial flower), enamelled in white with a slight tinge of blue, and defaced with the provincial arms surmounted by a Royal crown.

Suspender: A gold loop 21 mm in length.

Ribbon: A 38 mm ribbon of red, white, gold and red.

Bars: None

Postnominals: O.N.S.

Other: The insignia was designed by Christopher Cairns. The reverse of the insignia bears a three-digit number.

Number of Awards: 21

THE ORDER OF NEWFOUNDLAND AND LABRADOR

Origins: Founded by an act of the Legislative Assembly of Newfoundland and Labrador and given Royal assent on 24 May 2001. The concept for the order was initially developed in the late 1990s. The order consists of one level. The lieutenant governor of the province is chancellor of the order as well as an ex-officio member.

Criteria: Awarded for outstanding achievement or contribution in any field. Residents and former long-term residents of the province of Newfoundland and Labrador are eligible for the order. A maximum of eight people may be appointed to the order per year.

Appointments are made by the lieutenant governor on the advice of the Advisory Council of the Order of Newfoundland and Labrador, which is chaired by the Chief Justice of Newfoundland and Labrador and includes the clerk of the executive council, the president of Memorial University, and four other members appointed by the lieutenant governor-in-council (in effect, the provincial cabinet). Nominations are sought from the general public.

Order of
Newfoundland and Labrador

Insignia: The insignia, 54 mm wide, is a stylized rendering of the pitcher plant (the provincial floral emblem). The dark grey petals are made of labradorite (calcium sodium aluminum silicate), the provincial mineral, and are edged in gold. This is defaced with the arms of Newfoundland and Labrador surmounted by a Royal crown. It is one of the few orders in the world whose insignia is made from stone.

Suspender: A gold loop 21 mm in length.

Ribbon: The ribbon is 35 mm, edged with 5 mm of green. A 5 mm central blue stripe is bordered on either side by 4 mm of white, 2 mm of gold and an additional 4 mm of white.

Bars: None

Postnominals: O.N.L.

Other: A three-digit number is engraved on the reverse.

Number of Awards: 9

CHAPTER 11

Bravery Decorations

Prior to the establishment of the Order of Canada in 1967, and dating back to pre-Confederation times, Canadians were eligible for a variety of British bravery and gallantry awards. These included — but were not limited to — the Victoria Cross, the George Cross, the Albert Medal, the George Medal, the Queen's Commendation for Brave Conduct, and the various levels of the Order of the British Empire for gallantry. Nongovernmental organizations, such as the Royal Life Saving Society of Canada and Royal Canadian Humane Association, have also long possessed separate awards of lifesaving.

The earliest Canadian bravery award was the Government of Canada Medal "for Gallant and Humane Services Rendered in Life Saving from Shipwrecked Vessels." Established in 1868 by the minister of Marine and Fisheries, Peter Mitchell — who was himself the owner of a shipping company as well as a noted Father of Confederation and a former premier of New Brunswick — the medal was issued in gold and silver. The sparingly bestowed medal appears to have fallen into disuse by 1913; in total, only six gold and eleven silver medals were issued. Although obscure, this was the first uniquely government-sanctioned Canadian decoration for bravery. As the broader British honours system grew to include more bravery decorations for civilians, the need for such Canadian awards temporarily diminished.

During the years that Canada used the British honours system, Canadians became familiar with a number of awards. The George Medal, established in 1940 by King George VI, and the King's (or Queen's) Commendation for Brave Conduct became the primary forms of recognition accorded to Canadian civilians who had displayed exemplary bravery. These awards were also bestowed upon members of the Royal Canadian Navy, the Canadian Army and the Royal Canadian Air Force. Less frequently used in the Canadian context was the Order of the British Empire. Although it was primarily a military and civilian award for meritorious service, provisions had been made at the time of its establishment for the order to be used also as a junior bravery award. Even at times when all other British honours were prohibited, provisions were made for the continuance of bravery awards. Under the British honours system, Canadians received ten George Crosses,[13] seventy-seven George Medals, twenty-two British Empire Medals for Gallantry and numerous Queen's Commendations for Brave Conduct.

The small number of British bravery and gallantry awards is somewhat deceiving. From 1894 until 2001 the Royal Canadian Humane Association awarded nearly 6,000 bravery medals. (At various times, members of the Royal Canadian Navy, Canadian Army and Royal Canadian Air Force were permitted to wear the RCHA Bravery Medals along with their service medals.) In many ways, the RCHA Bravery Medals were the first indigenous Canadian awards for bravery.

The RCHA, which was modelled on the British Royal Humane Association, awarded medals in gold, silver and bronze. These bravery

awards made up for the absence of a Canadian bravery or lifesaving medal. The association would receive nominations from the general public, and a special committee would then decide on what awards were to be made. The medals were usually presented by the governor general or a lieutenant governor.

The Royal Canadian Humane Association ceased to operate in 2001; for more than a century it had rewarded bravery, but by the early 1990s it had become obvious that the three Canadian bravery awards instituted in 1972 were now fulfilling that mandate.

Royal Canadian Humane
Association Bravery Medal
Far left: Obverse
Left: Reverse

Canada's three bravery awards find their immediate origins in the Order of Canada Medal of Courage. The Medal of Courage was originally intended to serve as a Canadian version of the George Medal, but Prime Minister Lester Pearson also wanted to continue to use the Victoria Cross and George

Cross as part of the broader Canadian honours system. By March 1968, however, Pearson had reconsidered this arrangement and decided that the Canadian government should no longer make recommendations for Canadians to receive British bravery awards,[14] leaving the Medal of Courage as the only bravery award available to Canadians. It was suddenly required to replace not only the George Medal, but also the Victoria Cross, the George Cross and the Queen's Commendation for Brave Conduct, not to mention the myriad of service-specific bravery awards such as the Distinguished Service Cross, Military Cross and Distinguished Flying Cross.

Within a short period of time "it was decided ... that the Medal of Courage which was incorporated into the Order of Canada would not allow sufficiently for the recognition of acts of bravery."[15] A variety of solutions was considered. In the summer of 1968 the secretary to the governor general, Esmond Butler, suggested that the Medal of Courage be divided into three grades within the Order of Canada. This idea was quickly discarded, however, in the face of opposition from the Department of National Defence and the Royal Canadian Mounted Police.[16] It was agreed instead that "the Order of Canada should be persuaded to leave the field of bravery awards."[17] To this end, the Working Group on Honours — a subcommittee of the Decorations Committee — prepared a proposal for three separate bravery awards: a Hero's Cross, a Medal of Courage and a Canadian Life-Saving Medal. All would be separate from the Order of Canada.[18] This proposal for three separate decorations emerged in October 1968, and over the next three years would be refined into the Cross of Valour, Star of Courage and Medal of Bravery, although the exact names of each award were not to be devised until late 1971.

Although it took nearly four years to establish the Canadian bravery decorations, there was definitely a sense of urgency to the effort — the backlog of bravery award nominations extended back to 1965. (The last George Medals to be awarded to Canadians were presented in 1964 to Sergeant Joseph Lessard and Lieutenant Colonel Paul Mayer. After that, Ottawa requested that the practice be discontinued.) The Queen's Commendation for Brave Conduct continued to be awarded until 1968, yet even this was insufficient to recognize all acts of bravery.

Events aboard HMCS *Kootenay* in October 1969 helped to expedite the creation of the Canadian bravery decorations. The *Kootenay* suffered a catastrophic explosion in her engine room, and the ensuing fire threatened the entire ship. Through the selfless actions of a few, many lives — and the ship itself — were saved. The stories of Chief Warrant Officer Vaino Partanen and Sergeant Lewis Stringer — both of whom died on the *Kootenay*, Partanen while trying to report the situation and Stringer as a result of smoke inhalation he suffered while he cleared the galley — became widely known, as did the exemplary conduct of the remainder of the *Kootenay*'s crew. There were calls in the press for the men to be awarded the Medal of Courage, which was not practical as the government had already decided to abolish the Medal of Courage and replace it with a new series of decorations. The question of honours for the sailors persisted, however, and the subject was even brought up in Parliament. On 30 December 1971, D.W. Groos, the member for Victoria, asked "would [the PM] use his influence to speed [the awards] up as they are now more than two years overdue?"[19] Prime Minister Pierre Trudeau told the House that the new system was under consideration, knowing full well that the CV, SC and MB were in the final stages of preparation.

On 28 July 1971, Cabinet met to discuss the proposed restructuring of the Canadian honours system, which included the creation of the three bravery decorations. Cabinet did not spend much time on the bravery awards, being more fixated on the new structure of the Order of Canada and the brand new Order of Military Merit. The Decorations Committee proposed that the highest level of bravery decoration should be called the Kootenay Cross (in French, *le Croix de Kootenay*). The second level of bravery decoration was initially given a variety of names: the Laurentian Star, the Star of the North and the Cross of Courage. All of these ideas were poorly received, and while the overall proposal for three bravery decorations was approved, the name of the first and second degrees of the decoration were left "to be decided," while the third was designated the Medal for Bravery, or the MB.[20]

The Queen approved the new bravery decorations on 10 May 1972, and they came into effect on 1 July of that year. The three decorations were designated the Cross of Valour, the Star of Courage and the Medal of Bravery. The first awards were gazetted on 28 July 1972. Appropriately, the first Crosses of Valour, Stars of Courage and Medals of Bravery were awarded to crewmen of HMCS *Kootenay*.

Recipients of the Canadian Bravery Decorations are chosen by the Canadian Decorations Advisory Committee. This committee consists of up to ten members: the clerk of the Privy Council, the secretary to the governor general, the deputy minister of Canadian Heritage, the deputy minister of National Defence, the deputy minister of Transport, the commissioner of the Royal Canadian Mounted Police, and up to four other members — usually members of the armed forces — appointed by the governor general.

In 1997 the original letters patent constituting the Canadian Bravery Decorations were repealed and replaced with a revised version. These minor changes pertained to the membership of the Canadian Decorations Advisory Committee, and they included provisions for an extra person to be appointed to the committee by the governor general (increased from three to four), as a consequence of the removal of the Dominion Fire Commissioner. Other changes were related to the change in designation of the under-secretary of state (now the deputy minister of Canadian Heritage).

When Australia established its bravery decorations in 1975, it used the same structure — and almost the same criteria — as the Canadian Bravery Decorations. The British also learned from the Canadian example: in 1974 they established the Queen's Gallantry Medal, which is junior to the George Medal. Thus Britain now has a series of bravery awards (the George Cross, George Medal and Queen's Gallantry Medal) that is partially modelled upon the Canadian experience.

All three decorations were designed by Bruce Beatty. When his original drawings were presented to the Decorations Committee for approval, the committee was pleased, but it insisted that the Cross of Valour — which had originally been designed for wear on the breast — be changed to a neck decoration. This change was apparently made merely to make the decoration seem more "important." The drawings approved by the committee all utilized the same watered red ribbon, with no differentiation between them. As almost a last-minute augmentation, Beatty added two stripes of blue to the ribbon on the Star of Courage and three to that of the Medal of Bravery. All of the designs were subsequently approved by the Queen.

To date, the Cross of Valour has been awarded on only nineteen occasions, of which five were posthumous. It is awarded only for the most outstanding acts of bravery, and is comparable to the George Cross. The Star of Courage has been awarded 398 times, of which 76 were posthumous, and is similar to the George Medal in the United Kingdom. The Medal of Bravery has been awarded on 2,143 occasions. It is similar in calibre to the Queen's Gallantry Medal, the Order of the British Empire (for gallantry) and the Queen's Commendation for Brave Conduct. The Canadian Decorations Advisory Committee raised the ire of some when it sanctioned the award of the MB to 194 rescuers who were involved in the 1992 Westray coal mine disaster. This mass distribution was quite unprecedented in the history of Commonwealth bravery awards.

The Bravery Decorations have been awarded to a total of 30 non-Canadians.

Recipients of the Cross of Valour, the Star of Courage and the Medal of Bravery each receive a certificate bearing their name, the citation of their award and the signatures of the governor general and the secretary to the governor general.

The status of the bravery decorations has remained largely unchanged since the establishment of the Military Valour Decorations (Victoria Cross, Star of Military Valour and Medal of Military Bravery) in 1993. These new decorations are intended to recognize acts of valour demonstrated in the face of an enemy. While "the enemy" has been defined in broad enough terms to include service in situations short of war, no awards of the Military Valour Decorations have yet been made.

Cross of Valour obverse

THE CROSS OF VALOUR

Criteria: Awarded only for acts of the most conspicuous courage in circumstances of extreme peril.

Insignia: A gold cross of four equal limbs. The obverse is enamelled in translucent red with machine work in a lozenge pattern beneath. The entire insignia is edged with gold. In the centre of the cross, a gold maple leaf is surrounded by a gold laurel wreath. The reverse is plain, with the Royal cypher and Crown and the words *Valour — Vaillance.*

Suspender: At the top of the cross is a small ball, through which passes a circular ring attached to a 20 mm straight suspender. The Cross of Valour is worn around the neck for men and on a bow for women.

Ribbon: In light crimson, 38 mm wide. Recipients wear a miniature of the CV on their undress ribbon.

Bars: A gold maple leaf mounted to the 20 mm straight suspender (neck hanger). None has been awarded to date. Recipients of the bar would place two miniature CV insignias on their undress ribbon bar.

Postnominals: Recipients are entitled to the postnominals C.V.

Number of Awards: 19

Other: When the Cross of Valour was sanctioned in 1972, twenty-five insignia were ordered from Garrard and Company of London; the Chancellery is still using this original shipment. The frame is made of 18-karat gold, and the lower arm on the reverse was stamped with the 18-karat hallmark and maker's name. The recipient's name is engraved on the reverse of the Cross of Valour.

THE STAR OF COURAGE

Criteria: Awarded for acts of conspicuous courage in circumstances of great peril.

Insignia: A four-pointed silver star, with a maple leaf in each of the four angles. In the centre of the obverse is a gold maple leaf, surrounded by a gold laurel wreath. The reverse is plain, with the Royal cypher and crown and the word *Courage*.

Suspender: A small ball at the top of the star, through which passes a silver ring. The Star of Courage is worn on the left breast.

Ribbon: A crimson ribbon, 32 mm wide,

Cross of Valour reverse

*Cross of Valour
Left: Bar
Right: Lapel pin*

Prototype of the Cross of Valour

The Star of Courage
Top: Obverse
Middle: Reverse
Bottom Left: Lapel Pin
Bottom Right: Bar

with two 5 mm blue stripes set 2 mm from either edge.

Bars: A gold bar bearing a single maple leaf in the centre. A single gold maple leaf is worn in the centre of the undress ribbon for second awards.

Postnominals: Recipients are entitled to use the postnominals S.C., or É.C.

Other: Naming is engraved on the reverse below the word *Courage*. The first Stars of Courage were manufactured by Spink and Son of London. By the early 1980s the Royal Canadian Mint was striking them. They are hallmarked with "sterling" on the reverse of the lower arm of the star. In the mid-1980s Rideau of St. Laurent, Quebec, began making the star, and they are hallmarked with "Rideau STG" on the reverse of the lower arm of the star. Since 1997, the star has been manufactured by Birks and is hallmarked with "BIRKS STERLING" in two lines on the reverse of the lower arm of the star.

Number of Awards: 398 (2 to non-Canadians)

THE MEDAL OF BRAVERY

Criteria: Awarded for acts of bravery in hazardous circumstances.

Insignia: A circular silver medal. On the obverse is a single maple leaf surrounded by a laurel wreath. The reverse bears the Royal cypher and crown in the centre, surrounded by the words *Bravery — Bravoure*, with a six-leaf laurel flourish at the base.

Suspender: A straight suspender bar with a fleur-de-lys in the centre, mounted to the disc of the medal.

Ribbon: In light crimson, 32 mm wide, with three 3 mm blue stripes — one in the centre of the ribbon, the other two set 2 mm from either edge of the ribbon.

Bars: A silver bar bearing a single maple leaf in the centre. A single silver maple leaf is worn on the undress ribbon for second awards.

Postnominals: Recipients are entitled to use the postnominals M.B.

Other: Naming is engraved on the rim. On early issues, the date of award was engraved after the recipient's name. Initially the Medal of Bravery was made by Spink and Son of London. In the early 1980s the Royal Canadian Mint began striking the medal, after which the contract was awarded to Rideau of St. Laurent, Quebec, and then to Birks.

Number of Awards: 2,143 (26 to non-Canadians)

Medal of Bravery
Top: Obverse
Middle: Reverse
Bottom Left: Lapel pin
Bottom Right: Bar

CHAPTER 12

Military Valour Decorations

There is perhaps no more famous military decoration than the Victoria Cross. It has an almost universal recognition as the pre-eminent valour award. It also has an elegantly simple criteria:

> For most conspicuous bravery or some daring or pre-eminent act of valour or self-sacrifice or extreme devotion to duty in the presence of the enemy.[21]

The Victoria Cross was instituted by Queen Victoria on 5 February 1856. The designer remains unknown, although it is likely that the work was done by someone at Hancocks and Company of London,[22] and the original VC prototype was certainly made of sterling silver by Hancocks and Company. The appearance was deemed unsatisfactory, however, and bronze was procured. In fact, a very symbolic — and large — piece of bronze was used: that from a pair of bronze cannon that had been captured from the Russians in Sebastopol during the final battle of the Crimean War.

The quality of this bronze — which was Chinese in origin — was so inconsistent that the Victoria Cross had to be sand-cast rather than die-struck, as most medals were. The sand-casting technique is used to this day. The recipient's details are hand-engraved on the reverse, and the cross is fitted into a special presentation case. Occasionally, the citation for which the award is being made is printed on the silk lining of the case's interior.

Canadians have received a total of 94 of the 1,350 Victoria Crosses awarded between 1856 and 1982. The first was awarded to Alexander Dunn, a native of Upper Canada, who displayed outstanding valour during the famous Charge of the Light Brigade at Balaclava in the Crimean War. The second VC to be awarded to a Canadian was also the first conferred on a person of colour: William Hall of Nova Scotia received it for service in the Indian Mutiny while serving in the Royal Navy. Perhaps the most famous Canadian VC recipient is Billy Bishop, the noted Great War flying ace and later air marshal in the Royal Canadian Air Force. There is

Victoria Cross
Left: Obverse
Right: Reverse

little doubt that the Victoria Cross is firmly fixed in the Canadian symbolic lexicon.

Canada's military valour decorations do not only find their origins in the past; they are also very closely related to the Canadian Bravery Decorations instituted in 1972. All three awards (the VC, SMV and MMV) are presented for acts of valour in the presence of the "enemy," a term that is defined broadly enough to include mutineers, armed rebels and pirates. "Valour" is defined as an exemplary action demonstrated in the presence of the enemy, while "bravery" is an exemplary action demonstrated in a more general sense. Both require a significant level of personal risk.

Under the British system of honours, decorations for military valour included, amongst others, the Victoria Cross, the Distinguished Service Cross, the Military Cross, the Distinguished Flying Cross, the Distinguished Conduct Medal, the Military Medal, the Distinguished Service Medal and the Distinguished Flying Medal. These awards were regularly bestowed upon Canadians during the First and Second World Wars as well as the Korean War. Between the Korean War and the Gulf War of 1990–91, no military valour awards were granted to members of the Royal Canadian Navy, Canadian Army or Royal Canadian Air Force, although a number of bravery decorations and Meritorious Service Decorations were bestowed. The reason was that Canada was not involved in any armed conflict during that interval, and there was therefore little need for a separate series of military valour decorations; meanwhile, the broader bravery decorations instituted in 1972 were regularly awarded to members of the Canadian Forces.

Almost immediately after the establishment of the bravery decorations in 1972, questions were asked regarding the status of the Victoria Cross and whether or not Canadians would continue to be awarded it. Prime Minister Pierre Trudeau regularly dodged the question, always commenting that Canadians should receive "Canadian" decorations, but never stating definitively that the Victoria Cross was never to be awarded to a Canadian again. The country was, after all, not at war.

Throughout the late 1980s and early 1990s, veterans' groups — most notably the Royal Canadian Legion — and other civic-minded organizations such as the Monarchist League of Canada lobbied the government for the reinstatement of the Victoria Cross as Canada's premier decoration for military valour. This cause was supported by all parties in Parliament at the time, most notably the NDP, which was unanimously in favour. In 1987 Prime Minister Brian Mulroney assured members of the Royal Canadian Legion that the VC would become "the cornerstone of Canada's military valour decorations."

The question of creating a series of military valour awards had long been a topic of discussion for the Honours Policy Committee. In late 1990 the committee developed a proposal to establish a series of three military valour awards. It largely ignored the various calls for the reinstatement of the VC and instead proposed that three new military valour decorations be created: the Cross of Military Valour, the Star of Military Valour and the Medal of Military Valour.

Conveniently, in February 1991 a press leak resulted in a front-page article in *The Globe and Mail* that forced the Mulroney government to reconsider its decision. By October of that same year, Saskatchewan MP Doug Fee had introduced a private member's bill, the Victoria Cross Act, which sought to reinstate the decoration. After considerable lobbying by Fee, the bill received support from all parties in the House of Commons, and no member spoke against it.

At the direction of the Prime Minister's Office, the Honours Policy Committee re-examined the problem and decided to reinstate the Victoria Cross; at the same time two new decorations were to be established: the Star of Military Valour and Medal of Military Valour. These were based upon the Star of Courage and the Medal of Bravery respectively.

Such proposals for specific valour decorations for the military were not new. In 1966, shortly before the question of creating the Order of Canada came before Cabinet, the Department of National Defence had developed a proposal for the establishment of a "Cross of Courage" and a "Medal for Bravery."[23]

In the spring of 1993, Cabinet agreed to the creation of the Canadian VC, the SMV and the MMV, which were subsequently approved by the Queen on 2 February 1993, and award of the decorations was made retroactive to 1 January 1993.

Recipients of the awards are selected by the Military Valour Decorations Advisory Committee, which consists of six people, one appointed by the governor general and five appointed by the chief of the defence staff. The committee submits its recommendations to the chief of the defence staff, who then transmits them, upon approval, to the governor general. Under certain circumstances the governor general may delegate the power to award any of the Military Valour Decorations to field commanders, although their decisions are subject to the governor general's approval. Only members of the Canadian Forces and allied forces are eligible for the military valour decorations. Awards can also be cancelled or revoked by the governor general.

There are only a few differences between the original Victoria Cross and the Canadian Victoria Cross, the main one being that the Canadian cross can be revoked, whereas the British award, once bestowed, can never be rescinded. The term "enemy" is much more broadly defined for the Canadian VC as "a hostile armed force, [including] armed mutineers, armed rebels, armed rioters and armed pirates." Canada therefore does not have to be in a formal state of war for members of the forces to be eligible for the Canadian VC or other military valour decorations.

Canada is not the first country to duplicate the original VC; attempts have been made in a wide number of Commonwealth countries. The government of New Zealand, for instance, established the New Zealand Cross on 10 March 1869, by an order-in-council of the governor. This served as a colonial version of the Victoria Cross; it did not represent some great stride towards national independence in the realm of honours, but was rather a result of the fact that colonial troops were ineligible to receive the Victoria Cross at this time, and the New Zealand authorities wished to reward gallant soldiers who had served in the Maori Wars (1860–1872). The New Zealand Cross had effectively been phased out by the early twentieth century, the last award being made in 1910.

The most ignominious attempt to duplicate the VC was made by Ugandan dictator Idi Amin, who instituted a "Cross of Valour" that was practically identical in design and criteria to the VC, with the exception that President Amin's effigy replaced the lion and crown on the VC's obverse. Not surprisingly, Amin himself was one of the recipients!

Australia instituted the Australian Victoria Cross (identical to the British VC) in January 1991, two years before the Canadian VC was instituted. Indeed, actions by the Australian government to create the Australian Victoria Cross and the Australian Star of Gallantry and Medal for Gallantry helped to spur the development of the Canadian military valour decorations. Whereas Australia had used the Order of Canada, Cross of Valour, Star of Courage and Medal of Bravery as the basic structure for its system of honours established in 1975, Canada in turn borrowed Australia's reinstatment of the Victoria Cross and two other gallantry awards as the basis for its own.

The insignia of the Canadian VC differs from the British issue in one aspect only: instead of the motto *For Valour* that appears on the obverse of the British cross, the Canadian version bears the same saying in Latin: *Pro Valore*. The Canadian modifications to the VC were made by Bruce Beatty, who also designed the Star of Military Valour and the Medal of Military Valour.

As no awards of the military valour decorations have yet been made, no certificate has been designed or printed; however, the insignia for the Star of Military Valour and Medal of Military Valour have been manufactured. It can be expected that the design and layout of the certificates will be similar to those used for the three Canadian bravery decorations. Certificates will likely include the citation for the award, name of the recipient and the signature of the governor general.

THE VICTORIA CROSS (CANADA)

Criteria: Awarded for the most conspicuous bravery, a daring or pre-eminent act of valour or self-sacrifice, or extreme devotion to duty in the presence of the enemy.

Insignia: A bronze straight-armed cross pattée with raised edges, measuring 38 mm across. The obverse depicts a lion guardant standing upon the Royal crown, and below the crown a scroll bears the inscription *Pro Valore*. The reverse is plain with raised edges, and the date of the act of valour is engraved in the centre of the reverse (inside the raised circle).

Suspender: A small semicircle with a hole in the centre is located on the uppermost arm of the cross. Through this passes a small bronze link, connected to a "V" below a straight bar ornamented with laurel leaves. On the reverse of the bar is engraved the rank, name and unit of the recipient.

Ribbon: A crimson ribbon, 38 mm wide.

Victoria Cross
Top: Obverse
Bottom: Reverse

Bar for the Victoria Cross

*Star of Military Valour
obverse*

Recipients wear a single miniature of the VC on their undress ribbon.

Bars: Additional awards of the VC are signified by a bronze bar ornamented with laurel leaves.

Postnominals: Recipients are entitled to the postnominals V.C.

Other: Although no Canadian Victoria Crosses have been awarded to date, it is believed that arrangements have been made for the decoration to be made by Hancocks of London from the same bronze cannon metal used to make the British, Australian and New Zealand VCs.

Number of Awards: 0

THE STAR OF MILITARY VALOUR

Criteria: Awarded for distinguished and valiant service in the presence of the enemy.

Insignia: A four-pointed gold star, with a maple leaf in each of the four angles. In the centre of the obverse is a gold maple leaf in a red enamelled field, surrounded by a silver laurel wreath. The reverse is plain, with the Royal cypher and crown and the words *Pro Valore*.

Suspender: A small ball at the top of the star, through which passes a gold ring. The Star of Military Valour is worn on the left breast.

Ribbon: A crimson ribbon, 32 mm wide. Set 2 mm from either edge is a white stripe, 5 mm wide.

Bars: A gold bar bearing a single maple leaf in the centre. A single gold maple leaf is worn in the centre of the undress ribbon for second awards.

Postnominals: Recipients are entitled to use the postnominals S.M.V. or É.V.M.

Other: The rank, name and unit of the recipient are engraved on the reverse below the *Pro Valore* motto. A silver hallmark is impressed on the lower arm of the reverse.

Number of Awards: 0

Star of Military Valour reverse

THE MEDAL OF MILITARY VALOUR

Criteria: Awarded for an act of valour or devotion to duty in the presence of the enemy.

Insignia: A circular gold medal; on the obverse is a single maple leaf surrounded by a laurel wreath. The reverse bears the Royal cypher and crown in the centre, surrounded by the words *Pro Valore*.

Suspender: A straight suspender bar with a fleur-de-lys in the centre, mounted to the disc of the medal.

Ribbon: A crimson ribbon, 32 mm wide, with three 3 mm white stripes — one in the centre of the ribbon, the others set 2 mm from either edge of the ribbon.

Bars: A gold bar bearing a single maple leaf in the centre. A single gold maple leaf is worn on the undress ribbon for second awards.

Medal of Military Valour obverse

Medal of Military Valour reverse

Medal of Military Valour
Left: Lapel pin
Right: Bar

Postnominals: Recipients are entitled to use the postnominals M.M.V., or M.V.M.

Other: The rank, name and unit of the recipient are engraved on the rim. A silver hallmark is impressed on the side of the suspender.

Number of Awards: 0

CHAPTER 13

Meritorious Service Decorations

The meritorious service decorations, which include the Meritorious Service Cross and the Meritorious Service Medal, serve as junior awards to the Order of Canada, Order of Military Merit and Order of Merit of the Police Forces, which are typically used to recognize a lifetime of service. These decorations reward service, or a specific achievement, that falls short of that normally required for admission to one of the national orders. Whether one is awarded the cross or the medal is determined by the calibre of the specific achievement or service rendered.

The military division of the Meritorious Service Cross is similar to the Distinguished Service Order, which was awarded to Canadian officers from the Anglo-Boer War until the Korean War. The civilian division compares with the Commander level of the Order of the British Empire. The military division of the Meritorious Service Medal, however, bears little relation to its British predecessor of the same name; the British Meritorious Service Medal was typically awarded to senior noncommissioned officers who had served more than twenty years in the armed forces. It was also infrequently used as a junior gallantry award. In contrast, both the military and civil divisions of the Canadian Meritorious Service Medal are awarded for deeds similar to that recognized by the Officer and Member level of the Order of the British Empire. Although considered intermediate awards, both the cross and the medal are awarded sparingly.

The origins of the meritorious service decorations can be found in the Canada Medal, which was instituted in 1943 but was never awarded. The Canada Medal was initially intended to be a junior service award for special service of a high degree of merit, such as the discharge of special duties above and beyond the recipient's ordinary work, or highly meritorious performance of ordinary duties where this has entailed work of an especially trying nature or the display of a high degree of initiative and forethought.[24]

Originally the Canada Medal was supposed to be instituted along with a five-levelled Canadian order — similar in structure to the Order of the British Empire — but when the government of the day refused to allow creation of such an order, the Canada Medal was quickly elevated to a senior award that would be conferred upon foreign heads of state and corporals alike. Needless to say, this arrangement was entirely impractical, and although the medal remained an official award from 1943 until 1967, it was never awarded. Initially, the Canada Medal was to be called the Canadian Meritorious Award, and in 1944 there was a further proposal for a Meritorious Service Star.[25]

Left: Prototype of the Meritorious Service Cross
Centre: Prototype of the Forces Meritorious Service Decoration
Right: Prototype of the Forces Meritorious Service Medal

Shortly before the creation of the Order of Canada, the minister of National Defence, Paul Hellyer, tabled a proposal before Cabinet that called for the creation of a comprehensive set of Canadian military awards. The proposal sought to establish two awards for meritorious service, the Forces Meritorious Decoration and the Forces Meritorious Medal, both of which were designed to recognize exceptionally meritorious service over a period of time or in a specific deed.[26] The entire proposal was shelved at the request of Prime Minister Lester Pearson, who was far more interested in getting his Cabinet to agree to the establishment of the Order of Canada, and who did not want to overload them with honours proposals.

Following the establishment of the Order of Military Merit in 1972, members of the Canadian Forces were, on the whole, happy with their new awards. At the most senior level, however, there was still a desire to create an award for meritorious service rendered in a specific deed. Neither the Order of Canada nor the Order of Military Merit could be used for this purpose, and while the country had recently adopted a set of three bravery awards, there was still considered to be a significant gap in the honours system.

Throughout the late 1970s the Government Working Group on Honours examined the shortcomings of the Canadian honours system. Its report of July 1980 called for the creation of the Meritorious Service Cross, along with a variety of other additions.

On 15 September 1982, Prime Minister Pierre Trudeau approved the Canadian Forces Honours Policy. The report indicated that there was a need for an intermediate award, to be ranked below the Order of Military Merit, to recognize "short-term outstanding achievement."[27] The military division of the Meritorious Service Cross was founded on 11 June 1984, when the Queen signed the letters patent.

The civil division of the Meritorious Service Cross and both divisions of the Meritorious Service Medal were created in part due to problems experienced by the Advisory Council of the Order of Canada. Since its inception, the council had complained that there was no junior honour to the Order of Canada. There had also been constant worries about the practice of awarding the Order of Canada in recognition of a single achievement — something that had been done in a number of instances, most specifically for Olympic medallists. The addition of a civil Meritorious Service Cross and Meritorious Service Medal was seen by members of the Honours Policy Committee (the successor to the Working Group on Honours) as an appropriate solution. Thus, some nine years after the establishment of the Meritorious Service Cross, the letters patent were amended on 6 June 1991.[28]

Recipients of the MSC and MSM are selected by either the Civil or Military Advisory Committee of the Meritorious Service Decorations. The committee consists of a person appointed by a special advisory committee, a person appointed by the governor general (or the governor general herself), and five members of the Canadian Forces (selected by the chief of the defence staff). The Civil Advisory Committee consists of a justice of the Supreme Court of Canada (who serves a three- year term), the secretary to the governor general, the clerk of the Privy Council, the deputy minister of Canadian Heritage, the deputy minister of Foreign Affairs, and four other members appointed by the governor general (for a three-year term). Both of the advisory committees are set up along the same lines as the Advisory Council of the Order of Canada.

The MSC and MSM are awarded with certificates bearing the name of the recipient, the citation of the award and the signature of the governor general.

The Meritorious Service Cross
Top: Obverse
Centre: Reverse
Bottom: Lapel pin

THE MERITORIOUS SERVICE CROSS

Criteria: Award of the Cross's military division is open to all ranks of the Canadian Forces — or allied forces — for the performance of a military deed or military activity, in a highly professional manner or of a very high standard, that brings benefit or great honour to the Canadian Forces.

The civil cross is awarded to Canadian citizens, Commonwealth and foreign citizens for the performance of a deed or activity, in an outstandingly professional manner or of an uncommonly high standard, that brings considerable benefit or great honour to Canada.

Insignia: Designed by Bruce Beatty, the insignia is identical for both the military and civilian divisions, consisting of a Greek silver cross with splayed and convexed ends, surmounted with the Royal crown. At the centre of the obverse is a maple leaf surrounded by a circle, and between the arms of the cross there is a laurel wreath. In the centre of the reverse is the Royal cypher and, surrounded by a double circle, the words *Meritorious Service Méritoire*. The name of the recipient is on the reverse of the suspension bar, and the date is engraved on the reverse of the top arm. Until the mid-1990s the MSC was made from sterling silver; it is now made of rhodium plated to look like silver.

Suspension: A straight graduated bar attached to the top of the crown.

Ribbon: For the military version, the ribbon is 32 mm wide and blue in colour, with a white strip 6 mm wide centred on the outer third of each side of the ribbon. The civilian version is similar, but with an additional 2 mm white stripe down the centre.

Bars: Subsequent awards of the cross are recognized with a silver bar with a maple leaf in the centre. A silver maple leaf is worn on the undress ribbon to represent a second award.

Postnominals: Recipients are entitled to use the postnominals M.S.C.

Other: The MSC can be awarded for deeds retroactive to 11 June 1984 (the date the Meritorious Service Cross was created).

Number of Awards: 84 Military Division, 30 Civil Division (including one civil MSC to a non-Canadian and 17 military MSCs to non-Canadians)

THE MERITORIOUS SERVICE MEDAL

Criteria: Award of the military division of the Meritorious Service Medal is open to all ranks of the Canadian Forces (or allied forces) for the performance of a military deed or military activity, in a highly professional manner or of a very high standard, that brings benefit or honour to the Canadian Forces.

The civil award is given to Canadian citizens, Commonwealth and foreign citizens

Meritorious Service Cross Ribbon — Civil

Meritorious Service Cross Ribbon — Military

Meritorious Service Medal obverse

Meritorious Service Medal
Top: Reverse
Bottom: Lapel pin

Meritorious Service Cross
Ribbon — Civil

The Meritorious Service Cross
Ribbon — Military

for the performance of a deed or activity, in a highly professional manner or of a very high standard, that brings benefit or honour to Canada.

Insignia: Like the MSC, the medal is designed by Bruce Beatty and is identical for both military and civilian recipients, consisting of a circular silver medal surmounted by the Royal crown. The obverse bears the design of the Meritorious Service Cross; the reverse bears the Royal cypher and, within a double circle, the words *Meritorious Service Méritoire.* The medal is named on the edge. Until the mid-1990s, the MSM was made from sterling silver; it is now rhodium plated to look like silver.

Suspension: A small silver ring which passes through the top of the crown.

Ribbon: The military version has a blue ribbon, 32 mm wide. Centred on the outer third of either side of the ribbon is a white stripe 6 mm wide, with a 1 mm wide blue stripe in its centre. The civilian ribbon is similar, but with the addition of a 2 mm white stripe down the centre of the ribbon.

Bars: Subsequent awards of the medal are recognized with a silver bar with a maple leaf in the centre. A silver maple leaf is worn on the undress ribbon to represent a second award.

Postnominals: Recipients are entitles to use the postnominals M.S.M.

Other: The MSM can be awarded for deeds retroactive to 11 June 1984 (the date the

Meritorious Service Cross was created). The year of award is engraved on the reverse just below the crown.

Number of Awards: 150 Military Division, 229 Civil Division (18 civil division MSMs to non-Canadians and 8 military division MSMs to non-Canadians)

Bar for the Meritorious Service Cross and the Meritorious Service Medal

CHAPTER 14

War, Operational and Service Medals

War service medals are perhaps the most familiar awards to the general public. Most people can recall a father or grandfather polishing his medals, and in most cases these were war medals. With the increase in the number of peacekeeping missions and Canada's involvement in military operations conducted by international organizations, however, the scope of contemporary war service medals has been broadened to include operational service medals and service medals.

Although medals commemorating service in battle are known to date back to the time of Elizabeth I and the defeat of the Spanish armada, these were not medals intended for wear. Instead, the British Naval General Service Medal and Military General Service Medal — both established in 1848 — have served as the primary models for war and operational service medals throughout the Commonwealth. They were largely retroactive awards, for battles dating back to 1793 and including the War of 1812. While a few earlier issues, such as the Sutlej Medal, are of a similar design, the former two medals were the most widely awarded.

The Naval and Military General Service Medals — although not awarded solely for service in North America — were the first modern-style medals awarded to Canadians or to others for service in what is now Canada. The first British medal awarded for service in Canada was the North West Canada Medal, instituted in September 1885 for those who had served in suppressing the second Riel rebellion. The obverse of the medal displayed a youthful Queen Victoria, while the reverse featured a wreath of maple leaves and the inscription "North West Canada 1885." It was an austere design, but it set a precedent in Canada as the first true Canadian military service medal. More than 5,000 were awarded, almost all of which went to members of the Canadian militia, the North West Mounted Police and Canadian transport officials. It was largely a Canadian expedition, one in which very few British officials were involved.[29]

*Military General
Service Medal
Left: Obverse
Right: Reverse*

Indeed, the striking of the medal was initiated by Canada's governor general, Lord Lansdowne. On 19 May 1885, Lansdowne suggested to the British government that a medal recognizing service in the North West Rebellion should be struck, as it "would have an excellent effect upon the spirit of the Canadian forces."

Just over two months later, on 22 June 1885, the British government agreed that such a medal could be struck, on the condition that the cost be borne by the Canadian government.[30] Lansdowne was elated with this news, although much less satisfied that the Canadian government was to be saddled with the bill. He viewed the cost as inconsiderable, given the "results which would follow from the free gift of the medal." It was ultimately agreed that the imperial government would pay for the honour.

The governor general even took an interest in the design: "The obverse will, I assume, represent the Queen's head, and the reverse might be engraved with a design distinctive of the Dominion."[31] And Lansdowne later suggested that the reverse of the medal "should be ornamented with a wreath of Maple leaves, in the centre of which the words 'The North West 1885' might be impressed." While the governor general developed the concept, it was Allan Wyon of the Royal Mint who completed the formal designs.

The Canadian government, never having been involved with the striking of an official military medal, briefly considered having the medal struck in bronze, although Lansdowne insisted that silver be used. The Canadian government was clearly unaware that bronze medals were usually reserved for native troops in India.

An order-in-council was approved on 16 February 1887, after Queen Victoria authorized the design and striking of the medal; thus Canada's first military medal was born.

North West
Canada Medal
Left: Obverse
Right: Reverse

The design and purpose of such war service medals has remained largely the same since the striking of the North West Canada Medal, with minor variations. Even the eighteen-month period that it took to get the medal approved is comparable to the time it takes to have a modern Canadian award developed from a rough concept to completed design.

The next medal with a connection to Canada was the Canada General Service Medal, sanctioned in 1899 by Queen Victoria for those who had served in the 1866 and 1870 Fenian Raids as well as in the 1870 Red River Rebellion. The obverse depicted Queen Victoria, while the reverse contained a spreading wreath of maple leaves and the Canadian Red Ensign. Most significantly, the ribbon comprised three equal stripes: red, white and red — possibly taken from the flag used by the Royal Military College of Canada, founded in 1876. To some degree, it is from this flag, ribbon and medal that Canada gained its official colours and, ultimately, the Maple Leaf flag.

There was another tradition inaugurated with the Canada General Service Medal: the creation of medals thirty years or more after the actual event: the first Fenian Raids had taken place thirty-three years before. Similarly, the Korea Volunteer Service Medal was not issued until 1991, more than forty years after the Korean War.

It was not until the 1990s that the Canadian government would begin instituting new medals on a regular basis. Prior to 1990, aside from the Canadian Forces Decoration and United Nations Service Medals, there were no Canadian medals for operational services such as peacekeeping or for service with NATO or other international organizations.

While the Second World War yielded the Canadian Voluntary Service Medal and the Korean War a special Korean War Medal, these were the only uniquely Canadian awards used within the broader British honours system in Canada. Although the British government had given Canada permission to use the British Naval General Service Medal and Military General Service Medal, this offer was never accepted.

Attempts were made throughout the late 1950s and early 1960s to establish a modern Canadian General Service Medal. The Canadian Forces were involved in the International Commission for Supervision and Control in Indo-China, and there was a desire amongst some at the Department of National Defence to recognize their service. Regulations were created and designs drawn up, always to be thwarted by the Minister of National Defence or a senior elected official. The most detailed of these proposals emerged in June 1957: it called for the creation of a circular silver medal with the Queen's portrait on the obverse and on the reverse an anchor, crossed swords and an eagle, superimposed on a maple leaf and circumscribed by the words *General Service Général*. In many respects, this proposal served as the prototype for the Special Service Medal that was instituted in 1984 but not actually awarded until the early 1990s.

Aside from the new South-West Asia Medal, Campaign Service Star and General Service Medal, all of Canada's existing war and operational service medals were designed by Bruce Beatty. There are a variety of common elements amongst all the medals, be it an effigy of the Queen or the use of the crown, Royal cypher and a variety of maple leaf motifs. It is only most recently, with the South-West Asia Medal, that Canada has returned to using allegorical figures on the reverse of medals as opposed to the name of the medal or service. Similarly, the General Campaign Star and the General Service Medal return Canada to more traditionally designed awards.

The following section outlines the war and operational service medals that Canadians have been eligible for since 1967. The Canadian Voluntary Service Medal, the Newfoundland Voluntary Service Medal and the Canadian Korea War Medal are not included, as they were intended to be integrated into the broad-

er Commonwealth honours system, while awards since 1967 are purely domestic.

Left: Canada General Service
Medal obverse
Right: Canada General Service
Medal reverse

THE SPECIAL SERVICE MEDAL

Origins: The medal was originally instituted in 1984, following nearly three years of work; the medal received initial approval, but was then set aside. The original medal was to be struck in cupro-nickel and have a straight suspender bar that would be separately attached, while the individual bars were to be riveted to the medal, similar to the way bars are attached to the British General Service Medal. The original regulations indicated that each medal was to be named, and this remained in place until the regulations were changed in 1992 — however, no medal was ever officially named. Recipients were also to receive a special certificate of award with the medal, but none has been issued.

Special Service Medal obverse

The medal was revived in 1991, around the same time that the Korea Volunteer Service Medal and the Gulf and Kuwait Medals were being developed. The only difference between the regulations of 1984 and those issued in 1992 was that the 1984 regulations related more to the administration of the medal than to the medal itself. Each bar is authorized by an order-in-council, and as of 2005, seven bars have been authorized, although one — Jugoslavija — was subsequently revoked and never issued. The medal is awarded to members of the Canadian Forces, and can be awarded posthumously.

Special Service Medal reverse

Insignia: A circular silver medal 36 mm in diameter, made of a copper and zinc alloy and plated in rhodium. The obverse bears a single maple leaf surrounded by a laurel wreath, while the reverse depicts the Royal cypher and crown in the centre, circumscribed with the words *Special Service Spécial.* The medal was designed by Bruce Beatty.

Prototype of the Special Service Medal

Pakistan Bar

Peace Bar

Criteria: Awarded for special service in a specific theatre; the criteria vary according to the bar. The medal is never issued without a bar.

Pakistan 1989–90. The recipient must have given a minimum of ninety days' service with the Mine Awareness and Clearance Training Program in Pakistan, during the period beginning on 15 March 1989, and ending on 29 July 1990, under the auspices of the United Nations. This bar was created in 1992 and can now be exchanged for the United Nations Special Service Medal.

Peace — Paix. The recipient must have served an aggregate of 180 days of honourable service in peacekeeping operations, from the beginning of international peacekeeping operations in November 1947 through 21 July 2001. The service cannot have been recognized by any other award in, or accepted by, the Canadian system of honours. The list of missions for which this bar can be awarded consists of every UN peacekeeping mission and international mission that Canada has been involved in.

Essentially, this bar was awarded to those members of the Canadian Forces who participated in peacekeeping missions, yet did not meet the minimum requirement to qualify for the UN Service Medal. One could not receive the UN medal for a particular mission and also receive the Peace bar for the same mission. This bar was created in 1992, and the criteria were subsequently revised in 1995. On 21 June 2001, this bar was superseded by the Canadian Peacekeeping Service Medal.

Alert. The recipient must have served an aggregate of 180 days of honourable service on the posted strength of Canadian Forces Station Alert, or have performed honourable service with a military force operationally deployed to or at CFS Alert, since it began its operation on 1 September 1958. This bar was first created in 1992 and the criteria were revised in 1995.

Alert Bar

NATO+OTAN. The recipient must have served an aggregate of 180 days of honourable service within the North Atlantic Treaty Organization's area of responsibility, defined as the territory of any of the parties in Europe or North America, the Algerian departments of France, or the territory of Turkey or the islands under the jurisdiction of any of the parties in the North Atlantic north of the Tropic of Cancer. A person must have been under NATO command for 180 days in order to qualify for this bar. The award is also given to those serving within forces deployed on vessels or aircraft of any of the parties, when in or over these territories or any other areas in Europe in which occupation forces of any parties were stationed, or the Mediterranean Sea or the North Atlantic area north of the Tropic of Cancer, since NATO's establishment on 1 January 1951. The bar was first created in 1992, and the criteria were revised in 1995.

NATO + OTAN Bar

Humanitas. Awarded to those who have performed an aggregate of thirty days of honourable service outside Canada sine 11 June 1984, in support of any humanitarian operation conducted in response to a disaster or human conflict, including rescue, relief and reconstruction operations. The service cannot be acknowledged by the award of any other honour that is part of the Canadian honours system. This award includes the following missions: February 1985, Ethiopia, medical teams and relief

Humanitas Bar

supplies; September 1985, Mexico, earthquake relief; November 1985, Colombia, relief supplies after the mudslide; June 1988, Ethiopia, famine relief; December 1988, Armenia, provision of relief supplies; September 1988, Jamaica, relief supplies; October 1989, Montserrat and Nevis, relief supplies and medical assistance; March 1991, Turkey and Iraq, post–Gulf War medical assistance to Kurds; August 1991, Ethiopia, famine relief; January 1992, Commonwealth of Independent States, humanitarian assistance; September 1992, Florida, humanitarian relief after a hurricane; October 1992, Bahamas, humanitarian relief following a hurricane; July 1994, Rwanda, humanitarian relief to refugees. This bar was established in 1993, and the criteria were revised in 1997.

Ranger Bar

Ranger. Awarded for an aggregate of four years of honourable service as a Canadian Ranger, performing the duties involved with providing a military presence in support of Canadian sovereignty. Eligible service includes reporting unusual activities, collecting local data of significance to support military operations, supplying local expertise or assistance and advice, acting as a guide or advisor in search and rescue activities, and completing a minimum of three Ranger Patrol Exercises within Canada or its territorial and contiguous waters since 1947. This bar was created in 1999.

Suspender: A straight bar suspender.

Ribbon: A Canadian Forces green ribbon 32 mm wide, edged on either side with 5 mm of red and 5 mm of white.

Bars: Individual bars 32 mm long are sewn onto the ribbon. To date, seven bars have been approved: the six described above (Pakistan 1989–90, Peace—Paix, Alert, NATO+OTAN, Humanitas and Ranger) and Jugoslavija. The Jugoslavija bar was subsequently revoked and replaced by the European Community Monitoring Mission in Yugoslavia Medal. A small silver, gold or red maple leaf is worn on the undress ribbon to indicate a second, third or fourth award, respectively.

Postnominals: None

Number of Awards:
Pakistan 1989–90 50
Peace — Paix 2,267
Alert 7,113
NATO+OTAN 62,341
Humanitas 674
Ranger 2,411

Other: The medal is issued in a white, rectangular cardboard box, with the name of the medal in black letters on the lid.

THE KOREA VOLUNTARY SERVICE MEDAL

Origins: Many members of the Royal Canadian Navy, Canadian Army and Royal Canadian Air Force who served in Korea did not accumulate the requisite amount of service to qualify for the Queen's Korean War Medal, and so they were only awarded the United Nations Korea Service Medal. For many years there had been complaints that, while those who served during the Second World War had received a Voluntary Service Medal, Korean War veterans had not.[32] Forty years after the event, a Voluntary Service Medal was approved; basically, anyone who

Korea Voluntary Service Medal
obverse

*Korea Voluntary Service Medal
reverse*

received the United Nations Korea Service Medal received the new Korea Voluntary Service Medal.

Criteria: Awarded to a former member of the Royal Canadian Navy, the Canadian Army or the Royal Canadian Air Force who was a member of the Canadian armed forces during all or part of the period beginning on 27 June 1950, and ending 27 July 1954, and was in Korea, Japan, Okinawa or in Korean waters; was either on strength of an army unit of formation in Korea for at least one day, was on active service for at least twenty-eight days on board a ship, or flew one sortie over Korea or Korean waters in the Yellow Sea or Sea of Japan; or accumulated at least twenty-eight days' service in the above mentioned areas.

Insignia: A circular silver-coloured medal 36 mm in diameter, made of a copper and zinc alloy and plated in rhodium. The obverse bears a crowned effigy of Her Majesty, circumscribed by the words *Elizabeth II Dei Gratia Regina*, with the word *Canada* at the base of the medal. The reverse of the medal bears the inscription *Korea Volunteer 1950–1954 Volontaire Corée* contained within a laurel wreath, with a maple leaf centred at the bottom. The medal was designed by Bruce Beatty.

Suspender: A straight suspender, 32 mm wide.

Ribbon: A yellow ribbon 32 mm wide, bordered on either edge with a stripe 7 mm wide in United Nations blue. Down the centre there is a red stripe 6 mm wide, upon which is centred a 2 mm white stripe.

Bars: None

Postnominals: None

Number of Awards: 18,289

Other: The medal was issued in a white, rectangular cardboard box. It could be issued posthumously.

THE GULF AND KUWAIT MEDAL

Origins: In August 1990, Iraq invaded its neighbour Kuwait, an act that was immediately met with international indignation and outrage. Within a relatively short period of time a coalition had been formed — led by the United States and aided by Great Britain, Saudi Arabia, Canada, Italy, and a variety of other partners — which sought to liberate Kuwait. Close to 5,000 members of the Canadian armed forces were dispatched to the Persian Gulf. The majority were centred at a base in Bahrain, or on board HMCS *Athabaskan, Terra Nova, Huron* and *Protecteur* in the Persian Gulf. Canadian CF-18s also flew sorties over Iraq.

Gulf and Kuwait Medal obverse

Criteria: Awarded to members of the Canadian Forces (or those connected with it) who served a minimum of thirty days' cumulative service between 2 August 1990, and 27 June 1991, in Bahrain, Qatar, Kuwait, Iraq or any country in the immediate vicinity in which members of the coalition forces were based. The medal and bar was awarded to those who served in the theatre of operations between 16 January 1991, and 3 March 1991.

Gulf and Kuwait Medal reverse

Insignia: A circular, silver-coloured medal, 36 mm in diameter, made of a copper and zinc alloy and plated with rhodium. The obverse bears a crowned effigy of Her Majesty, circum-scribed by the words *Elizabeth II Dei Gratia Regina*, with the word *Canada* at the base of the medal. The reverse of the medal bears the inscription *The Gulf and Kuwait 1990–1991 Le Golfe et Kuwait* contained within a laurel wreath, with a maple leaf centred at the bottom. The medal was designed by Bruce Beatty.

Suspender: A straight suspender, 32 mm wide.

Ribbon: The ribbon is 32 mm wide; a central stripe, 8 mm wide and sand in colour, is flanked by a 5 mm navy blue stripe, a 2 mm scarlet stripe (to represent the army), and a 5 mm light blue stripe (to represent the air force).

Bars: A plain silver bar with a maple leaf in the centre.

Postnominals: None

Number of Awards: 4,436 medals (3,184 with bar, 1,252 without)

Other: Originally, the ribbon specified for this medal was to be the same as that used on the British Gulf War Medal. The manufacturer of the ribbon informed the Canadian government of this coincidence, and the design was slightly altered by reversing the two shades of blue. The medal could be issued posthumously, and was given in a white, rectangular cardboard box.

Gulf and Kuwait Medal Bar

THE SOMALIA MEDAL

Origins: In January 1991 the dictator of Somalia, Siad Barre, was overthrown and the country descended into chaos. As the situation deteriorated and the international community called for a cease-fire, the United Nations sent in a fifty-person observer team (UNOSOM) to monitor the situation. As the situation deteriorated further and starvation proliferated, the UNOSOM mission disintegrated. The UN Security Council subsequently adopted Resolution 794, which authorized "the use of all necessary means to establish as soon as possible a secure environment for humanitarian relief operations in Somalia." Operation Restore Hope and the United Task Force were authorized. The Canadian Airborne Regiment, which had been on notice, was dispatched to Somalia. What transpired there resulted in the death of one Somali youth and the disbandment of the Canadian Airborne Regiment. A small group of Canadian soldiers was implicated in the death of the Somali youth, and scandal erupted.

Somalia Medal obverse

Initially, the Canadian government did not intend to issue a medal in light of the "Somalia Incident." As it became apparent that the failings in the theatre were more a reflection of significant structural problems within the upper levels of the Canadian Forces and the Department of National Defence, the focus shifted away from the actual soldiers involved in the murder and onto the senior members of the Canadian Forces. The award was instituted to recognize members of the Canadian Forces who were involved in the Somalia Joint Task Force's Operation Deliverance. The mission's primary goal was to ensure peace and order in the capital city and other major centres, as well as to aid in the widespread distribution of food to the famine- and war-ravaged country.

Somalia Medal reverse

The medal was sanctioned, but unlike previous Canadian medals, the regulations required "honourable" service. Thus, those directly implicated in the killing of the Somali teenager were prohibited from receiving the medal.

Criteria: Awarded to members of the Canadian Forces who obtained a minimum of ninety days of honourable service (or sixty days if ordered out) in the Somalia Democratic Republic, the Republic of Kenya, or within 200 nautical miles of the coast of Somalia, between 16 November 1992 and 30 June 1993.

Insignia: A circular, gold-coloured medal 36 mm in diameter. The obverse bears three maple leaves, in fess and overlapping, above which is inscribed the word *Canada* and below which appear two sprigs of laurel leaves. The reverse depicts the Royal cypher and crown, circumscribed by the words *Somalia Somalie 1992–1993*. The medal was designed by Bruce Beatty.

Suspender: A small, undetailed claw protrudes from the top of the medal, through which a gold ring and the ribbon pass.

Ribbon: The ribbon is 32 mm wide. On either edge is a 5 mm stripe in United Nations blue. Superimposed on a central, 22 mm white stripe, is a series of five stripes, each of which is 2.5 mm wide. From left to right, these stripes are sand, navy blue, scarlet, light blue and sand.

Bars: None

Postnominals: None

Number of Awards: 1,408

Other: Early diagrams of the medal did not include the word *Canada*, and the medal was originally supposed to have a straight suspender bar. The straight suspender bar was changed to a ring on account of cost. The medal was issued in a white, rectangular cardboard box.

THE PEACEKEEPING SERVICE MEDAL

Origins: The Peacekeeping Service Medal was established in part so that Canadian peacekeepers would receive an award from Canada, besides the service medals from the United Nations, NATO and others that they would usually receive. The medal was established to acknowledge the award of the 1988 Nobel Peace Prize to all UN peacekeepers. In that same year, the Department of National Defence considered creating a special medal for those who had served in peacekeeping operations, but it was decided at the time that no medal should be struck, as those who had participated in UN missions and completed the requisite period of service had already been awarded one of the UN service medals. To award two medals for one action is contrary to the Canadian honours policy, and as this would have happened in the majority of cases, the plan was shelved.

In late 1996 a private member's bill was introduced into the House of Commons by Jack Fraser, O.M.M., M.S.C., C.D. Parliament subsequently passed an act sanctioning the creation of this medal, making it the only medal in the Canadian honours system that was established through an act of Parliament.

The Canadian medal is more accessible to peacekeepers, given that it is awarded for thirty days' service, or about a third of that required for most UN peacekeeping service

Peacekeeping Service Medal
obverse

Peacekeeping Service Medal
reverse

medals. Those who had previously not quali-fied for a UN medal or the Special Service Medal with the Peace bar thus became eligible for the new medal. Peacekeeping is one of the most significant activities undertaken by the Canadian Forces today, and it was seen as fit-ting that a Canadian medal of this type be issued. Civilians can also be awarded the medal, although it is primarily awarded to members of the Canadian Forces.

Criteria: A minimum of thirty days' cumula-tive peacekeeping service as a member of a force under the auspices of the United Nations, or with another recognized interna-tional peacekeeping force.

Insignia: A circular medal made of an oxidized silver-coloured alloy. The obverse depicts the three Canadian peacekeeper figures that top the Peacekeeping Monument in Ottawa, and this is circumscribed by the words *Peacekeeping — Service de la Paix,* together with two maple leaves. The reverse bears the Royal cypher and crown superimposed upon a maple leaf, sur-rounded by two sprigs of laurel. The word *Canada* appears at the base. The medal was designed by Bruce Beatty; the obverse design is taken from the Canadian Peacekeeping Memorial in Ottawa, which was designed by Jack Harman.

Suspender: A straight bar suspender, bearing a maple leaf on the post that connects the bar to the medal.

Ribbon: A ribbon 32 mm wide with a central 8 mm stripe of United Nations blue, flanked by 4 mm stripes of white, red and green.

Bars: None

Postnominals: None

Number of Awards: Approximately 69,543 to date. A total of 125,000 personnel are eligible, and the number grows each year.

Other: The obverse of the medal was originally intended to be the side that depicted the maple leaf and Royal cypher. Rather suddenly, after pressure from the Peacekeeping Veterans' Association, this was changed so that the side depicting the peacekeeping monument became the obverse. The medal was issued in a white, rectangular cardboard box.

THE SOUTH-WEST ASIA SERVICE MEDAL

Origins: Following the terrorist attacks on New York and Washington on 11 September 2001, the international community rallied to root out the terrorist group Al Qaida, which was principally located in Afghanistan. The United States, Canada, the United Kingdom and other partners subsequently invaded Afghanistan and overthrew the pro–Al Qaida Taliban government. The South-West Asia Service Medal was awarded to those who were involved in these operations.

Criteria: Awarded to members of the Canadian Forces who were posted, attached to or working with a Canadian or allied unit, or a formation deployed outside Canada that was participating in, or providing direct support on a full-time basis to, operations conducted in southwest Asia for a period of at least nine-

South-West Asia Service Medal obverse

South-West Asia Service Medal reverse

South-West Asia Service Medal Bar

ty days after 11 September 2001. Those who served thirty days in a theatre received a bar.

Insignia: A circular, nickel-plated medal, 36 mm in diameter. The obverse bears the effigy of Her Majesty the Queen, wearing the King George IV State Diadem, circumscribed with the words *Elizabeth II Dei Gratia Regina.* At the base is the word *Canada,* flanked by a pair of maple leaves. On the reverse is a hydra, a multiheaded creature from Greek mythology, transfixed by a Canadian sword and circumscribed by the Latin phrase *Adversus Malum Pugnamus* ("We are fighting evil"). This concept was designed by Captain Carl Gauthier, while the formal artwork was created by Cathy Bursey-Sabourin, the Fraser Herald.

Suspender: A straight bar suspender connects to the medal by a cluster of proportionate olive leaves.

Ribbon: The ribbon is 32 mm wide, with a central white stripe 12 mm wide, flanked on either side by 4 mm of black, 2 mm of red, and 4 mm of sand.

Bars: The Afghanistan bar is awarded to individuals who served for a period of thirty days while deployed in the theatre of operations after 11 September 2001.

Postnominals: None

Other: The medal is issued in a red, rectangular cardboard box.

Number of Awards: 7,497 (7,200 with the Afghanistan bar, 297 without)

THE GENERAL CAMPAIGN STAR

Origins: The practice of issuing a campaign star for service in a war zone or warlike situation can be traced back to the British East India Company, which issued a campaign star for its various engagements in Gwalior, Maharajpoor and Punnir in 1844. This tradition was continued with the 1914 and 1914–15 Campaign Stars, issued to those who served in action during the early days of the First World War. A total of eight campaign stars were awarded during the Second World War, including the 1939–45 Star, the Atlantic Star, the Air Crew Europe Star, the Pacific Star, the Burma Star, the Africa Star, the Italy Star and the France and Germany Star. The main requirement to receive these various stars was a minimum period of service in a defined theatre of war. The practice of issuing a star to recognize war or warlike service is a tradition that continues in other Commonwealth countries such as India and Kenya.

In this tradition, the recently inaugurated General Campaign Star was created to recognize service in warlike situations. The existing Canadian honours system did not adequate recognize such service, as the Special Service Medal was never intended to be used in such situations. All General Campaign Stars are issued with a bar to specify the operation being reognized. It is possible to earn more than one bar.

Criteria: The criteria vary depending on what bar is awarded with the star.

Allied Force Bar. This bar is to be awarded to aircrew who flew at least five sorties over enemy territory during Operation Allied Force between 24 March and 10 June 1999. As

General Campaign Star obverse

General Campaign Star reverse

*General Campaign Star
Allied Force Bar*

*General Campaign Star
ISAF + FIAS Bar*

Canadian honours policy precludes dual recognition, some recipients must exchange their previously awarded NATO Medal for the General Campaign Star.

ISAF+FIAS Bar. This bar is to be awarded to those who have served at least thirty days in Afghanistan as part of the Canadian contribution to the International Security Assistance Force (ISAF), since 24 April 2003.

Insignia: A four-pointed gold star, 44 mm wide, representing the four cardinal points of a compass. The obverse contains a wreath of maple leaves with the Royal crown at the top. The blades and hilts of two superimposed crossed swords form four additional points to the star, and over this are superimposed an anchor and a flying eagle. On the reverse, within a raised circle, are the Royal cypher ensigned by the Royal crown, a plain space for engraving, and three maple leaves on one stem. This concept was designed by Captain Carl Gauthier, while the formal artwork was created by Cathy Bursey-Sabourin, the Fraser Herald.

Suspender: A small gold ring passes through a ball at the tip of the star.

Ribbon: A ribbon 32 mm wide, with a green central stripe 12 mm wide, flanked on either side by 2 mm of white and a further 8 mm of red.

Bars: The star is always issued with a bar. There are currently two bars: Allied Force and ISAF+FIAS.

Postnominals: None

Other: The star is based upon the 1914–15 Star awarded to Canadians and other Commonwealth troops for service in the First World War. Each star will be named on the reverse. The medal is issued in a burgundy rectangular box whose lid is impressed in gold with the Canadian Coat of Arms.

Number of Awards: 42 with Allied Force Bar, 4,282 with ISAF Bar

THE GENERAL SERVICE MEDAL

Origins: The idea to strike a new Canadian General Service Medal dates back to the 1960s, although it was largely abandoned when the Special Service Medal was approved in 1984. This version of the General Service Medal is a companion to the General Campaign Star, the General Service Medal being reserved for operational support, while the General Campaign Star is for service in theatre.

Criteria: The criteria varies depending upon which bar is mainly awarded with the medal. The General Service Medal is awarded to those who are outside an area of operation, but performing a support role to operations in the presence of an armed enemy. This medal can be awarded to both military and civilian personnel.

Allied Force Bar. The Allied Force bar to the medal is to be awarded to those who provided direct support of Operation Allied Force in Aviano and Vicenza, Italy, for at least thirty days during the operation. As Canadian honours policy precludes dual recognition, some recipients must exchange their previously awarded NATO Medal for the General Service Medal.

General Service Medal obverse

General Service Medal reverse

General Service Medal Allied Force Bar

General Service Medal ISAF + FIAS Bar

ISAF+FIAS Bar. This bar to the medal is to be awarded to those members of the military who provided direct support from outside Afghanistan, in locations such as Camp Mirage and Turkey, for at least ninety days. Civilians eligible for recognition will be awarded the ISAF bar for thirty days' service in Afghanistan or ninety days' service outside the theatre.

Insignia: A silver-coloured circular medal of cupro-nickel, bearing a crowned effigy of Her Majesty Queen Elizabeth II on the obverse, circumscribed with *Elizabeth II Dei Gratia Regina* and *Canada*, separated by small crosses pattée. These crosses represent military valour and merit, and are of the shape used for the insignia of the Victoria Cross and the Order of Military Merit. On the reverse are two crossed swords, an anchor and a flying eagle; the entire device is surrounded by two branches of maple leaves which form a wreath, and this is surmounted by a Royal crown. The concept for this medal was designed by Captain Carl Gauthier, while the formal artwork was created by Cathy Bursey-Sabourin, the Fraser Herald.

Suspender: A straight bar suspender connects to the medal by a cluster of three overlapping maple leafs.

Ribbon: The ribbon is 32 mm wide, with a central red stripe 18 mm wide, on either side of which are 2 mm of white and a further 5 mm of green.

Bars: The medal is always issued with a bar. There are currently two bars: Allied Force and ISAF+FIAS.

Postnominals: None

Other: The medal is engraved with the name of the recipient on the edge of the medal. Each medal is issued in a burgundy rectangular box whose lid is impressed in gold with the Canadian Coat of Arms.

Number of Awards: 54 with Allied Force Bar and 804 with ISAF Bar

CHAPTER 15

United Nations Service Medals

The United Nations is perhaps the world's most widely recognized organization, its flag being universally recognized around the globe. Founded in 1945, the UN has served as a focal point for international diplomacy and peaceful co-operation amongst nations. The institution has gone to war on two occasions — the Korean War and the First Gulf War of 1990–91 — yet it is most widely known for its peace-keeping, observing and monitoring missions.

Under the auspices of the United Nations, forty-three separate medals have been issued for these missions. In nearly all of these cases, it is only the ribbon and not the physical metal medal that changes from one mission to another, the UN preferring to spend its valuable resources on the various missions and not on medals. In this sense, the UN medals are similar to the campaign stars issued during the Second World War.

The design of the various types of UN medals is relatively simple. The symbols employed on each medal are very similar, with only minor changes in wording or the suspension style used. Since the Korean War, the ribbons issued have generally been representative of the national colours of the country or countries in which the particular mission took place; early on it was discovered that there was a finite number of ways that blue and white could be used to make different ribbons. Even today, with thirty-eight different ribbons issued, it is difficult to develop new ribbon designs that are not easily mistaken for those that have already been issued. Indeed, some ribbons are shared between missions, while some UN medals have up to five different bars denoting different segments of a certain extended mission (Haiti).

The focal point of the UN's emblem is a map of the globe, centred on the North Pole and drawn using an azimuthal equidistant projection (one in which a straight line drawn from the centre to any point on the map will always represent the shortest distance between the two points), surrounded by olive branches. The pale blue colour used by the United Nations on its flag and in all UN medal ribbons — United Nations blue, less commonly known as Stettinius blue — was selected because no country used that colour in its national flag at that time. The UN emblem and colour scheme were designed by the United States State Department and were unveiled at the first UN Conference, held in San Francisco in 1945.[33]

The first United Nations medal, now known as the United Nations Korean Medal, was established in October 1950 for service in the Korean War. The United Nations Korean Medal was issued in eleven different languages (English, Amharic, Dutch, French, Greek, Italian, Korean, Spanish, Tagalog, Thai and Turkish). The UN Korean Medal was issued for twenty-four hours' service under United Nations command or in the immediate area. In all, 25,584 medals were issued to Canadians, while a total of 2,760,000 were awarded to all the countries that participated in the UN–led mission.

Despite the alacrity with which the UN Korean Medal was devised and approved, it would not be until the mid-1960s that a standard medal was sanctioned for other UN missions. The standard-issue UN medal — the United Nations Service Medal — was authorized by the secretary general on 16 February 1966 and is currently on issue. As noted above, the medal remains the same for each mission, while the ribbon differs, making this medal the most widely distributed multitheatre award ever issued. There are three types of UN medals — only the standard type is currently on issue — and to date the United Nations has issued them for forty-two missions, of which Canadians have been active in thirty-six.

Although the UN medals are created by the United Nations, it is not until the Canadian government approves them for wear and integrates them into the broader Canadian honours system that Canadians are permitted to wear them. And only medals issued for those missions that Canada is officially involved in are approved and integrated into the Canadian honours system. Once approved, the medals are considered "Canadian" awards.

This chapter will not recount the historical background behind each United Nations mission that has been recognized with a medal; such an undertaking has already been completed in such works as *In the Eye of the Storm* and *The Canadian Peacekeeper*. Instead, the goal of this chapter is to provide a broad overview of the criteria and basic events surrounding each mission.

There is no master register of record of every UN medal issued to Canadians, and precise numbers of medals issued for each mission are therefore difficult to obtain. This ambiguity is due in part to the fact that the medals are issued in theatre and the awards are recorded on each individual's record. The numbers quoted here represent a reasonably accurate estimate.

STANDARD ISSUE
UNITED NATIONS SERVICE MEDAL

Insignia: There are three types: the United Nations Korean Medal, the United Nations Emergency Force Medal and the United Nations Service Medal.

The United Nations Korean Medal is bronze and 35 mm in diameter. On the obverse, the UN emblem appears in bas-relief, while the reverse bears the legend, *For Service in Defence of the Principles of the Charter of the United Nations* — or, in French, *Pour la défense des principes de la charte des Nations Unies.*

The UNEF Medal is identical to the standard issue, although the letters *UNEF* appear on the obverse above the UN emblem.

The United Nations Service Medal "Standard Issue" is a circular bronze medal, 35 mm in diameter. On the obverse, the letters *UN* appear above the United Nations emblem. On the reverse, the words *In the Service of Peace* appear.

Suspender: The standard and UNEF medals have a small ball mounted on the top of the medal, through which passes a bronze mounting ring and ribbon. The Korea UN issue medal has a straight bar suspender and bar with *Korea* or *Corée* in bas-relief.

Ribbon: Varies for each mission.

Bars: A small silver numeral is worn on the ribbon for additional tours. These were approved in 1983. A number of bars have been issued, usually only on a temporary basis until a proper unique ribbon could be developed for a particular mission. For example, UN forces serving in the Congo were initially awarded a

Standard Issue United Nations Service Medal reverse

Standard Issue United Nations Service Medal silver numeral

United Nations Service Medal with the same ribbon as the UNTSO issue, but with a bar with *Congo* embossed on it to set it apart. A distinctive ribbon for the ONUC Congo mission was developed a few years later. The UN Special Service Medal and the UN medal for the various United Nations missions in Haiti are accompanied by special bars.

Other: The medals have been manufactured by upwards of twenty-five different firms around the world, and the quality of the metal sometimes varies. UN medals are not typically issued with a certificate, although unofficial "in-theatre" certificates are sometimes presented.

UNEF — UNITED NATIONS EMERGENCY FORCE, 1956–1967

Origins: After Egypt nationalized the Suez Canal in 1956, British, French and Israeli troops combined to launch an assault. In November of that year, the United Nations Emergency Force, headed by Canadian General E.L.M. Burns, was organized and dispatched to occupy the Canal Zone, enforce the cease-fire that had been declared, supervise the withdrawal of foreign troops from Egypt, and to act as a buffer between Egyptian and Israeli forces. At Egypt's request, the mission ended in June 1967.

Criteria: Awarded for ninety days' service with the UNEF between 7 November 1956 and 19 May 1967

Insignia: UNEF Medal

Ribbon: A 35 mm wide ribbon, primarily sand yellow in colour. Down the centre is a

UNEF Medal

stripe of United Nations blue, 9 mm wide, flanked on either side by 5 mm of sand, 1 mm of green, 1 mm of sand and 1 mm of dark blue. The remainder, to the edges, is sand.

Number of Awards: 9,963

UNTSO — UNITED NATIONS TRUCE SUPERVISION ORGANIZATION IN PALESTINE, 1948–PRESENT

Origins: The UN's first peacekeeping initiative, UNTSO was set up in June 1948 to oversee a cease-fire between Israel, Egypt, Jordan, Lebanon and Syria. Subsequently, it has carried out various tasks in the region, including the containment of hostilities and the enforcement of truces after the Suez crisis of 1956 and the Six-Day War of 1967. UNTSO continues to support and co-operate with UN missions (UNDOF and UNIFIL) in the region and has provided observers to help set up several other missions: UNGOMAP, UNIMOG, UNIKOM, and UNPROFOR.

UNTSO Medal

Criteria: Awarded for ninety days of consecutive service with UNTSO

Insignia: "Standard issue" UN Medal

Ribbon: A ribbon 35 mm wide in UN blue, superimposed with 1 mm white stripes inset 6 mm from either edge.

Number of Awards: 920

UNOGIL Medal

UNMOGIP Medal

UNOGIL — UNITED NATIONS OBSERVER GROUP IN LEBANON, 1948– 1958

Origins: At the request of Lebanese President Camille Chamoun, the Security Council formed this observer group in June 1958 to ensure that unauthorized personnel, arms and other materiel did not enter the country during its civil war. The mission, primarily staffed by U.S. troops, ended in December of the same year.

Criteria: Awarded for 30 consecutive days' service between 11 June and 9 December 1958

Insignia: "Standard issue" UN Medal

Ribbon: Same as for UNTSO

Number of Awards: 77

UNMOGIP — UNITED NATIONS MILITARY OBSERVER GROUP IN INDIA AND PAKISTAN, 1948–1979

Origins: Following the partition of India and Pakistan and the granting of independence to the two states, violence broke out between them over the princely state of Jammu and Kashmir. UNMOGIP was established in January 1949 to oversee the cessation of hostilities and observe the cease-fire line drawn through the region, which was divided between the two countries.

Criteria: Awarded for 180 consecutive days of service with the UNMOGIP between 20 January 1948 and 20 January 1979.

Insignia: "Standard issue" United Nations medal

Ribbon: The ribbon is 35 mm wide. The outer edges are marked by a 4 mm stripe of UN blue and a 0.5 mm stripe of white. In the centre is a 26 mm band in various shades of green — starting with 4 mm of dark green, and growing progressively lighter in both directions until the white stripes are reached.

Number of Awards: 501

ONUC — OPERATION DES NATIONS UNIES AU CONGO (UNITED NATIONS OPERATION IN THE CONGO), 1960–1964

Origins: In the summer of 1960, the Congo gained its independence from Belgium, an event marked by the mutiny of the Congolese army and an attempt by the Katanga province to secede. Although it was no longer a Belgian colony, the government in Brussels dispatched troops to the Congo. At Prime Minister Lumumba's request, the UN Security Council created ONUC to help maintain order, offer technical assistance, and oversee the withdrawal of the Belgian troops. ONUC's mandate was later broadened: it was to prevent civil war from breaking out, reunite the country and prevent foreign military and civilian personnel from getting involved in the crisis outside the UN's purview. The mission was concluded in June 1964.

ONUC Medal

Criteria: Awarded for ninety consecutive days of service with the ONUC

Insignia: "Standard issue" United Nations medal

Ribbon: A 35 mm wide ribbon, with a central band of dark green (21 mm) flanked by stripes of white (2 mm) and dark blue (4 mm).

Other: Originally, this medal was hung from the same ribbon that was used for the UNTSO and UNOGIL medals, with the addition of a small bronze Congo bar. This was replaced in 1963 by the current ribbon.

Number of Awards: 1,900

UNTEA — UNITED NATIONS TEMPORARY EXECUTIVE AUTHORITY IN WEST NEW GUINEA, 1962–63

Origins: In August 1962, an agreement was reached whereby the Netherlands would transfer control over West New Guinea to Indonesia. During the transition period, the territory was to be administered by the United Nations, which established UNTEA in October of that year. UNTEA and a UN Security Force were given the task of ensuring an orderly transfer. The mission was completed in April 1963.

UNTEA Medal

Criteria: Awarded for ninety consecutive days' service with UNTEA

Insignia: "Standard issue" United Nations medal

Ribbon: A ribbon, predominantly light blue, 35 mm wide. Down the centre are three stripes, each 3 mm wide, in dark green, white, and light green.

Number of Awards: 13

UNYOM — UNITED NATIONS YEMEN OBSERVER MISSION, 1963–64

UNYOM Medal

Origins: Established in July 1963, after a coup in Yemen, to oversee and certify that the disengagement agreement between Saudi Arabia and the United Arab Republic was put into practice. The mission ended in September 1964.

Criteria: Awarded for sixty consecutive days of service

Insignia: "Standard issue" United Nations medal

Ribbon: A 35 mm ribbon, with a central stripe in various shades of brown, bordered by stripes of white, light yellow and UN blue (2 mm).

Number of Awards: 30

UNFICYP — UNITED NATIONS PEACEKEEPING FORCE IN CYPRUS, 1964–PRESENT

Origins: The peacekeeping force was organized in March 1964 to prevent violence from breaking out between Greek and Turkish Cypriots. After a military coup on the island, Turkey invaded Cyprus; UNFICYP's mandate was expanded to include supervision of the UN–sponsored cease-fire and occupation of a buffer zone between the Greek Cypriot

UNFICYP Medal

UNIPOM Medal

territory to the south and that of the Turkish Cypriots in the north.

Criteria: Awarded for ninety consecutive days of service with the UNFICYP

Insignia: "Standard issue" United Nations medal

Ribbon: The ribbon is 35 mm wide and predominantly UN blue in colour. A central 9 mm strip of white is bordered on either side by 1 mm of dark blue.

Number of Awards: 32,980

UNIPOM — UNITED NATIONS INDIA-PAKISTAN OBSERVER MISSION, 1965–66

Origins: UNIPOM was established in September 1965 after fighting broke out between India and Pakistan during the summer of that year. The mission's observers were dispatched to the border (except within the state of Jammu and Kashmir, which was UNMOGIP's responsibility) to oversee a cease-fire, as well as the return of troops from both sides to pre–5 August 1965 lines. The mission ended in March 1966.

Criteria: Awarded for ninety consecutive days of service with UNIPOM

Insignia: "Standard issue" United Nations medal

Ribbon: The same as that issued for UNMOGIP. The ribbon is 35 mm wide. The outer edges are marked by a 4 mm stripe of UN blue and a 0.5 mm stripe of white. In the centre is a 26 mm band in various shades of green — starting with 4 mm of dark green, and growing progressively lighter in both directions until the white stripes are reached.

Other: Same ribbon as that used for UNMOGIP

Number of Awards: 112

UNEFME — UNITED NATIONS EMERGENCY FORCE MIDDLE EAST, 1973–1979

Origins: Also known as UNEF II. Set up in October 1973 to uphold the cease-fire between Egypt and Israel after the Yom Kippur War and to occupy the buffer zones established under agreements made between the two sides on 18 January 1974, and 4 September 1975. The mission concluded in July 1979.

Criteria: Awarded for ninety consecutive days of service with UNEFME

Insignia: "Standard issue" United Nations medal

UNEFME Medal

Ribbon: The ribbon is 35 mm wide, with a 9 mm stripe of UN blue at either edge. Down the centre is 2 mm of light yellow, flanked by 1 mm stripes of dark blue and additional 6 mm bands of light yellow.

Number of Awards: 11,500

UNDOF Medal

UNDOF — UNITED NATIONS DISENGAGEMENT OBSERVER FORCE (GOLAN HEIGHTS), 1974–PRESENT

Origins: Established in 1974 to supervise the cease-fire between Israel and Syria and the disengagement of the two countries' forces, as well as to establish a buffer zone to be patrolled by the UN.

Criteria: Awarded for ninety consecutive days of service with UNDOF

Insignia: "Standard issue" United Nations medal

Ribbon: The central stripe of this 35 mm ribbon is 1 mm wide and red in colour, and it is flanked on either side by 4 mm of UN blue, 1 mm of black, 3 mm of white, and 9 mm of maroon.

Number of Awards: 12,425

UNIFIL — UNITED NATIONS INTERIM FORCE IN LEBANON, 1978–PRESENT

Origins: Established in March 1978 after Israel's invasion of Lebanon, this mission's task was to confirm the withdrawal of Israeli forces from southern Lebanon, to restore stability between the two nations, and to help restore the Lebanese government's authority over its territory.

Criteria: Awarded for ninety consecutive days of service with UNIFIL

Insignia: "Standard issue" United Nations medal

UNIFIL Medal

Ribbon: A ribbon 35 mm wide, with edges in UN blue (9 mm each) and a central strip of green (11 mm). The green is separated from the blue by 1 mm stripes of white, red and white.

Number of Awards: 117

UNIIMOG — UNITED NATIONS IRAN-IRAQ MILITARY OBSERVER GROUP, 1988–1991

Origins: Established in August 1988, after the Iran–Iraq War, to oversee the cease-fire and the withdrawal of all forces to within the respective nations' internationally recognized boundaries. The mission ended in February 1991.

Criteria: Awarded for ninety consecutive days of service with UNIIMOG

Insignia: "Standard issue" United Nations medal

Ribbon: A 35 mm ribbon with a central stripe (17 mm) of UN blue, one edge is marked by a trip of 3 mm stripes (moving from outside in) green, white and red, and the other side is marked by a trio of 3 mm stripes, black, white and red.

Number of Awards: 581

UNIIMOG Medal

UNTAG — UNITED NATIONS TRANSITIONAL ASSISTANCE GROUP (NAMIBIA), 1989–90

Origins: Established in April 1989 to ensure that Namibia's transition to independence

UNTAG Medal

ONUCA Medal

from South Africa was orderly and that free and fair elections, under the supervision and control of the UN, were held. This mission concluded in March 1990.

Criteria: Awarded for ninety consecutive days of service with UNTAG

Insignia: "Standard issue" United Nations medal

Ribbon: A 35 mm wide ribbon with a central stripe of 17 mm yellow, bordered on each side by 8 mm of UN blue. The yellow centre of the ribbon is divided by five 1 mm stripes: black, yellow, red, green and royal blue.

Number of Awards: 401

ONUCA — UNITED OBSERVER GROUP IN CENTRAL AMERICA, 1989–1992

Origins: Established in December 1989 to ensure that the governments of Costa Rica, El Salvador, Guatemala, Honduras and Nicaragua had ceased to provide aid to irregular (i.e., para-military) forces and insurrectionists, and that none of these countries was being used to launch attacks on any of the others. The mission ended in January 1992.

Criteria: Awarded for ninety consecutive days of service with ONUCA

Insignia: "Standard issue" United Nations medal

Ribbon: A 35 mm ribbon edged with 6 mm of royal blue and 7 mm of UN blue. The centre is divided by alternating 1 mm stripes of green and white (five green and four white)

Number of Awards: 350

UNIKOM — UNITED NATIONS IRAQ-KUWAIT OBSERVER MISSION, 1991–PRESENT

Origins: Established in April 1991 to monitor a demilitarized zone along the Iraq–Kuwait boundary and patrol the Khor Abdullah waterway.

Criteria: Awarded for ninety consecutive days of service with UNIKOM

Insignia: "Standard issue" United Nations medal

Ribbon: A 35 mm wide sand ribbon divided down the centre by a 4 mm stripe of UN blue.

Number of Awards: 605

UNIKOM Medal

UNAVEM — UNITED NATIONS ANGOLA VERIFICATION MISSION, 1988–1997

Origins: Established in December 1988, originally to ensure that Cuban troops were withdrawn from Angola. UNAVEM's mandate was altered in May 1991; now known as UNAVEM II, its new role was to monitor the cease-fire called for under the peace accords that had been signed at that time and to supervise elections.

UNAVEM Medal

With the renewal of fighting between government troops and UNITA rebels, UNAVEM entered a third phase (UNAVEM III), during which it was tasked with demobilizing the UNITA forces, restoring order and overseeing new elections. The mission was concluded in June 1997.

Criteria: Awarded for ninety consecutive days of service with the UNAVEM

Insignia: "Standard issue" United Nations medal

Ribbon: A 35 mm ribbon with a 9 mm central stripe in UN blue, bordered on either side by 1 mm of black, 2 mm of white, 2 mm of red and 8 mm of yellow.

Number of Awards: 60

MINURSO — UNITED NATIONS MISSION FOR THE REFERENDUM IN WESTERN SAHARA, 1991–PRESENT

MINURSO Medal

Origins: Established in May 1991 to oversee a referendum through which the people of Western Sahara were to choose between integration with Morocco or independence.

Criteria: Awarded for ninety consecutive days of service with the MINURSO

Insignia: "Standard issue" United Nations medal

Ribbon: A 35 mm ribbon, with a central stripe 27 mm wide in sandy brown, bordered on either side by 4 mm of UN blue.

Number of Awards: 140

ONUSAL — UNITED NATIONS OBSERVER MISSION IN EL SALVADOR, 1991–1995

Origins: Established in May 1991 to monitor agreements ending the civil war between the government of El Salvador and the Frente Farabundo Martí para la Liberación Nacional (FMLN). This mission was expanded in January 1992 to include monitoring the cease-fire and supervising the demobilization of the warring forces, and maintaining order during the period while the national police force was phased out and replaced by a new civilian police force. ONUSAL also supervised the 1994 elections. Upon completing its tasks, the mission was concluded in April 1995.

Criteria: Awarded for ninety consecutive days of service with ONUSAL

Insignia: "Standard issue" United Nations medal

Ribbon: A 35 mm wide ribbon, with a 7 mm wide central stripe of white, bordered on either side by 7 mm of dark blue and 7 mm of UN blue.

Other: The medal was established by the UN in January 1992.

Number of Awards: 55

ONUSAL Medal

UNPROFOR Medal

UNPROFOR — UNITED NATIONS PROTECTION FORCE IN THE FORMER YUGOSLAVIA, 1992–1995

Origins: Established on an interim basis in February 1992 to create a stable environment in which an overall settlement of the Yugoslavian crisis could be negotiated. UN troops were assigned to ensure that areas designated as "UN Protected Areas" became and remained demilitarized and to remove the threat of armed attack in these regions. UN police monitors were assigned to supervise local police forces, primarily with an eye toward preventing human rights abuses. UNPROFOR also helped the UN's humanitarian agencies of the UN with the return of all displaced persons who so desired. The mission's mandate was extended several times: to reopen the Sarajevo airport for humanitarian purposes; to establish a security zone around Sarajevo and its airport; to protect convoys of released detainees in Bosnia and Herzegovina; to monitor arrangements for the complete withdrawal of the Yugoslavian Army from Croatia; to oversee the demilitarization of the Prevlaka peninsula and the removal of heavy weapons from neighbouring areas of Croatia and Montenegro; to monitor compliance with a ban on military flights; and to establish a UN presence in Macedonia. UNPROFOR also monitored a cease-fire between the Bosnian government and Bosnian-Croat forces in February 1994, and another between the Bosnian government and Bosnian Serb forces, which became effective on 1 January 1995. On 31 March 1995, UNPROFOR was replaced with three separate but interrelated peacekeeping operations: UNCRO (United Nations Confidence Restoration Operation in Croatia), UNPRE-DEP (United Nations Preventive Deployment

Force), both under the auspices of UNPF (United Nations Peace Forces). In January 1996, the UNPF mission was phased out.

Criteria: Awarded for ninety consecutive days of service with UNPROFOR

Insignia: "Standard issue" United Nations medal

Ribbon: A 35 mm wide ribbon with, from left to right: a 3 mm stripe of UN blue, 6 mm stripe of olive green, 3 mm of UN blue, 1 mm of white, 9 mm of red, 1 mm of white, 3 mm of UN blue, 6 mm of brown, and 3 mm of UN blue.

Number of Awards: 6,650

UNAMIC — UNITED NATIONS ADVANCED MISSION IN CAMBODIA, 1991–92

Origins: Established in October 1991 to liaise between the four warring factions in Cambodia in matters related to the cease-fire and to launch a mine-awareness training program. UNAMIC's mandate was later broadened to include training in mine clearance and to launch a program to remove landmines. The mission's mandate expired in March 1992, when the United Nations Transitional Authority in Cambodia was established.

Criteria: Awarded for ninety consecutive days of service

Insignia: "Standard issue" United Nations medal

UNAMIC Medal

Ribbon: A 35 mm ribbon, with a central 3 mm white stripe, bordered on either side by 4 mm of dark blue, 1 mm of yellow, 4 mm of red and 7 mm of UN blue.

Number of Awards: 7

UNTAC — UNITED NATIONS TRANSITIONAL AUTHORITY IN CAMBODIA, 1992–93

UNTAC Medal

Origins: This mission succeeded UNAMIC, and its role was to supervise the ceasefire agreed to in October 1991, to oversee the withdrawal of foreign forces and the demobilization of armed forces from the four parties, to temporarily assume civil administrative duties, to ensure that the police and other bodies respected human rights, to repatriate and resettle refugees and displaced persons, and to organize and supervise elections. After the elections, the mission was terminated on 15 November 1993, its place to be taken by the United Nations Military Liaison Team (UNMLT). Consisting of twenty military observers, this team's six-month mandate was to monitor the situation, help the government deal with military loose ends related to the Paris peace agreement, and to report to the secretary general on matters affecting security in Cambodia. UNMLT was established for a single period of six months. UNMLT military observers are eligible to receive the UNTAC medal.

Criteria: Awarded for ninety consecutive days of service with the UNTAC

Insignia: "Standard issue" United Nations medal

Ribbon: A 35 mm ribbon, with a 3 mm central stripe of white, bordered on either side by 1 mm of red, 4 mm of UN blue, 1 mm of dark blue and 10 mm of dark green.

Number of Awards: 465

UNOSOM — UNITED NATIONS OPERATION IN SOMALIA, 1992–93

Origins: UNOSOM was established in April 1992, when fifty unarmed uniformed military observers were dispatched to Mogadishu to monitor the cease-fire there. They were to be stationed along the line that divided the Somali capital into two zones. The mission was also to protect distribution centres and the port of Mogadishu and to escort supply convoys throughout the vicinity. They were also to provide security for United Nations personnel, equipment and supplies at the airport in Mogadishu. On 28 August, the Security Council authorized the posting of four more UN security units to UNOSOM, to protect humanitarian aid convoys and distribution centres throughout Somalia.

UNOSOM Medal

As ongoing fighting interfered with relief efforts, the Security Council on 3 December authorized UNOSOM and UNITAF — the Unified Task Force spearheaded by the United States — to work together, using any means necessary, to ensure a stable environment for humanitarian and relief efforts to operate. Once UNITAF's task was accomplished, military command was assumed by the UN. Meanwhile, UNOSOM remained in charge of its original political and humanitarian mandates. In March 1993, UNOSOM II was created. Like UNITAF, it was authorized to use force if necessary to create a secure environment to distribute humanitarian aid. In February 1994, after several violent incidents and attacks on United Nations soldiers, UNOSOM II's mandate was updated to exclude the use of coercion. Unable to make satisfactory progress, UNOSOM II was withdrawn in early March 1995.

Criteria: Awarded for ninety consecutive days of service with UNOSOM

Insignia: "Standard issue" United Nations medal

Ribbon: A 35 mm ribbon, with a central stripe (11 mm) in UN blue, bordered on either side by 2 mm of olive green and 10 mm of light yellow.

Number of Awards: 343

ONUMOZ — UNITED NATIONS OPERATION IN MOZAMBIQUE, 1992–1994

Origins: Established in October 1992, ONUMOZ's mandate was to monitor the cease-fire, the withdrawal of foreign forces and the disbandment of unofficial armed forces; to secure transportation routes; to monitor elections; and to assist humanitarian aid operations. Having fulfilled its mandate, the mission was wound down in January 1995.

Criteria: Awarded for ninety consecutive days of service

Insignia: "Standard issue" United Nations medal

ONUMOZ Medal

Ribbon: A 35 mm ribbon, with a 15 mm wide central stripe of light blue, bordered on each side by 5 mm of white and 5 mm of green.

Number of Awards: 45

UNOMUR — UNITED NATIONS OBSERVER MISSION IN UGANDA-RWANDA, 1993–94

Origins: Established in June 1993, UNO-MUR's mission was to monitor the border between Uganda and Rwanda and ensure that no military materiel — primarily in the form of weapons and ammunition — reached Rwanda. The mission was concluded in October 1994.

Criteria: Awarded for 180 consecutive days of service with UNOMUR

Insignia: "Standard issue" United Nations medal

UNOMUR Medal

Ribbon: A 35 mm wide ribbon with a central 9 mm stripe of light blue, bordered on each side by 1 mm of white, 4 mm of black, 4 mm of yellow and 4 mm of red.

Number of Awards: 5

UNAMIR — UNITED NATIONS ASSISTANCE MISSION IN RWANDA, 1993–1996

Origins: Established in October 1993, UNAMIR's mandate was tasked with monitoring the cease-fire agreement, helping secure

UNOMIR Medal

the capital of Kigali, helping to remove mines, co-ordinate humanitarian aid efforts and protect and repatriate refugees. UNAMIR also helped protect human rights workers and the personnel of the International Tribunal for Rwanda, and helped establish a new national police force.UNAMIR's mandate concluded in March 1996.

Criteria: Awarded for ninety consecutive days of service with

Insignia: "Standard issue" United Nations medal

Ribbon: A 35 mm wide ribbon with a 9 mm wide central stripe of light blue, bordered on each side by 1 mm of white, 4 mm of black, 4 mm of green and 4 mm of red.

Other: The medal was established by the United Nations in December 1993.

Number of Awards: 375

UNMIH, UNSMIH, UNTMIH, MIPONUH, MICAH — UNITED NATIONS MISSIONS IN HAITI, 1993–PRESENT

Origins: This UN medal issue is perhaps the most complex, there being five separate bars and missions.

UNMIH Medal

UNMIH. Originally established on 23 September 1993, with the initial task of helping modernize Haiti's armed forces and establish a new police force. Haitian military authorities did not co-operate, preventing the mandate from being carried out. In 1995 a renewed UNMIH took over from the U.S.–led multinational force to maintain order, help create a civilian police force and oversee elections. Its mission ended in June 1996.

UNSMIH. UNMIH was succeeded in July 1996 by the United Nations Support Mission in Haiti (UNSMIH). Its mandate expired on 31 July 1997.

UNTMIH. The United Nations Transition Mission in Haiti was the third UN peacekeeping operations in Haiti. It existed from 30 July 1997 until 30 November 1997. Its role was to train the Haitian National Police (HNP).

MIPONUH. In December 1997, UNTMIH was succeeded by the United Nations Civilian Police Mission in Haiti (MIPONUH). Its mandate was to continue training the HNP.

MICAH. MIPONUH was succeeded by the International Civilian Support Mission in Haiti (MICAH) on 16 March 2000. The establishment of MICAH was approved by the General Assembly in Resolution A/54/193 of 17 December 1999. Its mandate is to reinforce the results its predecessors had yielded. It was also assigned to promote human rights and support the police and justice system.

Criteria: Awarded for ninety consecutive days of service with UNMIH, UNSMIH, UNTMIH, MIPONUH or MICAH.

Insignia: "Standard issue" United Nations medal. Bars were awarded to denote which mission or missions personnel served in.

UNMIH Bar

UNSMIH Bar

UNTMIH Bar

MIPONUH Bar

Various Haiti Bars

Ribbon: A 35 mm ribbon, consisting of (from left to right) stripes of UN blue, white (1 mm), royal blue (7 mm), red (7 mm), white (1 mm) and UN blue.

Number of Awards:
Single Bars: UNMIH, 902; UNSMIH, 820; MIPONUH, 102; UNTMIH, 112
Multiple Bars: UNMIH and UNSMIG, 756; UNSMIH and UNTMIH, 815

MINUGUA — UNITED NATIONS VERIFICATION MISSION IN GUATEMALA, 1994–1997

Origins: Established in September 1994 to verify the establishment of human rights in Guatemala. The mission was concluded in May 1997.

Criteria: Awarded for ninety consecutive days of service

Insignia: "Standard issue" United Nations medal

Ribbon: A 35 mm ribbon, with a central stripe of UN blue, flanked on either side by a group of five stripes in deep blue, white, green, white and deep blue.

Number of Awards: 64

MINUGUA Medal

MINURCA — UNITED NATIONS MISSION IN THE CENTRAL AFRICAN REPUBLIC, 1998–2000

Origins: After social unrest and army mutinies took place in the Central African Republic, MINURCA was formed to monitor the area and ensure that the truce agreements were put into operation. The mission was concluded in February 2000.

Criteria: Awarded for ninety consecutive days of service with MINURCA

Insignia: "Standard issue" United Nations medal

Ribbon: A 35 mm ribbon with a 5 mm central stripe of UN blue bordered on either side by five 3 mm stripes of yellow, green, red, white and dark blue. by 1 mm each of yellow, green, red, white and dark blue.

Number of Awards: 143

MINURCA Medal

UNPREDEP — UNITED NATIONS PREVENTATIVE DEPLOYMENT FORCE IN MACEDONIA, 1995–1999

Origins: UNPREDEP was created in March 1995 to carry out the work of UNPROFOR within the Former Yugoslav Republic of Macedonia. Its mandate was to monitor the borders and report any potential external threats to the country's stability. The mission was concluded in February 1999.

Criteria: Awarded for ninety consecutive days of service with the UNPREDEP

UNPREDEP Medal

Insignia: "Standard issue" United Nations medal

Ribbon: A 35 mm wide ribbon edged on each side by 7 mm of UN blue, 1 mm of white, 2 mm of red, 1.5 mm of yellow, 2 mm of red, 1.5 mm of yellow and a central red stripe measuring 5 mm wide.

Other: The medal was established by the UN in May 1996.

Number of Awards: 20

UNMIBH — UNITED NATIONS MISSION IN BOSNIA AND HERZEGOVINA, 1995–2002

Origins: UNMIBH was established in December 1995 to carry out a variety of law enforcement functions and create favourable conditions for elections to be held. The mission was concluded in December 2002.

Criteria: Awarded for ninety consecutive days of service with UNMIBH

Insignia: "Standard issue" United Nations medal

Ribbon: A 35 mm wide ribbon, with a central 6 mm stripe of white, bordered on either side by 7 mm of UN blue and 7 mm of green (on the left) or 7 mm of red (on the right).

Other: The medal was established by the UN in August 1996.

Number of Awards: 250

UNMIBH Medal

UNMOP — UNITED NATIONS MISSION OF OBSERVERS IN PREVLAKA (CROATIA), 1996–2002

Origins: Established in January 1996, the mandate of the mission was to monitory the demilitarization of the Prevlaka peninsula. The mission was concluded in December 2002.

Criteria: Awarded for ninety consecutive days of service with UNMOP

Insignia: "Standard issue" United Nations medal

Ribbon: A 35 mm ribbon with a central 5 mm yellow stripe, bordered on each side by 1 mm of pale blue, 4.5 mm of dark blue, 4.5 mm of UN blue and 5 mm of dark blue.

Other: The medal was established by the United Nations in May 1996.

Number of Awards: 27

UNMOP Medal

UNMIK — UNITED NATIONS INTERIM ADMINISTRATION MISSION IN KOSOVO, 1999–PRESENT

Origins: UNMIK was established on 10 June 1999, to act as a civil authority in Kosovo, to ensure the safe return of refugees and to prevent conflicts between parties from escalating.

Criteria: Awarded for ninety consecutive days of service with UNMIK

Insignia: "Standard issue" United Nations medal

UNMIK Medal

Ribbon: A 35 mm ribbon with a 15 mm central stripe of dark blue, bordered on either side by 1 mm of white and 9 mm of UN blue.

Other: The medal was established by the United Nations in September 1999.

Number of Awards: 155

UNAMSIL/UNOMSIL — UNITED NATIONS MISSION IN SIERRA LEONE, 1997–PRESENT

Origins: UNOMSIL was established in June 1998 to disarm and demobilize the former combatants in Sierra Leone's lengthy civil war. In October 1999 the UN established UNAMSIL, a much larger mission (with a maximum of 6,000 military personnel, including 260 military observers) designed to help enact the Lome peace agreement. At the same time, UNOMSIL was cancelled.

Criteria: Awarded for ninety consecutive days of service with the UNAMSIL

Insignia: "Standard issue" United Nations medal

Ribbon: A 35 mm ribbon, with a central 11 mm stripe of UN blue, bordered on either side by 4 mm each of green, white and dark blue.

Number of Awards: 8

UNOMSIL Medal

UNAMET AND UNTAET — UNITED NATIONS MISSION IN EAST TIMOR AND UNITED NATIONS TRANSITIONAL ADMINISTRATION IN EAST TIMOR, 1999–PRESENT

Origins: UNAMET was established in June 1999 to organize and conduct a referendum on whether the people of East Timor wished to separate from Indonesia. When the people voted for independence, violence broke out. In September, UNTAET was organized and dispatched to provide security and maintain order, develop civil institutions and lay the groundwork for self-government.

Criteria: Awarded for ninety consecutive days of service with the UNAMET/UNTAET

Insignia: "Standard issue" United Nations medal

Ribbon: A 35 mm ribbon, with a 7 mm central stripe of white, bordered on either side by 2 mm of yellow, 2 mm of red and 10 mm of UN blue.

Other: The medal was established by the United Nations on 9 December 1999.

Number of Awards: approximately 30

UNAMET Medal

MONUC — UNITED NATIONS ORGANIZATION MISSION IN THE DEMOCRATIC REPUBLIC OF THE CONGO, 1999–PRESENT

Origins: The primary assignment of this mission, established on 24 February 2000, is to

MONUC Medal

liaise between the armed forces of all five parties to the Lusaka Cease-Fire Agreement signed in July of that year, to investigate violations of the agreement, and aid in the release of all prisoners of war.

Criteria: Awarded for ninety consecutive days of service with MONUC

Insignia: "Standard issue" United Nations medal

Ribbon: A 35 mm with a 9 mm wide central stripe of dark blue, bordered on either side by 2 mm of yellow and 11 mm of UN blue.

Other: Medal established by UN on 2 May 2000

Number of Awards: 22

UNMEE — UNITED NATIONS MISSION IN ETHIOPIA AND ERITREA, 2000–PRESENT

Origins: The mission was created on 15 September 2000. Its primary task is to monitor the cease-fire between Ethiopia and Eritrea.

Criteria: Awarded for ninety consecutive days of service with the UNMEE

Insignia: "Standard issue" United Nations medal

Ribbon: A 35 mm ribbon with a 2 mm central stripe of green, bordered on either side by 6.5 mm of sand and 10 mm of UN blue.

UNMEE Medal

Other: Medal established by the UN in January 2001

Number of Awards: 680

UNSS — UNITED NATIONS SPECIAL SERVICE, 1974–PRESENT

Origins: Created to recognize military and civilian police personnel who have served the UN in capacities other than in established peacekeeping missions or at UN Headquarters.

Criteria: Awarded for ninety consecutive days of service

Insignia: "Standard issue" United Nations medal

Ribbon: A 35 mm ribbon, with a broad central stripe of UN blue bordered on either edge by 5 mm of white.

UNSS Medal

Other: Awards can be made for service dating back to 1974. The UN approved this medal in June 1995. To identify the theatre in which the medal was earned, a bar is sometimes added with the name of the country or the UN organization (UNHCR, UNSOM etc.). The medal was created by the United Nations in June 1995.

Number of Awards: 247

UNHQ Medal

UNHQ — UNITED NATIONS HEADQUARTERS SERVICE, 1974–PRESENT

Origins: Created to recognize military personnel who hold staff positions at UN Headquarters in New York.

Criteria: Awarded for ninety consecutive days of service at UN Headquarters

Insignia: "Standard issue" United Nations medal

Ribbon: A 35 mm ribbon, entirely of UN blue

Other: Awards can be made for service dating back to 1974. The UN approved this medal on 16 June 1997.

Number of Awards: 235

CHAPTER 16

North Atlantic Treaty Organization Medals

As a founding member of the North Atlantic Treaty Organization, Canada has played a small but significant role in the organization since its establishment in 1948. Beginning in the early 1990s, when civil war broke out in the Federal Socialist Republic of Yugoslavia, NATO has increasingly become involved in peacemaking and peacekeeping missions.

The vast majority of these missions have been sponsored and carried out under a resolution of the United Nations Security Council, part of a growing trend for peacekeeping and peacemaking operations to be sanctioned by the United Nations, yet carried out by organizations such as NATO.

The six NATO medals that have been awarded to Canadians and accepted by the Canadian government are similar to the various United Nations peacekeeping medals in that the design of all six is uniform, and they are differentiated only by their ribbons and in some cases, by the bars awarded with them.

NATO Medal certificate

NATO Medal, Former Yugoslavia, obverse

NATO Medal, Former Yugoslavia, reverse

THE NATO MEDAL, FORMER YUGOSLAVIA

Origins: After Slovenia, Croatia and Macedonia seceded from the Federal Socialist Republic of Yugoslavia, Bosnia and Herzegovina also voted late in 1991 for independence from Yugoslavia. But much of the Bosnian Serb population, who would represent a minority of the new republic's population, refused to separate. A bloody civil war commenced. In 1995, NATO became involved in the Bosnian war, initially in support of the United Nations, along with the Western European Union. The alliance monitored and enforced UN sanctions, enforced the no-fly zone over Bosnia and provided support for the UN Protection Force (UNPROFOR). NATO also played a key role in carrying out air strikes that ended the siege on Sarajevo.

In December 1995 the governments of Bosnia, Croatia and Serbia were brought together in Dayton, Ohio, to negotiate, and a peace treaty was signed. On 20 December, a NATO-led multinational force — the Implementation Force, or IFOR — was deployed in Bosnia and Herzegovina to bring about and maintain an end to hostilities and to separate the armed forces of Bosnia's two newly created entities, the Federation of Bosnia and Herzegovina and the Republika Serpska. These goals were attained by June 1996. Later that year, IFOR was succeeded by SFOR (Stabilization Force), which was also deployed as part of the Dayton peace accord. This peacekeeping operation, 20,000 strong, is assigned to maintain and enforce security to "enable the country to rebuild after the devastation of years of conflict." SFOR is composed of sixteen NATO members and thirteen partner countries.

Because this was the first large-scale NATO peacekeeping operation, it was decided to issue a service medal similar to those the UN awarded to peacekeepers. The medal for the Former Yugoslavia was the first NATO medal instituted, and was created by the alliance's secretary general on 20 December 1994.

Criteria: Awarded for thirty days' continuous or accumulated service on the land, at sea or in the air spaces of the former Yugoslavia, Albania, the former Republic of Macedonia, or the Adriatic Sea (the theatre of operations); or ninety days' continuous or accumulated service in the territories of Italy, Greece, Hungary and Austria, in direct support of the NATO operations in the former Yugoslavia (the adjacent area). The service must have been rendered between 1 July 1992 and 31 December 2002.

Insignia: Standard NATO Service Medal: a bronze medal, 36 mm in diameter, bearing the NATO star, surrounded by a wreath of olive leaves, on the obverse. The reverse bears the motto *In the Service of Peace and Freedom*, a laurelled bar, and *Au service de la paix et de la liberté*, encircled by the words *North Atlantic Treaty Organization — Organisation du Traité de l'Atlantique Nord.*

Suspender: A bronze ring passes through the top of the medal, through which the ribbon passes.

Ribbon: NATO blue, 36 mm wide, with a 4 mm white stripe set 4 mm from each edge.

Bar: A plain bronze bar with *Former Yugoslavia* or *Ex-Yougoslavie* centred in bas-relief. A bronze numeral 2 is worn on the ribbon of the medal for an additional 180 days' service in the theatre of operation, or 540 days' service in the adjacent area as defined above. Further service would be recognized by a numeral 3, and so forth. Tour numerals are worn below the bar.

Postnominals: None

Other: Medals are manufactured by Eekellers-Centini of Belgium. They are issued in a rectangular blue plastic case — some issues bear the NATO star, while others are plain. This medal was replaced by the NATO Non–Article 5 Medal for operations in the Balkans on 1 January 2003.

Number of Awards: more than 12,000

THE NATO MEDAL, KOSOVO

Origins: Throughout the 1990s the situation in the Balkan states — in what was formerly the Federal Socialist Republic of Yugoslavia — deteriorated significantly. In 1998, protest erupted in Kosovo, and Serbian police reacted with excessive force, while members of the Kosovo Liberation Army (KLA) began a series of terrorist raids on Serb targets and civilians. More than 250,000 residents of Kosovo were displaced by the violence, and the UN passed a series of resolutions designed to yield a political solution. The government of the Federal Republic of Yugoslavia (essentially Serbia) refused to cease its actions, and NATO, authorized by the United Nations, undertook Operation Allied Force — an extensive bombing campaign that struck targets throughout Yugoslavia. In June 1999, after eleven weeks of bombing, the Yugoslavian government

NATO Medal, Kosovo

relented and agreed to allow an International Security Force (KFOR) into Kosovo.

Shortly thereafter, a UN resolution called for the deployment of an effective international civil and security presence in Kosovo — this represented an official endorsement of the KFOR mission. The mission itself had many objectives, although it was primarily charged with establishing a lasting end to hostilities.

Criteria: Awarded for thirty days' continuous or accumulated service on the land, at sea or in the air space of Kosovo and other territories of the Federal Republic of Yugoslavia, Albania, the former Republic of Macedonia, and the Adriatic and Ionian seas (the theatre of operations); or for ninety days' continuous or accumulated service in the territories of Italy, Greece and Hungary, in direct support of the NATO operations in Kosovo (the adjacent area).

Aircrew who flew in fifteen sorties in the airspace of Kosovo and the other territories of the Federal Republic of Yugoslavia during Operation Allied Force between 24 March 1999 and 10 June 1999, also qualify. Aircrew who completed fewer than fifteen sorties may combine the number of completed sorties with other qualifying service between 13 October 1998 and 31 December 2002 to qualify.

Insignia & Suspender: The standard NATO Service Medal

Ribbon: NATO blue, 36 mm wide, with a 6 mm white stripe in the centre and edged on either side with 2 mm of white.

Bar: A plain bronze bar with *Kosovo* centred in bas-relief. A bronze numeral 2 is worn on the ribbon of the medal for an additional

180 days' service in the theatre of operation, or 540 days' service in the adjacent area as defined above. Further service would be recognized by a numeral 3. Tour numerals are worn below the bar.

Postnominals: None

Other: Medals are manufactured by Eekellers-Centini of Belgium. They are issued in a rectangular blue plastic case — some issues bear the NATO star, while some bear a map of Kosovo. This medal was replaced by the NATO Non–Article 5 Medal for the Balkans on 1 January 2003. Those who qualified for this medal for service with Operation Allied Force may now exchange it for the General Campaign Star or General Service Medal.

Number of Awards: more than 2,200

THE NATO MEDAL, FORMER YUGOSLAV REPUBLIC OF MACEDONIA

Origins: After the disintegration of the Federal Socialist Republic of Yugoslavia in the early 1990s, Macedonia declared its independence. In 1993, it joined the UN under the name "the Former Yugoslav Republic of Macedonia." In the wake of the influx of Albanian refugees from Kosovo in 1999, Macedonia's ethnic Albanian population began to lobby for more rights and a constitutional position. Initially, the Macedonian government responded coldly to these requests, and in early 2001 the National Liberation Army, an ethnic Albanian group closely related to the Kosovo Liberation

NATO Medal, Former Yugoslav Republic of Macedonia

Army, launched a mortar attack on a Macedonian police station. The conflict escalated, and Macedonian security forces engaged the NLA throughout early 2001. A tentative political solution was arrived at in August 2001, and President Trajkovski of Macedonia asked NATO troops to disarm the NLA and other ethnic Albanian groups. Operation Essential Harvest was launched on 22 August 2001, and it began in earnest on 27 August. Approximately 3,500 NATO troops engaged to disarm the NLA and its weapons. The operation lasted until 26 September 2001.

Criteria: Awarded for twenty-five days' continuous or accumulated service on the land, or in the airspace of the former Yugoslav Republic of Macedonia between 1 June 2001 and 27 August 2001 (the period prior to Operation Essential Harvest); or between 27 August 2001 and 27 September 2001 (during the operation); or for thirty continuous or accumulated days of service between 27 August 2001 and 31 December 2002.

Insignia & Suspender: The standard NATO Service Medal

Ribbon: A NATO blue ribbon 36 mm wide, edged with 3 mm of white. A pair of 4 mm white stripes are superimposed on the blue, set 7 mm from either edge.

Bars: There is no bar to this medal.

Postnominals: None

Other: Medals are manufactured by Eekellers-Centini of Belgium. They are issued in a rectangular blue plastic case, bearing either the NATO star or an outline map of Macedonia on the lid.

Number Awarded: 297

THE ARTICLE 5 MEDAL FOR OPERATION EAGLE ASSIST

Origins: After the terrorist attacks on the United States on 11 September 2001, NATO launched Operation Eagle Assist, under which the alliance was to assist the United States and demonstrate its resolve against terrorism. Deployment was authorized on 12 October 2001 and was completed on 16 May 2002.

Criteria: Awarded for thirty days' continuous or accumulated service in the area of operation between 12 October 2001 and 16 May 2002. The area of operation was defined as North American airspace for which NORAD was responsible.

Article 5 Medal for Operation Eagle Assist

Insignia & Suspender: The standard NATO Service Medal

Ribbon: A blue ribbon 36 mm wide, with a central 5 mm white stripe superimposed with a thin gold thread.

Bars: All NATO medals for Operation Eagle Assist are awarded with a plain bronze bar with *Article 5* centred in bas-relief.

Postnominals: None

Other: Medals are manufactured by Eekellers-Centini of Belgium. They are issued in a

rectangular blue plastic case, bearing the
NATO star on the lid.

Number Awarded: 60

THE ARTICLE 5 NATO MEDAL FOR
OPERATION ACTIVE ENDEAVOUR

Origins: After the terrorist attacks on the
United States on 11 September 2001, NATO
launched Operation Active Endeavour, the
purpose of which was to provide a NATO
presence and demonstrate the alliance's resolve
in the Eastern Mediterranean. A standing
naval force was deployed on 26 October 2001.
This mission is ongoing.

Criteria: Awarded for thirty days' continuous
or accumulated service in the international
waters of the Mediterranean Sea, and the airspace above it.

Insignia and Suspender: The standard NATO
Service Medal

Ribbon: A NATO blue ribbon 36 mm wide.
Inset 5 mm from each edge is a 5 mm white
stripe, bisected by a single thin gold thread.

Bars: All NATO medals for Operation Active
Endeavour are awarded with a plain bronze
bar with *Article 5* centred in bas-relief.

Postnominals: None

Other: Medals are manufactured by Eekellers-
Centini of Belgium. They are issued in a rectangular blue plastic case, bearing the NATO
star on the lid.

*Article 5 NATO Medal for
Operation Active Eneavour*

Number Awarded: 260 (only HMCS *Toronto* participated)

THE NON–ARTICLE 5 NATO MEDAL FOR OPERATIONS IN THE BALKANS

Origins: This medal replaces the NATO Medal for the Former Yugoslavia, the NATO Medal for Kosovo and the NATO Medal for the Former Yugoslav Republic of Macedonia. It was introduced to reduce the number of NATO medals awarded for service in the Balkans. This medal was first issued on 1 January 2003, at the same time as the other three were phased out.

Non–Article 5 NATO Medal for Operations in the Balkans

Criteria: Awarded for thirty days' continuous or accumulated service in the area of operation (the Balkans Joint Operational Area), commencing 1 January 2003. Service in adjacent areas no longer qualifies, as it had under previous NATO medals for service in the Balkans.

Insignia: The standard NATO Service Medal

Suspender: A bronze ring passes through the top of the medal, through which the ribbon passes.

Ribbon: A blue ribbon 36 mm wide, with a central 4 mm white stripe superimposed with a 1 mm silver thread.

Bars: All NATO medals for Non–Article 5 Operations in the Balkans are awarded with a plain bronze bar with *Non Article 5* centred and in bas-relief.

Postnominals: None

Other: Medals are manufactured by Eekellers-Centini of Belgium. They are issued in a rectangular blue plastic case, bearing the NATO star on the lid.

Number Awarded: approximately 500

CHAPTER 17

International Mission Medals

Since the end of the Second World War, Canada has participated in a wide variety of international organizations and commissions. These have ranged from such entities as the North Atlantic Treaty Organization and the United Nations to the Commonwealth, the European Union and the Francophonie. With this increased international involvement, Canada's military has frequently been called upon to help in monitoring, truce-making, peacekeeping and peacemaking missions.

The six international mission medals that have been awarded to Canadians and recognized by the Canadian government are similar to the various UN and NATO medals. With the exception of the International Force East Timor Medal, all are the product of an international or regional organization and not a specific country. The International Force East Timor Medal is an Australian medal, allowed by the Australian government to be awarded to non-Australian forces involved in the INTERFET mission. The most recent international mission medal to be issued comes from the European Union, and is issued as part of the European Union Security Defence Policy Group, which is essentially the military operational wing of the European Union. The medal is sanctioned by the EU and has been approved by the Canadian government with its various bars.

Unfortunately, the international mission medals have tended to be of marginal quality and are symbolically drab. The 1973 International Commission for Supervision and Control in Vietnam Medal became affectionately known as the "Cracker Jack" or "tin pot" medal, on account of its shiny gold appearance and light weight.

As with the quality of these medals, there is no consistency with regard to the issue of award certificates. While certificates were issued with the 1973 ICCS medal, they have generally not been issued with other international mission medals.

International Commission for Supervision and Control Service Medal obverse

International Commission for Supervision and Control Service Medal reverse

THE INTERNATIONAL COMMISSION FOR SUPERVISION AND CONTROL SERVICE MEDAL

Origins: Following the end of the Second World War, instability in French Indochina (Vietnam, Laos and Cambodia) grew into a full-fledged conflict as the Viet Minh waged a war of independence against French forces. In July 1954 a conference was held in Geneva, and accords were signed. Three separate commissions were established, one each for Laos, Cambodia and Vietnam. The accords further divided Vietnam into two separate parts, North and South. The International Commission for Supervision and Control (ICSC) was charged with supervising the cease-fires and the withdrawal of French military personnel, facilitating the return of refugees to their homes and patriating of civilian and military prisoners. The commission was quite literally intended to supervise and control the implementation of the Geneva accords.

At the direction of the commission's Indian delegation, a medal was authorized by the ICSC in February 1961, although approval from the Department of National Defence did not come until March 1962. Even then, the department was still considering whether or not to institute a Canadian General Service Medal rather than allow Canadian personnel to accept medals from international organizations. The General Service Medal project was never approved, therefore the ICSC medal was sanctioned.

Criteria: Awarded for ninety days' service — consecutive or cumulative — as a member of the Commission between 7 August 1954 and 28 January 1973. Persons killed while serving with the commission were automatically awarded the medal posthumously.

Insignia: A circular antiqued bronze medal, 34 mm in diameter, bearing the crossed flags of Canada and Poland, with the arms of India in the centre and the dove of peace at the point where the flags cross, circumscribed by the words *International Commission for Supervision and Control*, with the word *Peace* at the base. The reverse bears a map of Indochina with the names of the three countries — Vietnam, Laos and Cambodia.

Suspender: A floral motif connects the mounting suspender to the medal: the suspender through which the ribbon passes appears as shoots of bamboo.

Ribbon: A 32 mm wide ribbon of three equal stripes: dark green, white and red. The green represents India, the white peace and the red Canada and Poland.

Bars: None

Other: The medal was made by Barton's Jewelers of Bangalore, India. The recipient's name and rank were impressed on the rim in block capitals, and the impression was then filled with white paint. Unlike other international organizational medals, the ICSC medal was of a relatively high quality. The medal was issued in a black leatherette box, which was delivered covered in brown paper and tied up with a purple ribbon. This award was superseded by the ICCS Medal.

Number of Awards: 1,550

International Commission of Control and Supervision, Vietnam obverse

International Commission of Control and Supervision, Vietnam, Canadian Issue obverse

THE INTERNATIONAL COMMISSION OF CONTROL AND SUPERVISION, VIETNAM

Origins: Following the Paris Peace Conference, the U.S.–led war in South Vietnam came to an end and American forces began pulling out. The International Commission of Control and Supervision (ICCS) was charged with monitoring the cease-fire and facilitating the exchange of prisoners. This mission was the successor to the International Commission for Supervision and Control (ICSC).

Criteria: Awarded for ninety days' service, consecutive or cumulative, as a member of the commission between 28 January 1973 and 31 July 1973. Persons killed while serving with the ICCS were automatically awarded the medal posthumously.

Insignia: A brilliant, gold-coloured circular medal, 36 mm in diameter, bearing the national emblems of the four countries involved (Canada, Hungary, Poland and Indonesia), circumscribed by the words *International Commission of Control and Supervision.* The reverse bears a laurel wreath with the words *Service — Vietnam — 17-1-1973* on three separate lines.

Suspender: An eyelet is mounted on the top of the medal, through which passes a rounded rectangular clip that attaches the medal to a straight mounting bar.

Ribbon: A 36 mm wide ribbon consisting of eight alternating 4 mm stripes of red and white, with a central 4 mm stripe of green.

Bars: None

Postnominals: None

Other: In the early 1990s, at the direction of then Minister of External Affairs Joe Clark, this medal was issued to civilians involved in the mission. The civilian issue made in Canada is of a much higher quality; members of the Canadian Forces who received the original medal could apply to exchange their award for the Canadian issue.

Beyond the quality, the Canadian issue differed from the original 1973 version in a number of ways. The medal is thicker, it has a solid, straight suspender bar and claw, and the reverse features a maple leaf above the words *Vietnam 17-1-73*. This revamped Canadian issue was designed by Bruce Beatty and manufactured by Rideau of St. Laurent, Quebec. It was issued in a black leatherette case whose lid was embossed with the viceregal lion.

Number of Awards: 384

THE MULTINATIONAL FORCE AND OBSERVERS MEDAL

Origins: The multinational force in the Sinai was created as part of the Camp David Accord of 1979, which established peace between Egypt and Israel. The force is funded by the United States, Egypt, Israel, Japan and Germany. Canadians have been involved with the multinational force since 1986. The purpose of the mission is to "observe, verify and report" on the status of the area.

International Commission of Control and Supervision, Vietnam reverse

International Commission of Control and Supervision, Vietnam, Canadian Issue reverse

ICCS Certificate

Multinational Force and Observers Medal obverse

Multinational Force and Observers Medal reverse

Criteria: Awarded for six months' service with the Multinational Force and Observers stationed in the Sinai.

Insignia: The medal is bronze in colour and 34 mm in diameter; a stylized dove of peace, holding an olive branch, is in the centre. The medal is circumscribed with the words *Multinational Force & Observers*. The reverse is plain and bears the words *United in Service for Peace.*

Suspender: A straight suspender bar is connected to the medal by a small ring, which passes through an eyelet on the top of the medal.

Ribbon: The ribbon is orange in colour, 36 mm wide, with a central 10 mm white stripe flanked on either side by 3 mm of dark green.

Bars: Silver numerals are added for additional tours.

Postnominals: None

Other: This medal continues the tradition of "Cracker Jack"–style awards. Each medal was issued in a plastic box and was accompanied by a miniature medal.

Number of Awards: 1,105

EUROPEAN COMMUNITY MONITOR MISSION MEDAL (YUGOSLAVIA)

Origins: In late June 1991, Slovenia and Croatia declared independence from Yugoslavia. Six days later the Yugoslav National Army (JNA) marched into Slovenia. On 8 July the Brioni Agreement came into force, effectively ending hostilities in Slovenia. Part of the agreement called for the European Community to establish a monitor mission to observe and report on the withdrawal of the JNA. As the conflict in the former Yugoslavia spread, the monitor mission grew to include Croatia and Bosnia and Herzegovina. The main task was to "monitor political, humanitarian, security, military and economic developments in the countries of the Western Balkans and deliver valid, firsthand reporting to the EU Council of Ministers and to the participating states." In December 2000 the name of the mission (which is still active) was changed to the European Union Monitor Mission (EUMM). EUMM consists of approximately 120 monitors spread throughout the Balkans.

European Community Monitor Mission Medal (Yugoslavia) obverse

Criteria: Awarded for ninety days' service (consecutive or cumulative) as part of the European Community Monitor Mission in Yugoslavia. The mission began on 8 September 1991, and is current.

Insignia: A circular, oxidized silver-coloured medal, 36 mm in diameter. In the centre is a map of Yugoslavia defaced with the words *EC Monitor Mission*. The map is circumscribed by twelve European Community stars. The reverse bears a large dove of peace in flight, holding an olive branch in its beak.

European Community Monitor Mission Medal (Yugoslavia) reverse

Suspender: A small eyelet is mounted on the top of the medal, through which passes a silver ring and the ribbon.

Ribbon: The ribbon is 36 mm wide and consists of eleven stripes of varying sizes. Either edge has 2 mm of blue, 3 mm of white, 3 mm of red, 3 mm of blue, 2 mm of yellow. The central stripe, measuring 10 mm wide, is blue. A circular emblem of the obverse of the medal is worn on the undress ribbon.

Bars: None

Postnominals: None

Other: This medal cancelled the award of the Jugoslavija bar to the Special Service Medal. It was issued in a dark blue leatherette box, impressed with the EU emblem in yellow, accompanied by an undress ribbon, a miniature and a lapel pin.

Number of Awards: 78

INTERNATIONAL FORCE EAST TIMOR MEDAL

Origins: In August 1999 the people of East Timor — a former Portuguese colony that had been invaded by Indonesia in 1975 — voted to become independent from Indonesia. Following the UN–monitored vote, Indonesian militia groups went on a rampage and drove more than 200,000 people from their homes. On 15 September 1999, the United Nations Security Council passed a resolution approving the creation of INTERFET. With the permission of the Indonesian government, INTERFET was authorized to restore peace and security in East Timor, to protect and support UNAMET in its tasks and to facilitate humanitarian aid efforts. The force was led by Australia, and sixteen other nations, including Canada, participated. The mission lasted from October 1999 until April 2000.

International Force East Timor Medal obverse

Criteria: The Canadian criteria for the INTERFET Medal is a minimum of thirty days' cumulative service in the area of operations — defined as East Timor, the sea adjacent to East Timor to a distance of twelve nautical miles, or the staging base at Darwin, Australia.

Insignia: An oxidized, silver-coloured medal, 38 mm in diameter, the obverse bearing a dove holding an olive branch within its beak, overlaying a map of East Timor and circumscribed by the words *International Force East Timor*. There is also an olive branch at the base of the medal. The reverse is plain and circumscribed with the words *Together as One for Peace in East Timor*. The highlights of the medal are polished.

Suspender: A straight bar 32 mm wide, attached to the medal with an Australian Federation star.

Ribbon: The ribbon is 32 mm wide, with a 2 mm central red stripe, flanked on either side by 4 mm of green, 7 mm of white and 4 mm of blue.

Bars: None

Postnominals: None

Other: Although the medal was officially issued to Canadians unnamed, the reverse is plain to allow for engraving. This medal is quite unusual in that it is an Australian award that was awarded to Canadians. The Queen — as Queen of Australia — approved the creation of the International Force East Timor Medal on 25 March 2000, at Government House, Canberra.

Number Awarded: 760

International Force East Timor Medal reverse

EUROPEAN SECURITY AND DEFENCE POLICY SERVICE MEDAL

Since the early 1990s the European Union has taken an increasingly active role in various international missions, both within Europe and beyond. These actions have been taken within the framework of the European Security and Defence Policy, which is administered by the Council of the European Union. To recognize those personnel participating in ESDP missions, the European Union authorized the striking of a standard ESDP medal, to which various service bars are attached. To date, five bars have been created for this medal: EUPM, Artemis, Concordia, Proxmia and Althea. With the exception of Proxmia, all have been awarded to Canadians.

Insignia: The standard ESDP medal is an oxidized, silver-coloured medal, 35 mm in diameter. The obverse bears 12 five-pointed stars around the circumference of the medal. These stars symbolize the unity of Europe. The reverse is plain except for the three words *Pro Pace Unum* (united for peace) on three lines in the centre.

Suspender: A small ball is mounted on the top of the medal, through which passes a silver-coloured ring and the ribbon.

Ribbon: A 36 mm ribbon made up of three equal stripes, of yellow and EU blue.

Postnominals: None

Other: Medals are manufactured by Eekellers-Centini of Belgium. A letter *E* is impressed on the reverse mounting ball on the top of the medal. The medals are issued in a rectangular blue plastic case. The lid is marked with a circle of twelve stars and the name of the mission (e.g., *Artemis*) and *ESDP Service Medal.*

EUROPEAN UNION POLICE MISSION (EUPM)

Origins: The European Union Police Mission (EUPM) in Bosnia Herzegovina commenced on 1 January 2003 and follows from the United Nations International Police Task Force, which had been active in Bosnia to maintain the rule of law and assist with the fostering of peace and order. Approximately 500 police officers from thirty-two countries make up the mission.

Criteria: Awarded for thirty days' continuous or accumulated service as part of the European Union Police Mission in Bosnia Hercegovina, after 1 January 2003.

Bar: A silver-coloured bar, 36 mm wide and 6 mm tall, bearing the word *EUPM*. Silver numerals can be worn to signify additional tours. A small version of this bar is worn on the undress ribbon.

Number Awarded: 6

OPERATION ARTEMIS

Origins: In the summer of 2003, increasing unrest in the Democratic Republic of the Congo and an impending humanitarian disaster prompted the European Union to assist the United Nations mission (MONUC) to evacuate people and provide supplies to local

European Secutity and Defence Policy Service Medal with Artemis Bar obverse

European Security and Defence Policy Service Medal with Artemis Bar reverse

residents. The mission began on 30 May 2003, and concluded on 1 September 2003. The Canadian name for the operation was Operation Caravan, while the European Union designated it Operation Artemis.

Criteria: Awarded for thirty days' continuous or accumulated service on land or in the airspace of the Democratic Republic of the Congo as part of Operation Artemis between June and July 2003.

Bar: A silver-coloured bar, 36 mm wide and 6 mm tall, bearing the word *Artemis*. Silver numerals can be worn to signify additional tours. A small version of this bar is worn on the undress ribbon.

Number Awarded: 53

OPERATION CONCORDIA

Origins: The Former Yugoslav Republic of Macedonia has been host to several international missions. After it achieved independence from the Federal Socialist Republic of Yugoslavia in the early 1990s, tensions began to rise between Macedonians and ethnic Albanians living the country. From 1992 until 1995 the United Nations Preventative Deployment Force was charged with ensuring the integrity of the country's borders, this responsibility was assumed by NATO in 1995. As a result of the Kosovo war in neighbouring Yugoslavia, there were increasing calls by ethnic Albanians (most notably the National Liberation Army, which was closely associated with the Kosovo Liberation Army) living in Macedonia for greater autonomy and rights.

Throughout early 2001, Macedonian security forces engaged the National Liberation Army. After a number of actions, a tentative truce was reached. Following the cease-fire, President Trajkovski of Macedonia requested that NATO disarm the National Liberation Army and other ethnic Albanian groups. This mission began in August 2001 and lasted until the end of September 2001, although NATO forces remained in Macedonia until 31 March 2003.

At that time, at the request of President Trajkovski and authorized by a UN Security Council resolution, the European Union launched Operation Concordia. The purpose of this mission was to provide a stable and secure environment and to allow for the implementation of the August 2001 Ohrid Framework Agreement, which set out to promote democracy, foster better relations between the various ethnic groups living in the Former Yugoslav Republic of Macedonia, and improve relations between Macedonia and the EU.

More than 400 military personnel from twenty-six countries participated in the mission, which ended on 15 December 2003. The first medals were presented on 20 September 2003.

Criteria: Awarded for thirty days' continuous or accumulated service on the land, at sea or in the airspace of the former Yugoslav Republic of Macedonia between 31 March 2003 and 15 December 2003.

Bar: A silver-coloured bar, 36 mm wide and 6 mm tall, bearing the word *Concordia*. Silver numerals can be worn to signify additional tours. A small version of this bar is worn on the undress ribbon.

Number Awarded: 5

OPERATION ALTHEA

Origins: As the number of NATO troops involved in SFOR in Bosnia and Herzegovina was reduced in December 2004, EUFOR began taking on more responsibility. The long-term goals of this mission are to ensure a peaceful and multiethnic Bosnia and Herzegovina that co-operates peacefully with its neighbours, and to encourage eventual EU membership.

The Canadian name for this mission is Operation Boreas.

Criteria: Awarded for thirty days' continuous or accumulated service on the land, at sea or in the airspace of the Bosnia and Herzegovina after 2 December 2004.

Bars: A silver-coloured bar, 36 mm wide and 6 mm tall, bearing the word *Althea*. Silver numerals can be worn to signify additional tours. A small version of this bar is worn on the undress ribbon.

Number Awarded: 69

CHAPTER 18

The Canadian Forces Decoration

T he Canadian Forces Decoration is one of the most widely recognized awards in the Canadian honours system. In its modern form, the tradition of awarding long service medals was initiated with the creation of the Royal Navy Long Service and Good Conduct Medal in 1830. This medal was originally awarded for twenty-one years' service in the ranks of the Royal Navy. Later, the British Army instituted a similar medal, and throughout the late Victorian era and following the First World War a wide variety of long service medals and decorations was created by the British government for use throughout the British Empire. The Canadian Forces used these awards until just after the Second World War, when the Canadian Forces Decoration (CD) was established.

Prior to the CD, Canadian service personnel had been eligible for any one of eight separate long service awards, depending on which service they were enrolled in and what rank they held. There was the RCN Long Service Medal, the Royal Canadian Navy Voluntary Reserve (RCNVR) Long Service Medal and the RCNVR Officer's Decoration for members of the navy. The army had the Army Long Service and Good Conduct Medal, the Efficiency Medal and the Efficiency Decoration. Those in the air force were eligible for the RCAF Long Service and Good Conduct Medal or the Air Efficiency Award.

Brooke Claxton, the Canadian minister of Defence from 1946 until 1954, had a keen interest in honours and awards and was the central supporter of plans for a unique Canadian long service award. Clerical staff at the Department of National Defence had long complained that administering the various separate long service awards was time-consuming and complex, and plans for a separate Canadian long service award emerged from DND in 1947.

Through Order-in-Council 6335, Cabinet approved the establishment of the Canadian Forces Decoration on 15 December 1949, and a submission was forwarded to King George VI. The King approved the creation of the CD on 8 March 1950. After 1949, the CD superseded all of the above listed awards.

*Left: George VI
Canadian Forces
Decoration obverse
Above: Reverse*

*Left: Efficiency Decoration, George VI issue
Right: Efficiency Medal, Elizabeth II issue*

*Left: Army Long
Service and Good
Conduct Medal,
George VI issue
obverse. Above:
Reverse*

*Left: Royal
Canadian Navy
Long Service and
Good Conduct
Medal obverse
Above: Reverse*

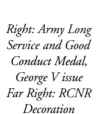

*Right: Army Long
Service and Good
Conduct Medal,
George V issue
Far Right: RCNR
Decoration*

*Left: Air Efficiency
Award obverse
Above: Reverse*

*Left: Royal Canadian
Air Force Long
Service and Good
Conduct Medal
Above: Reverse*

When it was instituted, the CD was unique in that it was awarded to all ranks, from enlisted soldiers to flag and general officers. Under the British system there had been a tradition of differentiating between those with long service in the ranks and those who were long-serving officers. Reserve officers in the army were typically awarded the Efficiency Decoration, known as the Territorial Decoration in the United Kingdom (officers in the regular army received no long service awards), while non-commissioned officers were awarded the Efficiency Medal (for reservists) or Canadian Army Long Service and Good Conduct Medal (for members of the regular force). This situation was similar for the Royal Canadian Navy and Royal Canadian Air Force, both of which possessed their own long service awards. Thus, under the previous system, officers received long service "decorations" — and were therefore entitled to postnominals — while noncommissioned officers received long service "medals," which did not entitle the recipient to postnominals.

Another feature of the CD was that, with it, the period of service required to receive a long service award was standardized. Until now, the period of service varied depending on what service the recipient had spent the majority of his or her time in. A leading seaman in the Royal Canadian Navy had to serve fifteen years to receive the Royal Canadian Navy Long Service and Good Conduct Medal, while a leading seaman in the Royal Canadian Naval Voluntary Reserve only had to serve twelve years to receive the RCNVR Long Service and Good Conduct Medal. A similar situation existed in the other services, where the period of service to qualify for a long service medal varied widely between ten and twenty years. This system of multiple awards was complex and laborious to administer.

Proposals for a uniquely Canadian long service award emerged from the Awards Co-ordination Committee in November 1946, although the idea originated shortly after the Royal Canadian Naval Voluntary Reserve and Royal Canadian Naval Reserve were unified into the Royal Canadian Navy (Reserve) and considered creating a single long service award for both the regular and reserve services.

Initially, two new awards were to be established: a Canadian Long Service Medal, for award to regular members of the Canadian Armed Forces, and a Canadian Forces Long Service Decoration, for award to those in the reserve force. Both were to be awarded for fifteen years' long service and good conduct. No differentiation was to be made on the basis of rank — only whether one was a member of the regular or reserve force. The Cabinet Defence Committee approved the CD on 15 October 1947, and designs were subsequently drawn up. By December 1949, plans for the Canadian Long Service Medal and Canadian Forces Long Service Decoration were merged into one award: the Canadian Forces Decoration.

This new plan set out that a differentiation was to be made between those in the regular forces and those in the reserve. For recipients in the regular Armed Forces, the insignia were to be made of silver gilt (gold in colour), as were the clasps. The ribbons were to be red, with three thin, evenly spaced white stripes. For those in the reserve Armed Forces, the insignia and clasps were to be of silver, while the ribbons were to be red with a single thin white stripe.

The plans for this differentiation were dropped in June 1950, however, and the original plan for the regular Armed Forces CD was extended to the reserve Armed Forces. One of the reasons why the reserve Armed Forces CD was shelved was the perceived similarity between the ribbon of the reserve CD and the ribbon of the Order of the British Empire (military division), which was bordered on each side by thin grey stripes with a single grey stripe in the centre.

The CD was designed by Warrant Officer Barry Reddy. Early versions did not bear the King's effigy on the obverse or reverse. When he was presented with the first drawing in April 1948, George VI noted that the new decoration did not include this feature. This disappointed him, as he had always taken such a keen interest, not only in the Canadian armed forces, but also in Canada itself. The King's private secretary noted these "observations" and conveyed them to the governor general. The omission of the effigy was not made out of disrespect (his Royal cypher was included), but once it was clear that the King had taken such an interest in the new decoration, a new design was created. Reddy redesigned the medal to include the King's effigy on the obverse. (Earlier versions bore a design of maple leaves, beavers, dams and the aurora borealis.)

The new award was announced on 15 July 1950, and most newspapers carried sketches of it. On 7 June 1951, at Rideau Hall, the first Canadian Forces Decoration was presented to Viscount Alexander of Tunis, the governor general, by Brooke Claxton, the minister of National Defence. At the same time, nine other CDs were given to Lord Alexander for presentation to King George VI, Queen Elizabeth, Queen Mary the Queen Mother, Princess Elizabeth, Princess Margaret, the Duke of Gloucester, the Princess Royal, Lady Patricia Ramsay and Princess Alice. All of these members of the Royal family were serving members as colonels in chief of Canadian regiments.

Following the death of King George VI in February 1952, the design of the CD was altered to bear the effigy of Queen Elizabeth II on the obverse, while the reverse remained the same, save the removal of King George's Royal cypher. Further alterations were also made to the medal: the suspender was changed from a bar bearing the word *Canada* to an opening, with a maple leaf, at the top of the medal. The new method of suspension was designed by Bruce Beatty. The material from which the medal is struck was also changed, from silver gilt to tombac. These changes were made in an effort to reduce costs. Some recipients of the King George VI CD also claimed that the suspension bar tended to break off, although there is little evidence of the medal being fragile. While the King George VI CD bears the Royal cypher on the reverse, the Queen Elizabeth II issue does not. When the first Queen Elizabeth II issue was struck, the Royal Canadian Mint acciden-

tally used George VI's cypher on the reverse. The problem was detected, and the medals were destroyed. Subsequently, the Queen's cypher (EIIR) was left off the reverse.

Left: Canadian Forces Decoration King George VI silver proof obverse
Right: Canadian Forces Decoration Queen Elizabeth II proof

Since the presentation of the first CD to Viscount Alexander in 1951, it has been a tradition that all Canadian governors general receive the medal, in their capacity as commanders-in-chief. Vincent Massey was the second governor general to receive the CD. Initially, to lend prestige to the new decoration, all members of the Royal family who were members of the Canadian Forces were automatically awarded the CD, even if they had not completed twelve years' service; since 1953 the award has not been automatic to members of the Royal family who serve as members of the Canadian Forces.

The Queen's CD is of the King George VI type and is engraved *HRH the Princess Elizabeth*. Prince Phillip's CD is of the Elizabeth II type, and is engraved *HRH the Duke of Edinburgh*. It was not until June 1954 that the first Elizabeth II type of the CD was struck.

Although it was originally planned to present the Canadian Forces Decoration with a certificate signed by the governor general, this plan was never carried out, and no official certificate is issued when the award is presented.

Current Canadian Forces Decoration obverse

THE CANADIAN FORCES DECORATION

Origins: The Canadian Forces Decoration was created as a Canadian replacement for a variety of British long service awards that were bestowed upon Canadians for service in the Royal Canadian Navy, Canadian Army and Royal Canadian Air Force.

Criteria: Awarded to officers and noncommissioned members of the Canadian Forces who have completed twelve years of service. The last eight years of claimed service must have been "good" in order to qualify for the CD.

Insignia: There have been two separate issues. The **King George VI type** is decagonal in shape, 36.5 mm in diameter, made from .800 silver and gilded. The obverse bears an uncrowned effigy of King George VI and the words

Georgivs VI D : G : Britt : OMN : Rex Fid : Def.
The reverse bears a naval crown at the top, three
maple leaves and an albatross, representing the
three elements of the armed forces. The Royal
cypher is superimposed over this motif. The
word *Service* is embossed on a scroll at the base,
bordered on either side by a fleur-de-lys.

The **Elizabeth II type** is decagonal in
shape, 36.5 mm in diameter and made from
tombac.[34] The obverse bears an uncrowned
youthful effigy of Queen Elizabeth II and the
words *Elizabeth II Dei Gratia Regina* with the
word *Canada* at the base. The obverse is identical to that of the King George VI issue,
although without the Royal cypher.

*Current Canadian Forces
Decoration reverse*

Suspender: For the King George VI type, a rectangular bar bearing the word *Canada*,
attached to the medal by two scrolled arms
which are connected to the actual medal by a
single rivet. For the Elizabeth II type, there are
two scroll bars with a maple leaf at the base,
through which the ribbon passes. The medal is
struck from one piece of metal, whereas the
King George VI type was hand-assembled
from two pieces.

Ribbon: Red in colour, 39 mm wide, with
three equally spaced white stripes 1 mm wide.
Until 1967 the ribbon was a pale shade of red;
in recent years the red has been a deeper,
blood-red colour.

Bars: Awarded for an additional ten years' service. The first type of clasp is plain silver gilt,
and bears the older-style scalloped shield of the
Royal Arms of Canada surmounted by a Tudor
crown. The second type is a plain, gold-
coloured clasp bearing the shield of the Royal
Arms of Canada surmounted by a St. Edward's

*Pre-1957 Canadian Forces
Decoration clasp*

Slide-on CD Bar

Canadian Forces Decoration, rosette for undress ribbon

crown. Two holes are drilled into each side of the clasp so that it may be sewn onto the ribbon. Slip-on clasps also exist, although these were primarily used for award ceremonies. Recipients of clasps wear a silver rosette on the undress ribbon for each clasp awarded.

Postnominals: Recipients are entitled to use the postnominals C.D. after their names.

Naming: On the King George VI type, the rank and name of the recipient are engraved on the reverse of the *Canada* suspender bar. On the Elizabeth II type, the rank and name of the recipient are engraved in capitals around the edge of the medal. Early Queen Elizabeth issues have the lettering impressed.

Other: The CD is awarded in a brown, rectangular metal box whose lid is embossed with the Royal Arms of Canada. The interior is lined with black velvet and white or salmon-coloured satin. Until the early 1990s the CD was manufactured by the Royal Canadian Mint. There is one known prototype of the Elizabeth II issue that was made from silver gilt, although this was never awarded. All other Royal Canadian Mint issues were made from tombac. Those made by private firms have been made from a variety of materials.

Number of Awards: King George VI type, approximately 14,000; Queen Elizabeth II type, approximately 217,000; clasps, approximately 84,500

CHAPTER 19

The RCMP Long Service Medal

The RCMP Long Service Medal is the oldest continuously awarded long service medal in the Canadian honours system and one of the oldest in the Commonwealth. In the summer of 1925, Commissioner Cortlandt Starnes began to investigate how a special long service medal could be established. By 22 September of the same year he had submitted a memorandum to the minister of Justice, suggesting the creation of a Royal Canadian Mounted Police Officer's Decoration and a Royal Canadian Mounted Police Long Service Medal. The project seems to have received little attention; it was not until 30 September 1927 that Starnes submitted a secondary report which altered the proposed length of service from twenty-five years to twenty. Prime Minister William Lyon Mackenzie King gave his consent for the project, as did the governor general, Lord Willingdon, and on 5 December 1928 an order-in-council was issued creating the medal and decoration. The decoration was to be awarded to officers who had fulfilled twenty-five years of commissioned service, while the medal was to be awarded to officers, noncommissioned officers and constables upon completion of twenty-five years' service. It is likely that the decoration was meant to look something like the Colonial Auxiliary Forces Decoration.

Despite the adoption of an order-in-council, no further action was taken. The idea for a medal was revived in 1932 by Major General Sir James Howden MacBrien, the commissioner of the RCMP. A long-serving Canadian army officer, MacBrien had seen service in the Anglo-Boer War and in the First World War. Shortly after being appointed commissioner, he broached the topic with Prime Minister R.B. Bennett. MacBrien felt that the RCMP should have a long service medal similar to that awarded to members of the Canadian militia, but unlike Starnes he did not see a need for a separate officer's decoration. Bennett — who, it will be remembered, resumed the practice of submitting civilian honours lists — was a keen supporter of the proposal. On 14 January 1933, the old order-in-council that had created the Officer's Decoration and Long Service Medal was cancelled; a new one ordered that a Royal Canadian Mounted Police Long Service Medal be issued.

The medal was formally established by King George V on 6 March 1934. Already elated that the Canadian government was resuming civilian honours lists, the King was enthusiastic about the new medal.

Formal announcement of the medal's establishment came at Standish Hall in Hull, Quebec, on 26 April 1934, as Commissioner MacBrien informed the gathering that His Majesty the King had been pleased to approve the establishment of the medal. The first investiture took place in the Drill Hall at Cartier Square on 12 March 1935. The governor general, Lord Bessborough, invested seventy-one members and former members of the force.

Other parts of the British Empire, such as South Africa, Malta and Cyprus, had already established long service medals for their police forces; the Canadian request was not unusual, especially as the RCMP was one of the most respected police forces in the empire. A few members of the Royal North West Mounted Police had been awarded the Imperial Service Medal, but until 1935 there was no medal unique to the Canadian police.

The medal has borne the effigies of Canada's Sovereigns since King George V. In 1954, another order-in-council was adopted to establish a series of bars; these are awarded for twenty-five, thirty and thirty-five years of service.

The medal was designed by the staff at the Royal Canadian Mint, and it continues to be struck there. It is the only long service medal still being struck in silver. In 2004, a gold-and-silver bar with four stars was approved to recognize forty years of service. Each medal is awarded with a certificate bearing the recipient's name.

Left: Old RCMP Medal transmittal box
Above: Old RCMP Medal certificate

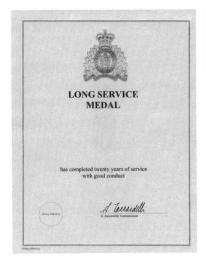

Current RCMP Long Service and Good Conduct certificate
Left: English. Right: French.

THE RCMP LONG SERVICE MEDAL

Origins: Part of the broader trend throughout the Commonwealth in the 1920s and 1930s of dominion and colonial governments establishing police long service medals. The criteria and design are similar to the Colonial Auxiliary Forces Long Service Medal, which was awarded to members of the Canadian Militia from 1901 until 1931.

Criteria: Awarded to any officer, noncommissioned officer or constable who bears an irreproachable character and has completed not less than twenty years of service.

Insignia: A circular silver medal, 36 mm in diameter. The obverse bears the youthful effigy of Queen Elizabeth II, circumscribed by the words *Elizabeth Dei Gratia Regina*. The reverse bears the Arms of the RCMP and is circumscribed with the words *For*

RCMP Long Service Medal
obverse

*RCMP Long Service Medal
reverse (English)*

*The RCMP Long Service Medal
reverse (French)*

*RCMP Long Service Medal
Bronze, Silver, and Gold bars*

Long Service and Good Conduct, or *Pour ancienneté et bonne conduite.*

There have been four different obverses: one for King George V, two for King George VI and one for Queen Elizabeth II. There have been three reverses: one bearing the RCMP arms with a Tudor crown (for the George V and George VI issues), and two bearing the St. Edward's crown (for the Elizabeth II issue, one in English and one in French).

Suspender: A straight, silver, claw-footed suspender bar 32 mm wide.

Ribbon: A blue ribbon, 32 mm wide, with a 3 mm yellow stripe set 6 mm from either edge. A bronze, silver or gold bar is worn on the ribbon to denote the award of any bars.

Bars: There are four types of bars: a bronze bar with a single star in the centre is awarded for twenty-five years of service; a silver bar with two stars equally spaced in the centre is awarded for thirty years of service; and a gold bar with three stars equally spaced is awarded for thirty-five years of service. These bars are usually hallmarked "18k" on the reverse. A gold-and-silver bar with four stars equally spaced is awarded for forty years of service. Only the bar for the longest service is worn on the ribbon.

Other: From 1934 until 1948 the medal was made of sterling silver (.925 silver). From 1948 until 1975 the medal was struck in .800 silver, which is more durable. Since 1975 the medal has been struck in sterling silver. All medals are named in block capitals. They were originally housed in a plain, white, rectangular cardboard box, but since the 1960s most have been issued in a square, blue leatherette case with a miniature version of the RCMP arms on the lid.

Number of Awards:
King George V Issue: 388
King George VI, 1st type (with Ind Imp): 384
King George VI, 2nd type: 329
Elizabeth II with older King George VI reverse: 482
Queen Elizabeth II made of .800 silver: 1,329
Queen Elizabeth II made of .925 silver: 14,203

RCMP Long Service Medal One-, Two-, Three-, and Four-Star Bars

RCMP Long Service Medal (King George V)

RCMP Long Service Medal (King George VI first type)

RCMP Long Service Medal (King George VI second type)

RCMP Long Service Medal (old reverse)

CHAPTER 20

Exemplary Service Medals

L ike the Canadian Forces Decoration and the RCMP Long Service
and Good Conduct Medal, the Exemplary Service Medals find
their origins in the myriad of long service awards once used
throughout the British Empire and Commonwealth. The closest relative
of the Exemplary Service Medals is the RCMP Long Service Medal, which
was established in 1934.

For nearly fifty years, the RCMP Long Service Medal was the only standardized official police award, and even then only members of the RCMP
were eligible for it. Individual police forces developed a patchwork of awards,
varying in criteria and design, none of which was officially recognized.

Since 1909, Canadians had been eligible for the King's Police and Fire
Service Medal, which was awarded for both gallantry and distinguished
service. While the gallantry issue of the King's Police and Fire Service
Medal was similar to the modern-day Medal of Bravery and Star of
Courage, the distinguished service issue was more like the Order of Merit
of the Police Forces or Meritorious Service Decorations. Although these
two awards were at the disposal of the Canadian government, only fifty
were ever awarded.

Other parts of the Commonwealth had established their own long
service awards. The first was New Zealand, which instituted the New
Zealand Police Long and Efficient Service Medal in 1868, more than
twenty-five years before New Zealand became a country. This was the first
official police long service medal to be issued with regularity. South Africa
followed suit, establishing a prison long service medal and police long
service medal in 1921 and 1922, respectively. Malta, Ceylon (Sri Lanka)
and Cyprus also had special police long service medals by the late 1920s.
One must therefore ask why it took so long for the various frontline services in Canada to call for the creation of their own awards.

The answer can be found in the Canadian government's reluctance to
award medals for civilian service, let alone to institute them, prior to 1967.
Indeed, the dearth of Canadian long service medals was not for lack of

trying. In 1958, for instance, the Canadian Association of Chiefs of Police asked the federal government if it would consider creating a Canadian Police Long Service Medal, and the reply was negative. The association then established its own award — the Canadian Association of Chiefs of Police Long Service Medal — which was awarded for twenty years of good service, but the award was not recognized by the government and was considered only a temporary measure.

Throughout the 1970s, and especially following the establishment of the Canadian Bravery Awards in 1972, the Canadian Association of Chiefs of Police regularly asked the government to reconsider the creation of a Canadian Police Long Service Medal. In 1976, shortly before the tenth anniversary of the creation of the Order of Canada, Cabinet was asked to consider the creation of such a medal. The proposal was finally accepted in 1980, and the Canadian Association of Chiefs of Police was invited to co-operate in the creation of the new award. Finally, on 12 August 1982, the Queen signed the letters patent creating the Police Exemplary Service Medal.

Although not initially part of the plan, the exemplary service medals program would eventually expand to include correctional services, fire services, the Canadian Coast Guard, emergency medical services, and most recently peace officers. Prior to this, only the various fire services had been recognized, and even then with unofficial awards that were provincially or locally sanctioned. The adoption of this series of exemplary service awards was rooted in part in a fear that each province and organization would institute its own awards, with varying criteria and designs, and then demand that they be

Above: Canadian Association of Chiefs of Police Long Service Medal
Right: Imperial Service Medal obverse
Below: reverse

incorporated into the broader Canadian honours system. To avoid this, officials at Government House and in the Privy Council Office encouraged the creation of a series of standardized national awards.

The exemplary service medals are awarded only to those public services in which the public servant — whether it be police officer, corrections guard, ambulance driver or firefighter — is working in potentially life-threatening environments. All of the medals require a minimum of twenty years of service in their respective organization. For each medal there is an advisory committee which submits lists of nominees to the governor general. These committees vary in composition; whereas the advisory committee for the Police Exemplary Service Medal is the Decorations Committee of the Canadian Association of Chiefs of Police and is therefore national in scope, there are separate committees in each province and territory for the Corrections Exemplary Service Medal and Fire Service Exemplary Service Medal. The committees for the Coast Guard and EMS versions of the medal, meanwhile, are more centralized, along the lines of the Police Exemplary Services Medals. These committees ensure that the minimum required service has been attained and they advise the governor general on matters concerning the award of the medals. They do not generally review submissions in the detailed manner that members of the Advisory Council of the Order of Canada do.

The term "exemplary service" — rather than "long service" — was used in the criteria because the award is not granted automatically upon completion of twenty years of service: one must also have a good record. Exemplary service is defined as "service characterized by good conduct, industry and efficiency that serves as a model for others." In extraordinary cases the medal may be awarded posthumously to persons who died in the performance of their duties. Until the late 1990s the names of those awarded the medal were published in the *Canada Gazette*. Recently, a practice of submitting the list of recipients to be tabled in the House of Commons every month has been initiated. Each medal is awarded with a certificate bearing the recipient's name.

All of the Exemplary Service Medals are of a similar design, featuring the maple leaf on the obverse and Royal cypher and crown on the reverse. The Coast Guard Exemplary Service Medal is slightly different in that it features a smaller maple leaf that is not cut out. With the exception of the Emergency Medical Services and Peace Officer's Exemplary Service Medals, all of the Exemplary Service Medals were designed by Bruce Beatty.

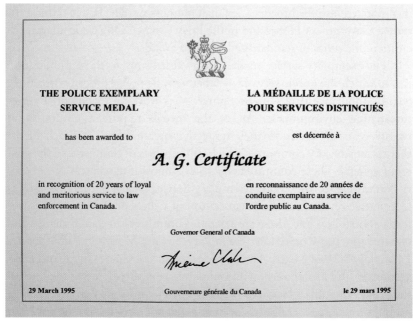

THE POLICE EXEMPLARY
SERVICE MEDAL

LA MÉDAILLE DE LA POLICE
POUR SERVICES DISTINGUÉS

has been awarded to

est décernée à

A. G. Certificate

in recognition of 20 years of loyal
and meritorious service to law
enforcement in Canada.

en reconnaissance de 20 années de
conduite exemplaire au service de
l'ordre public au Canada.

Governor General of Canada

29 March 1995

Gouverneure générale du Canada

le 29 mars 1995

Exemplary Service Medal certificate

Police Exemplary Service Medal
obverse

THE POLICE EXEMPLARY
SERVICE MEDAL

Origins: Largely based upon the Royal
Canadian Mounted Police Long Service
Medal and, by extension, the Canadian
Association of Chiefs of Police Long Service
Medal (now obsolete).

Criteria: Awarded to serving police officers
who have completed a minimum of twenty
years of full-time service with one or more recognized Canadian police forces, including
full-time police-cadet training, of such good
standard as to warrant an award, if such period of service, in whole or in part, has not been
recognized by any other official, national long
service and good conduct or efficiency decoration or medal. The award can be made retroac-
tively if the person was a serving police officer

on 1 August 1980 and meets the above-mentioned criteria. Members of the Royal Canadian Mounted Police who have been awarded the RCMP Long Service Medal and members of the Canadian Forces Military Police who have received the Canadian Forces Decoration are ineligible for the award. Bars may be awarded for ten years of additional service.

Police Exemplary Service Medal reverse

Insignia: A circular silver colour medal, 36 mm in diameter, with the obverse bearing a stylized maple leaf and the Scales of Justice, circumscribed with the words *Exemplary Services — Services Distingués*. The reverse bears the Royal cypher surmounted by a crown. Parts of the maple leaf not touching the inner edge of the medal are cut out.

Suspender: An inverted fleur-de-lys attached to a straight bar.

Ribbon: The same as used for the Canadian Association of Chiefs of Police Long Service Medal. Composed of five equal stripes — three blue and two yellow — the entire ribbon is 32 mm wide.

Bars: A plain, straight, silver bar bearing a maple leaf in the centre. A small silver maple leaf is worn on the undress ribbon to represent each bar awarded.

Other: Each medal is engraved on the rim with the name of the recipient (e.g., *W.G. MACDONALD*). The medal is presented in a black or blue rectangular case embossed with the Royal Arms of Canada or the viceregal lion. The interior of the case is lined with maroon velvet and white satin.

Number of Awards: 32,835

Corrections Exemplary Service
Medal obverse

Corrections Exemplary Service
Medal reverse

THE CORRECTIONS EXEMPLARY SERVICE MEDAL

Origins: In part based upon the Police Exemplary Service Medal. Earlier long service awards for corrections officials originated in South Africa with the creation of the Prisons Good Service Medal in 1921.

Criteria: Awarded to employees of the Canadian Correctional Service who have completed a minimum of twenty years of full-time paid service, not necessarily continuous, with one or more correctional services in Canada, of such good standing as to warrant an award. Ten of those years must be spent as a peace officer in an institution, parole office or probation office. No period of service that has been recognized by another long service medal shall be counted towards the award of the Corrections Exemplary Service Medal. Bars may be awarded for ten years of additional service. The recipient must have been an employee of the Canadian Correctional Service on or after 11 June 1984.

Insignia: A circular silver-coloured medal, 36 mm in diameter. The obverse bears a stylized maple leaf with a key and torch crossed over each other, circumscribed with the words *Exemplary Service — Services Distingués*. The reverse bears the Royal cypher surmounted by a crown. Parts of the maple leaf not touching the inner edge of the medal are cut out.

Suspender: An inverted fleur-de-lys attached to a straight bar.

Ribbon: Composed of five equal stripes — three green and two yellow — the entire ribbon is 32 mm wide.

Bars: A plain, straight, silver bar bearing a maple leaf in the centre. A small silver maple leaf is worn on the undress ribbon to represent each bar awarded.

Other: Each medal is engraved on the rim with the name of the recipient (e.g., *H. KIL-FOYLE*). The medal is presented in a black or blue rectangular case embossed with the Royal Arms of Canada or the viceregal lion. The interior of the case is lined with maroon velvet and white satin.

Number of Awards: 7,602

THE FIRE SERVICES EXEMPLARY SERVICE MEDAL

Origins: In part based upon the Police Exemplary Service Medal. Prior to the establishment of the Fire Services Exemplary Service Medal, several provincial governments awarded medals to firefighters for long service — most notably Ontario, Newfoundland, Nova Scotia and British Columbia. The Fire Services Exemplary Service Medal is also similar in criteria to the Colonial Fire Brigade Long Service Medal created in 1934 and the British Fire Brigade Long Service and Good Conduct Medal established in 1954, as these were the first standardized long service awards for members of the fire services.

Criteria: Awarded to persons who have completed twenty years as a member of the fire service, and whose service is of such good standard as to warrant the award. No period of service that has been recognized by another long service medal shall be counted towards

The Fire Services Exemplary Service Medal obverse

*Fire Services Exemplary Service
Medal reverse*

the award of the Corrections Exemplary Service Medal. Bars may be awarded for ten years of additional service. The recipient must have been a member of the fire service on or after 29 August 1985.

Insignia: A circular, silver-coloured medal, 36 mm in diameter. The obverse shows a stylized maple leaf bearing a fire hydrant and crossed axes, with a Maltese cross entered thereon, all of which is circumscribed with the words *Exemplary Service — Services Distingués*. The reverse bears the Royal cypher surmounted by a crown. Parts of the maple leaf not touching the inner edge of the medal are cut out.

Suspender: An inverted fleur-de-lys attached to a straight bar.

Ribbon: Composed of five equal stripes — three red and two yellow — the entire ribbon is 32 mm wide.

Bars: A plain, straight, silver bar bearing a maple leaf in the centre. A small silver maple leaf is worn on the undress ribbon to represent each bar awarded.

Other: Each medal is engraved on the rim with the name of the recipient (e.g., *R. EDWARDSON*). The medal is presented in a black or blue rectangular case embossed with the Royal Arms of Canada or viceregal lion. The interior of the case is lined with maroon velvet and white satin.

Number of Awards: 37,857

THE COAST GUARD EXEMPLARY SERVICE MEDAL

Origins: In part based upon the Police Exemplary Service Medal.

Criteria: Awarded to persons who have completed twenty years of service with the Department of Transport, ten years of which have been served with the Canadian Coast Guard in the performance of duties involving potential risk (as determined by the advisory committee). No period of service that has been recognized by another long service medal shall be counted towards the award of the Coast Guard Exemplary Service Medal. Bars may be awarded for ten years of additional service. The recipient must have been a employee of the Department of Transport on or after 25 October 1990.

Insignia: A circular, silver-coloured medal, 36 mm in diameter. The obverse bears the crest of the Canadian Coast Guard (a single maple leaf in *dexter* and two dolphins *sinister*, surrounded by a nautical rope tied at the base), circumscribed with the words *Exemplary Service — Services Distingués*. The reverse bears the Royal cypher surmounted by a crown.

Suspender: An inverted fleur-de-lys attached to a straight bar.

Ribbon: Composed of seven coloured stripes; flanking a central 3 mm white stripe on either side are a 3 mm blue stripe, a 7 mm yellow stripe and another 3 mm blue stripe.

Coast Guard Exemplary Service Medal obverse

Coast Guard Exemplary Service Medal reverse

Bars: A plain, straight, silver bar bearing a maple leaf in the centre. A small silver maple leaf is worn on the undress ribbon to represent each bar awarded.

Other: Each medal is engraved on the rim with the name of the recipient (e.g., *L. BIRINGER*). The medal is presented in a black or blue rectangular case embossed with the Royal Arms of Canada or the viceregal lion. The interior of the case is lined with maroon velvet and white satin.

Number of Awards: 278

THE EMERGENCY MEDICAL SERVICES EXEMPLARY SERVICE MEDAL

Origins: In part based upon the Police Exemplary Service Medal. This is one of the first medals in the world to recognize long service rendered by emergency medical personnel.

Criteria: Awarded to persons who have completed twenty years of service with a recognized pre-hospital emergency medical service, ten years of which have been service in the performance of duties involving potential risk. The recipient must have been employed with an emergency medical service on or after 31 October 1991. No period of service that has been recognized by another long service medal shall be counted towards the award of the Emergency Medical Services Exemplary Service Medal. Bars may be awarded for ten years additional service.

Emergency Medical Services Exemplary Service Medal obverse

Insignia: A circular, silver-coloured medal, 36 mm in diameter. The obverse bears a stylized maple leaf, superimposed with a star of life, which is in turn overlaid with a caduceus, all of which is circumscribed with the words *Exemplary Service — Services Distingués*. The reverse bears the Royal cypher surmounted by a crown. Parts of the maple leaf not touching the inner edge of the medal are cut out.

Emergency Medical Services Exemplary Service Medal reverse

Suspender: An inverted fleur-de-lys attached to a straight bar.

Ribbon: Composed of five equal stripes, three blue and two yellow. Superimposed over the centre of each blue stripe is a 2 mm orange stripe. The entire ribbon is 32 mm wide.

Bars: A plain, straight, silver bar bearing a maple leaf in the centre. A small silver maple leaf is worn on the undress ribbon to represent each bar awarded.

Other: Each medal is engraved on the rim with the name of the recipient (e.g., *H. DAAMEN*). The medal is presented in a black or blue rectangular case embossed with the Royal Arms of Canada or the viceregal lion. The interior of the case is lined with maroon velvet and white satin.

Number of Awards: 746

Peace Officer Exemplary Service Medal obverse

Peace Officer Exemplary Service Medal reverse

THE PEACE OFFICER EXEMPLARY SERVICE MEDAL

Origins: In part based upon the Police Exemplary Service Medal.

Criteria: Awarded to persons who have completed twenty years of service with a recognized organization: the Canadian Border Service Agency, Department of Citizenship and Immigration, Department of the Environment, Department of Fisheries and Oceans, Parks Canada and other federal or provincial organizations that employ peace officers. No period of service that has been recognized by another long service medal shall be counted towards the award of the Peace Officer Exemplary Service Medal. The recipient must have been employed as a peace officer on or after 22 September 1998.

Bars may be awarded for ten years of additional service.

Insignia: A circular, silver-coloured medal, 36 mm in diameter. The obverse bears a shield set on a vallary star, superimposed on a maple leave, all of which is circumscribed with the words *Exemplary Service — Services Distingués.* The reverse bears the Royal cypher surmounted by a crown. Parts of the maple leaf not touching the inner edge of the medal are cut out.

Suspender: An inverted fleur-de-lys attached to a straight bar.

Ribbon: Composed of a band of dark blue at the outer edge, flanked by a narrower band of light blue and then a band of gold with a single wide band of green at the centre. The entire ribbon is 32 mm wide.

Bars: A plain, straight, silver bar bearing a maple leaf in the centre. A small silver maple leaf is worn on the undress ribbon to represent each bar awarded.

Other: Each medal is engraved on the rim with the name of the recipient (e.g., *V. SINHA*). The medal is presented in a black or blue rectangular case embossed with the Royal Arms of Canada or the viceregal lion. The interior of the case is lined with maroon velvet and white satin.

Number of Awards: 0

The first list of recipients is expected to be released in the summer of 2005.

CHAPTER 21

The Queen's Medal for Champion Shot

Proficient marksmanship within the armed forces is a talent that continues to be universally recognized. In many countries marksmanship is recognized through the award of a badge worn on the uniform. Since the time of the French regime it has been tradition for the Crown to organize shooting competitions, both for the regular and reserve forces.

The British Army Best Shot Medal, which the Queen's Medal for Champion Shot is modelled after, was established on 30 April 1869. Although members of the Canadian militia shot at Wimbledon and later at Bisley, it was not until 1923 that Canadians were awarded the medal. The best-shot competition was first held at Bisley, in Surrey, England, and has subsequently been held at the Connaught Ranges in Ottawa. The medal was awarded to the winner of this annual shooting competition. From 1954 until 1967, a separate medal was awarded to members of the Royal Canadian Air Force: the Queen's Medal for Champion Shot of the Royal Canadian Air Force. The RCAF medal was discontinued after the unification of the Royal Canadian Navy, Canadian Army and Royal Canadian Air Force into the Canadian Forces in 1968. In 1968 the name of the Canadian edition of the Queen's Medal for Champion Shot of the Army was changed to the Queen's Medal for Champion Shot of the Military Forces. This medal was identical in appearance to the previously issued Queen's Medal for Champion Shot of the Army; the difference was that the competition was now open to members of all branches of the Canadian Forces.

On 10 July 1991 the current Queen's Medal for Champion Shot was established. This decision was in part made to incorporate the Queen's Canadian titles — and the word *Canada* — into the obverse of the medal, thereby differentiating it from the British issue. The medal, its administration and the Queen's Medal Competition remain essentially the same as the pre-1991 Queen's Medal for Champion Shot of the Military Forces. The idea of creating a separate Canadian award was in part prompted by the Australian government's establishment of a separate Australian Medal for Champion Shot in 1988.

Current Queen's Medal for Champion Shot obverse

Current Queen's Medal for Champion Shot reverse

THE QUEEN'S MEDAL FOR CHAMPION SHOT

Criteria: Awarded to the member of the Canadian Forces or RCMP who obtains the highest aggregate score in stages one and two of the Queen's Medal Competition. Two medals are awarded yearly, one to a member of the Canadian Forces (regular), and one to a member of either the Canadian Forces (reserve) or the RCMP.

Insignia: A silver-coloured circular medal, 36 mm in diameter. The obverse bears a crowned effigy of Queen Elizabeth II circumscribed by the legend *Elizabeth II Dei Gratia Regina*, with the word *Canada* at the bottom. The reverse depicts the figure of Fame rising from her throne, facing left, with a horn in her left hand. With her right hand she is crowning, with a laurel wreath, a warrior facing right. The warrior's weight is on his right foot, as his left foot is raised and resting on the dais to support — on his left knee — a target having three arrows in the centre. In his right hand he holds a bow and a quiver full of arrows.

The obverse was designed by Bruce Beatty, while the reverse — which is identical to the British issue instituted in 1869 — was designed by the noted English engraver J.B. Wyon. The name and rank of the recipient are engraved on the rim of the medal. Initially there were some problems with the naming, as it distorted the rhodium plating on the medal. The first award was made in 1992.

Suspension: The medal is suspended by a straight, single-clawed non-swivelling bar. The suspender was changed in 2002 in order to reduce costs. The current suspender is an inverted fleur-de-lys attached to a straight bar (identical to that used on the Exemplary Service Medals). This alteration to the medal was not approved by the Queen, and the appropriate changes have yet to be made through an order-in-council.

Ribbon: The ribbon is 32 mm wide and is predominantly red, edged with a group of 3 mm stripes in black, white and black.

Bars: Each medal is issued with a date bar indicating the year of award. Until 2002, the date bars were riveted to the suspension of the medal, as had been done with earlier issues; however, these bars are now simply sewn onto the ribbon of the medal.

If a recipient wins a later competition, he or she receives another bar bearing the year of award.

Postnominals: None

Other: The medal is presented in a black or blue leatherette case with a viceregal lion embossed in gold on the lid.

Number of Awards: 23

Proper Champion Shot Medal obverse

CHAPTER 22

Commemorative Medals

The tradition of presenting loyal subjects with commemorative medals can be traced back more than half a millennia to India's Pudukkottai state, where *khelats* were presented on special occasions. These *khelats* were not high honours, but emblems of recognition, and they served as a mechanism for recognition as well as a means of ensuring stability within the existing order.[35] While the bestowal of commemorative medals may have this effect today, it is certainly no longer the intention of such awards. They are, in effect, small tokens of thanks given by the sovereign on special occasions to deserving people, both civilian and military.

The British tradition of awarding commemorative medals — for wear — first emerged with Queen Victoria's Golden Jubilee in 1887. Special medals were struck in gold, silver and bronze and were awarded to people involved in the Jubilee procession and other government officials. In typical Victorian fashion, whether one was awarded the gold, silver or bronze Jubilee Medal was dictated by one's social rank. This entire affair was repeated in 1897 for Queen Victoria's Diamond Jubilee. In 1902, when Edward VII ascended to the throne, a special Coronation Medal was struck, this time in only silver and bronze, and for the first time the bulk of awards went to members of the army and navy: silver for officers and bronze for noncommissioned officers. The tradition was continued when King George V succeeded his father in 1911; this time the medal was struck in silver only, and one was not required to have been involved in the Coronation/Jubilee procession to receive it. Twenty-five years later, when George V celebrated his Silver Jubilee, another medal was struck — the first Silver Jubilee Medal to be struck. Two more coronation medals were eventually issued — one in 1937 for the coronation of King George VI and the other in 1953 for the coronation of Queen Elizabeth II.

Although a British award, Canadians were eligible for every one of these commemorative medals. The 1887 Golden Jubilee and 1897

Top left: Queen Victoria 1867 Jubilee Medal obverse. Bottom left: Queen Victoria 1867 Jubilee Medal reverse. Top right: Queen Elizabeth Coronation Medal 1953 obverse. Bottom right: Queen Elizabeth Coronation Medal 1953 reverse.

Diamond Jubilee Medals were awarded sparingly, and thus only a few Canadians received them, most notably Sir John A. Macdonald (1887) and Sir Wilfrid Laurier (1897). The 1935 Silver Jubilee, 1937 Coronation and 1953 Coronation Medals were awarded to a wide cross-section of Canadian society, from mayors to social workers, and thus there developed a tradition in Canada of not only recognizing senior officials, but also recognizing those who make a tangible difference at the local level.

In 1868 a special Confederation Medal (not intended for wear) was struck and awarded to the Fathers of Confederation and other dignitaries.

While it was a table medal, it was the first uniquely Canadian commemorative medal. The first Canadian commemorative medal intended for wear was struck in 1967 to commemorate the Centennial of Confederation. In 1917 there had been some muted discussion about striking a Golden Jubilee of Confederation Medal, although this idea was not well received in light of the ongoing world war. In 1967 there was no such impediment, and in many ways the Centennial Medal was the catalyst for the creation of a broader Canadian honours system.

The idea for the Centennial Medal came from the then under-secretary of state, Jean Miquelon, in 1963. Initially, the Department of National Defence wanted the medal to be awarded only to members of the armed forces. This idea was discarded, and it was decided that the as-yet-unnamed medal was to be open to all Canadians. On 22 January 1964, Paul Hellyer, the new minister of National Defence, gave his approval for the award of the medal to both military personnel and civilians.[36] The secretary of state, Maurice Lamontagne, received a letter from the Centennial commissioner in March 1964 outlining the commission's view that the issue of creating a commemorative medal was for the government and not the Centennial Commission.[37]

Hellyer and Lamontagne presented a joint memorandum to Cabinet on 11 May 1965, in which they outlined the insufficiency of the existing honours policy as embodied in Cabinet Directive 30 of 1956. The conclusion outlined that the Centennial Medal would appropriately recognize "the specially valuable service of many Canadian citizens."[38] The submission was discussed at the 20 May Cabinet meeting, although Prime Minister Lester Pearson pushed the project aside. "The Prime Minister indicated [at the 20 May meeting] he wished to discuss the proposal further with Mr. Lamontagne. Mr. Pearson was inclined to the view that the institution of the Centennial Medal should be linked to the establishment of the Canada Medal."[39] In other words, Pearson was more concerned with getting the nascent Order of Canada project off the ground than establishing a single medal.

Approval for the Centennial Medal was given at the same time as Cabinet approved the creation of the Order of Canada. The Commonwealth tradition of awarding commemorative medals was thus firmly established in Canada, and it is a tradition that continues to this day. Every Canadian commemorative and jubilee medal has been issued with a distinctive certificate.

1967 Centennial Medal obverse

1967 Centennial Medal reverse

THE CENTENNIAL MEDAL, 1967

Origins: The Centennial Medal finds its origin in the 1947 Independence Medals issued in India and Pakistan. Both of these countries inaugurated the tradition of striking commemorative medals on important national occasions not directly associated with the Sovereign.

Criteria: Awarded to Canadian citizens who were deemed to have made a significant contribution to their community, province or the country as a whole.

Insignia: A circular silver medal, 36 mm in diameter. The obverse bears a maple leaf superimposed with a Royal cypher, circumscribed with *Confederation Canada Confédération.* The reverse depicts the Royal Arms of Canada with the dates "1867–1967" in the base. The medal was struck from sterling silver by the Royal Canadian Mint. Issued unnamed, although those personally presented by the governor general and those awarded to Government House staff members were officially impressed in block capitals with the person's full name (e.g., *ESMOND BUTLER*). The medal was designed by Bruce Beatty.

Suspension: The medal is attached to a graduated, straight suspender bar.

Ribbon: The ribbon is 32 mm wide, with 5 mm of red on either edge and four equally spaced 1 mm stripes of red set against a white background.

Bars: None

Other: The medal was presented in a brown leatherette case (made of metal), its lid stamped with the Royal Arms of Canada in gold (the same kind of case in which the Canadian Forces Decoration is awarded). The medal was also accompanied by two undress ribbon bars. Several gold-plated specimens exist which were originally to be awarded to the Expo 67 commissioners, although there is no evidence that the awards were ever presented.

The medal was issued with a certificate printed on white bond paper, with the Royal Arms of Canada at the top in red and the name of the recipient typed below. Certificates were issued in English or French.

In the mid-1990s the Canadian Chancellery ran out of the original issue of the Centennial Medal struck by the Royal Canadian Mint. The contract to strike replacement issues was awarded to Henry Birks & Sons. The Birks issues, although struck in sterling silver, are distinguishable from the mint's original striking because they are slightly thinner and the upper bar on the reverse of the suspender is marked, in raised letters, *Birks Sterling.*

Number of Awards: 29,500 were awarded

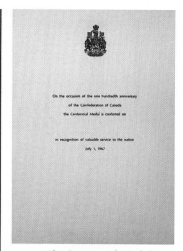

1967 Centennial Medal certificate

1967 Centennial Medal (Birks issue)

THE QUEEN ELIZABETH II SILVER JUBILEE MEDAL, 1977

Origins: Created as part of Queen Elizabeth's Silver Jubilee program in Canada, and following the tradition set when a special medal was struck for King George V's Silver Jubilee in 1935. The program was officially established on 6 February 1977.

Criteria: Awarded to Canadian citizens who

1977 Silver Jubilee Medal
obverse

1977 Silver Jubilee Medal
reverse

were deemed to have made a significant contribution to their community, province or the country as a whole. Recipients were selected by a variety of government officials, including elected politicians. Distribution is outlined below.

Insignia: A circular silver medal, 32 mm in diameter. The obverse bears a crowned effigy of Queen Elizabeth circumscribed by the words *Elizabeth II Dei Gratia Regina Fid Def.* The reverse bears a stylized maple leaf with the word *Canada* above and the dates 1952–1977 below, separated by the Royal cypher. The medal was struck from sterling silver by the Royal Canadian Mint. While the obverse was designed by the Royal Mint staff in London (and is identical to the British issue), the reverse was designed by the Canadian artist Dora de Pédry-Hunt.

Suspension: A footed claw, with a small hollow ball on top, through which a silver ring passes.

Ribbon: A 32 mm watered white ribbon, with a 1 mm blue stripe lining either edge and a central 1 mm red stripe bordered on either side by 1 mm of blue.

Bars: None

Other: The medal was presented in a small red cardboard box with a flip lid. The lid was impressed with the Royal cypher in silver, along with the dates 1952–1977. A grey/brown-coloured certificate was issued with each medal. The 1977 Jubilee logo was embossed in silver at the top of the certificate, and the name of the recipient typed in the middle. The signature of Jules Léger, the governor general, was printed in the upper right-hand corner. The award was issued unnamed, although those personally presented by the governor general and those awarded to Government House staff members were officially impressed in block capitals with the person full name (e.g., *JOHN R. MATHESON*).

Number of Awards: 30,000

Distribution:

Those in the Table of Precedence	1 each	1,225
Governor General's List		100
Lieutenant Governors' Lists	10 each	100
Prime Minister's Staff		15
Cabinet Ministers' Lists		300
Senior Civil Servants		240
Holders of VC, GC and CV	1 each	50
Order of Canada	1 each	1,000
Order of Military Merit	1 each	600
NWT & Yukon Territories		62
National Organizations		7,100
Special Groups		102
Public Service of Canada		2,700
Provincial Public Services		2,700
Education		1,000
Native Peoples		300
Municipal Officials (allocated depending on population)		1,796
Canadian Forces		7,000
Police		1,000
Firemen		300
Royal Canadian Mounted Police		650
Veteran's Organizations		1,000
Reserve *(extra medals for special issue and for use as replacements)*		560
TOTAL		**30,000**

RIDEAU HALL
OTTAWA

On the occasion of	À l'occasion du
the twenty-fifth Anniversary	vingt-cinquième anniversaire
of the accession of	de l'accession de
HER MAJESTY THE QUEEN	SA MAJESTÉ LA REINE
to the Throne	au Trône
the accompanying medal	la médaille ci-jointe
is presented to	est remise à

Joyce Turpin   CM   BEM

1952 ~ 1977

1977 Silver Jubilee Medal certificate

*Commemorative Medal for the
125th Anniversary of
Confederation, 1992, obverse*

THE COMMEMORATIVE MEDAL FOR THE 125TH ANNIVERSARY OF CONFEDERATION, 1992

Origins: Part of the 125th Anniversary of Confederation program — "Canada 125" — this medal is based upon the 1967 Centennial Medal. It was formally established on 7 May 1992.

Criteria: The medal was awarded to people who made a significant contribution to the well-being of their fellow citizens, their community or to Canada. Recipients were selected by a variety of government officials, including elected politicians (distribution is indicated below).

Insignia: A circular, silver-coloured medal, 36 mm in diameter. The obverse bears the Royal cypher surmounted by a crown, superimposed on a single maple leaf, circumscribed by the words *Confederation — Confédération*, with the dates 1867–1992 in the base. The reverse bears the shield of the Royal Arms of Canada encircled by the motto of the Order of Canada and surmounted by the viceregal lion, and circumscribed with the national motto *A Mari Usque Ad Mare* at the bottom. The medal is made of a copper-and-zinc alloy, rhodium-plated, issued unnamed, and was manufactured by a variety of private firms. This medal was designed by Bruce Beatty, and was based upon a revised version of the 1967 Centennial Medal.

Suspension: The medal is attached to a straight suspender which has a maple leaf in the centre.

Ribbon: The ribbon is 32 mm wide, white in colour, and edged on either side by a 4.5 mm stripe of blue, with five 1 mm red stripes equally spaced between the two blue stripes.

Bars: None

Other: The medal was issued in a blue cardboard box with the Royal Arms of Canada and the dates 1867–1992 stamped on the lid. Medals were awarded with a certificate printed on heavy white paper. The Royal Arms of Canada were printed at the top with the Canada 125 logo at the bottom. The name of each recipient was printed onto the certificate along with the signature of Ramon Hnatyshyn, the governor general.

Number Awarded: It was projected that 50,000 would be presented, but only 42,000 were issued due to problems with the program's administration and a lack of nominations.

Commemorative Medal for the 125th Anniversary of Confederation, 1992, reverse

Distribution:

Those in the Table of Precedence	1 each	1,500
Governor General's List		170
Lieutenant Governor's List	17 each	204
Prime Ministers' List		170
Cabinet Ministers' Lists	57 each	2,166
Senators' Lists	40 each	4,160
MPs' Lists	40 each	10,240
Holders of VC, GC and CV	1 each	18
Order of Canada Holders	1 each	2,500
Province and Territories (by population)		10,916
National Organizations		7,000
Special Groups		356
Public Service of Canada		5,000
Canadian Forces		4,000
Royal Canadian Mounted Police		1,000
Reserve *(extra medals for special issue and for use as replacements)*		600
TOTAL		**50,000**

THE COMMEMORATIVE MEDAL FOR THE
125TH ANNIVERSARY OF THE
CONFEDERATION OF CANADA
IS CONFERRED UPON

LA MÉDAILLE COMMÉMORATIVE
DU 125È ANNIVERSAIRE DE LA
CONFÉDÉRATION DU CANADA
EST CONFÉRÉE À

Joyce Bryant

in recognition of significant contribution to
compatriots, community and to Canada

en reconnaissance de sa contribution significative au bien-
être de ses compatriotes, sa communauté et au Canada

1867 – 1992

Gouverneur général du Canada

Governor General of Canada

*Commemorative Medal for the 125th Anniversary of Confederation, 1992,
certificate*

THE QUEEN ELIZABETH II GOLDEN JUBILEE MEDAL, 2002

Origins: Part of Queen Elizabeth II's Golden Jubilee program, the medal was formally established on 15 February 2002.

Criteria: Awarded to Canadian citizens who have made a significant contribution to Canada or to a particular province or territory, region or community within Canada, or who have made an outstanding achievement abroad that brings credit to Canada. Recipients were selected by a variety of government officials, including elected politicians (distribution is outlined below).

Insignia: A circular, gold-coloured medal, 32 mm in diameter. The obverse bears an effigy of Her Majesty Queen Elizabeth wearing the George IV diadem, circumscribed by the legend *Reine du Canada — Queen of Canada*. The reverse bears the Royal crown above a single maple leaf, upon which is superimposed the Royal cypher, all of which is circumscribed by *1952 — Canada — 2002*. The medal was struck by the Royal Canadian Mint and made from gold-plated bronze. It was designed by a committee at the Chancellery.

Suspension: A single loop (eyelet) through which a ring passes. The suspender was originally designed to consist of a claw, and this was approved by the Queen. The Chancellery changed the design to reduce costs.

Ribbon: The ribbon is 32 mm in width. The outer stripes of the ribbon are red and 2 mm wide, followed by 10 mm royal blue stripes, followed by 3 mm white stripes and a single

Queen Elizabeth II Golden Jubilee Medal, 2002, obverse

Queen Elizabeth II Golden Jubilee Medal, 2002, reverse

2 mm red stripe down the centre. Designed in the United Kingdom, this ribbon is the same as used for the British issue.

Bars: None

Other: The medal was issued in a blue cardboard box, with the Canadian Golden Jubilee logo (the Royal cypher EIIR with a flourish of maple leaves) stamped on the lid along with the numeral 50. Awards were accompanied by a white certificate bearing the Golden Jubilee Logo and the fiftieth anniversary of Canadian governors general logo at the bottom, with the recipients name laser printed in the centre.

Number Awarded: 46,000

On the occasion of — À l'occasion du
the fiftieth Anniversary — cinquantième anniversaire
of the accession of — de l'accession de
HER MAJESTY THE QUEEN — SA MAJESTÉ LA REINE
to the Throne — au Trône
the Golden Jubilee Medal — la Médaille du jubilé
is presented to — est remise à

Mr. Bruce Patterson, B.A., B.Ed., F.H.S.C.

CANADIAN GOVERNORS GENERAL 1952-2002 LES GOUVERNEURS GÉNÉRAUX CANADIENS

Queen Elizabeth II Golden Jubilee Medal, 2002, certificate

Distribution:

Those in the Table of Precedence		1,500
Governor General's List		170
Lieutenant Governors' Lists	20 each	1,000*
Prime Minister's List		170
Cabinet Ministers' Lists	10 each	360
Senators' Lists	20 each	2,100
MPs' Lists	20 each	6,020
Holders of VC, GC and CV	1 each	15
Order of Canada	1 each	2,900
Province and Territories (by population)		7,000
National Organizations/ Non-Governmental Organizations		10,000
Special Groups		356
Public Service of Canada		4,000
Canadian Forces		8,000
Royal Canadian Mounted Police		2,200
Reserve *(extra medals for special issue and for use as replacements)*		1,035
TOTAL		**46,470**

* Each lieutenant governor and territorial commissioner was allowed to nominate a minimum of twenty people; the remainder were allocated on the basis of provincial population. Thus the lieutenant governor of Ontario received more than 200 medals to distribute.

CHAPTER 23

The Canadian Memorial Cross

The Memorial Cross is in many respects the first uniquely Canadian award — that is, one that was instituted independently of any previously existing award, and one that applied to Canadians alone. Creation of the Memorial Cross was formally announced by Major General Sydney Chilton Mewburn in the House of Commons on 23 March 1919, and was later formalized by an order-in-council. Mewburn had initially created the Memorial Cross under the War Measures Act, but it was later thought more prudent to regulate the award through an order-in-council and not through the Routine Orders of the Canadian Expeditionary Force alone.

The Memorial Cross has remained largely unchanged since its institution on 1 December 1919, and along with the RCMP Long Service Medal and Canadian Forces Decoration it is the only award in the modern Canadian honours system that has been carried over from the pre-1967 (primarily British) system.

During the First World War the Memorial Cross was issued to the widows and mothers (if living) of every fallen soldier, sailor or airman. In cases where the widow or mother had died prior to receiving the cross, it would go to the father or eldest next of kin. The minister of Militia and Defence could also designate another recipient. The cross was even awarded to Newfoundlanders, a full generation before that Dominion joined Confederation.

The primary criteria for the award was that the soldier died in, or as a result of, service rendered during the First World War, while a member of one of His Majesty's armed services. Thus the mother of a Canadian who died while serving in the New Zealand Expeditionary Force would receive the cross. Similarly, if the family applied, provisions were made to allow Canadians who died in, or as a result of, service in other military forces to be issued the cross. Through this provision, a few examples of the mothers and wives of Canadians who died while serving in the United States Army during the First World War received the Memorial Cross.

The criteria for the Second World War Memorial Cross were almost identical to those used during the First World War, with the simple addition of airmen, merchant seamen and members of the Corps of Canadian Fire Fighters for Service in the United Kingdom.

The symbol of the Memorial Cross is a familiar one to many Canadians: a large replica of the Memorial Cross hangs in the Memorial Chamber of the Peace Tower at Parliament. Similarly, large versions of the King George V, King George VI and Queen Elizabeth II Memorial Crosses were cast in bronze and used on three of the four corners of the tomb of Canada's Unknown Soldier. Every year a "silver cross mother" lays a wreath at the National War Memorial in Ottawa on behalf of all mothers and wives who lost a loved one. The Memorial Cross insignia is based upon a three-quarter version of the Military Cross, with the addition of maple leaves on three of the four arms of the cross and a wreath that passes between each of the cross's arms.

The Memorial Cross was viewed as such a useful memento of remembrance that the practice was adopted by New Zealand. On 12 September 1947 King George VI approved the establishment of the New Zealand Memorial Cross. The criteria and design for this award are almost identical to those for the Canadian Memorial Cross. In place of the maple leaves at each end, however, New Zealand used fern leaves. The ribbon was purple. Like Canada, New Zealand continues to award the Memorial Cross, expanding the criteria to include peacekeeping and other international missions.

THE CANADIAN MEMORIAL CROSS (KING GEORGE V)

Criteria: Issued as a memento of personal loss and sacrifice on the part of the mother and widow (or eldest next of kin) of a sailor or soldier of Canada or Newfoundland who laid down his life for his country during the First World War, or who dies or died from causes attributable to service during the First World War.

Insignia: A silver cross patonce, equally proportioned, 32 mm in width. The cross is superimposed upon a wreath of laurel. The uppermost arm is surmounted by a Tudor crown, while the remaining three bear a maple leaf proper. The centre of the cross displays the Royal cypher GRI in raised letters. The reverse of the cross is engraved with the number, rank and name of the officer or soldier commemorated. The lower arm of the cross is normally stamped with a maker's mark and "sterling."

Suspender: A small silver eyelet is mounted on the upper most arm, through which passes a silver loop and the ribbon.

Ribbon: An ecclesiastical purple ribbon 10 mm wide and of varying lengths. The King George V–issue Memorial Cross was worn around the neck.

Other: The Memorial Cross was issued in a black case embossed with a Tudor Crown on the lid. The interior was of white satin and velvet.

Number of Awards: 65,000+
No exact figures for recipients exist; the number grew with time as more and more veterans of the Great War died as a direct result of illness or wounds attributed to the war. The manufacture and engraving of the Memorial Crosses were undertaken by a variety of firms, and thus there are no concrete figures.

THE CANADIAN MEMORIAL CROSS (KING GEORGE VI)

Criteria: Issued as a memento of personal loss and sacrifice on the part of the mother and widow (or in certain circumstances the father or eldest next of kin) of a sailor, soldier, airman,

*Canadian Memorial Cross
(King George V) obverse*

The Canadian Memorial Cross
(King George VI) obverse

E.29983
Rfn. R. ENGLEHART

Canadian Memorial Cross
reverse

merchant seaman or firefighter of Canada or Newfoundland who laid down his life for his country during the Second World War, or who dies or died from causes attributable to service rendered during the Second World War.

Insignia: A silver cross patonce, equally proportioned, 32 mm in width. The cross is superimposed upon a wreath of laurel. The uppermost arm is surmounted by a Tudor crown, while the remaining three bear a maple leaf proper. The centre of the cross displays the Royal cypher GVIR in raised letters. The reverse of the cross is engraved with the number, rank and name of the officer or soldier commemorated. The lower arm of the cross is normally stamped with a maker's mark and "sterling."

Suspender: A small silver eyelet is mounted on the uppermost arm, through which passes a silver loop and the ribbon. After January 1945 the Memorial Cross was mounted on a silver bar, 32 mm long and 5 mm wide, with flared edges, bearing maple leaves (in the same style as on the cross) at each edge.

Ribbon: An ecclesiastical purple ribbon 10 mm wide and of varying lengths. The King George VI issue Memorial Cross was worn around the neck. No ribbon was issued after January 1945.

Other: The Memorial Cross was issued in a black case, embossed with a Tudor crown on the lid. The interior was of white satin and velvet.

Number of Awards: 60,000+
As with those Memorial Crosses issued as a result of the First World War, no exact figures exist.

THE CANADIAN MEMORIAL CROSS (QUEEN ELIZABETH II)

Criteria: Issued as mementos of personal loss and sacrifice on the part of mothers and widows of personnel of the Canadian Forces who have laid down their lives for their country whilst in, or proceeding or returning from, an area of hostilities outside of Canada or who die of causes attributable to service in such areas, in consequence of any action undertaken by Canada under the United Nations Charter, the North Atlantic Treaty or any other instrument for collective defence that may be entered into by Canada.

*Canadian Memorial Cross
(Queen Elizabeth II) obverse*

Insignia: A silver cross patonce, equally proportioned, 32 mm in width. The cross is superimposed upon a wreath of laurel. The uppermost arm is surmounted by a Royal crown, while the remaining three bear a maple leaf proper. The centre or the cross displays the Royal cypher EIIR in raised letters. The reverse of the cross is engraved with the number, rank and name of the officer of soldier commemorated. The lower arm of the cross is normally stamped with a maker's mark and "sterling."

*Canadian Memorial Cross
(Queen Elizabeth II) reverse*

Suspender: A small eyelet is mounted on the upper most arm, through which passes a silver loop which is attached to another eyelet which is in turn mounted on a silver bar 32 mm long and 5 mm wide with flared edges, bearing maple leaves (in the same style as on the cross) at each edge.

Ribbon: None

Other: The Memorial Cross is issued in a rectangular black leatherette case, embossed on the with the Royal Arms of Canada, surrounded by a border of gold. The interior is lined with black velvet and off white satin. As of 2003 the case of issue is been impressed with a simple St. Edward's crown in gold, and no border.

Number of Awards: 1,200 +

Approximately 1,000 awards were given for the Korean War, and the balance for soldiers killed in United Nations Peacekeeping Missions — most recently for those killed in the South-West Asia (Afghanistan) operations. While an official award, the Memorial Cross is not ranked in the Order of Precedence. It is only since the Korean War that accurate records of the number of crosses issued have been maintained.

CHAPTER 24

Organizational Long Service Awards

The Canadian honours system includes two awards for service in nongovernmental associations that have a special relationship with the Crown. The Order of St. John has been active in Canada since 1883 and has been recognized by a Royal charter and included in the Canadian honours system (see Chapter 9 for a brief history).

The Canadian Corps of Commissionaires has been active in Canada since 1925. Initially composed primarily of veterans of the First World War, it has grown to become one of the main security service providers in Canada and many of its members are former members of the Canadian Forces. This close, though unofficial, relationship between the corps and the Canadian Forces led to the creation of a long service medal for members of the corps in 1948. The corps has provided, and continues to provide, services to many Canadian Forces bases and stations, as well as government buildings, hospitals and universities across Canada.

THE SERVICE MEDAL OF THE ORDER OF ST. JOHN

Origins: This medal was first approved in 1895, but was not instituted until 1898. The final design was approved by the chapter-general of the Order of St. John on 31 October 1899. This is the only award in the Canadian honours system that is conferred for long service in a volunteer organization.

Criteria: Awarded to members of the St. John Ambulance organization for twelve years' service, with a minimum of sixty hours' volunteer service per year. In other parts of the

*Service Medal of the
Order of St. John obverse*

*Service Medal of the
Order of St. John reverse*

Commonwealth, the medal has been awarded for ten or fifteen years of service. The medal can also be awarded for meritorious service, and in exceptional circumstances it is not necessary to have completed the nominal twelve years' service.

Insignia: A silver-coloured, circular medal 38 mm in diameter. The obverse depicts a veiled effigy of Queen Victoria, surrounded by the inscription *Victoria : D : G : Britt : Reg : F : D : Ind : Imp.* The effigy of Victoria was taken from a bust sculpted by her daughter, HRH Princess Louise. The reverse of the medal depicts the Royal Arms of the United Kingdom within a garter bearing the motto *Honi Soit Qui Mal y Pense.* Above this is a Tudor crown, and below it is the Prince of Wales' feathers. On either side is a badge of the order, each bearing a shield — the one on the left charged with the arms of the order, while the one on the right is charged with the arms of the Prince of Wales. The whole device rests upon a flourish of St. John's wort and is surrounded by the Latin words *Magnus Prioratus Hospitalis Sancti Johannis Jerusalem in Anglia.* Without question this is the most symbolically rich medal in the Canadian honours system.

Suspender: A double-toe claw suspender. On early issues the suspender is a separate piece riveted to the medal, while later issues (post-1960s) are struck with the suspender already attached. Prior to 1913 the medal was issued with a ring suspender.

Ribbon: Consists of five equal stripes, three watered black and two white, and is 38 mm wide.

Bars: A thin silver bar with sprigs of St. John's wort and a Maltese cross in the centre is awarded for each additional five years of service. A maximum of three five-year bars can be awarded. After twenty years of additional service, a gilt bar is awarded. Each additional five years of service is recognized with a gilt bar.

Postnominals: There are no postnominals for this medal.

Naming: The medals are issued unnamed. Prior to 1970, Canadian medals were usually named in a variety of styles.

Other: From 1898 through 1947, the medal was struck in sterling silver; from 1948 until 1960, in base metal that was silver plated; from 1960 through 1966, in silver-plated cupro-nickel; and since 1966, rhodium-plated base metal.

Number of Awards: 6,322

THE CANADIAN CORPS OF COMMISSIONAIRES LONG SERVICE MEDAL

Origins: The Corps of Commissionaires was created in 1859 in England as an organization dedicated to finding gainful employment for veterans of the Crimean War. Similarly, the Canadian Corps of Commissionaires was formed in Canada in 1925 with the purpose of finding employment for veterans of the First, and later the Second, World War. The Commissionaires continue to employ more than 15,000 Canadians.

A committee consisting of Major William Borrett, Colonel George Ross and Brigadier

Canadian Corps of Commissionaires Long Service Medal obverse

Canadian Corps of Commissionaires Long Service Medal reverse

General Georges Francoeur designed the medal, and it was approved by the Corps on 4 June 1947. At the request of the Canadian Corps of Commissionaires, the secretary of state approved the creation of two long service medals on 20 August 1948. The bronze Corps of Commissionaires Long Service Medal was awarded for ten years' service, while the silver medal was awarded for fifteen years. Recipients of the silver medal had to turn in their bronze ones (the two could not be worn simultaneously).

The regulations were changed in 1998 and the Corps of Commissionaires Medals were brought into conformity with other Canadian long service awards. The bronze Long Service Medal was abolished, and the length of service for the silver medal was reduced to twelve years (the same period of service required to be eligible for the Canadian Forces Decoration). The new Corps of Commissionaires Long Service Medal came into effect on 26 February 1998.

Awards of the medal are made by the national board of the Canadian Corps of Commissionaires on the recommendation of each division of the corps. The governor general has the authority to make extraordinary awards of the medal, if the twelve-year period of service has not been completed, for "special service to the Corps or for a record of exemplary service of such high standard as to merit the award of the medal."

Criteria: Awarded for twelve years of continuous or noncontinuous service in the Canadian Corps of Commissionaires.

Insignia: On the current version of the medal, the obverse is surrounded by a garter-style ribbon bearing the motto *Virtute et Industria*

("With courage and hard work"). At the centre is a natural maple leaf defaced with a crossed anchor, a sword and an eagle. (The eagle was added in 1998 after a design change by Lieutenant General René Gutknecht). Around the edge of the reverse are the words *The Canadian Corps of Commissionaires — Le Corps Canadien des Commissionnaires.* The medal has a top mounting bar that bears the words *Labor Omnia Vincit* ("Work conquers all").

Suspender: A small eyelet is affixed to the top of the medal, through this passes a small ring and a larger ring.

Ribbon: A 32 mm wide ribbon consisting of a central stripe of maroon, bordered on either side by 6 mm of white, bordered in turn by 3 mm of dark blue.

Bars: A silver bar adorned with a maple leaf is awarded for each five years of additional service. A maximum of three bars can be awarded to any one individual.

Postnominals: None

Naming: Issued unnamed. Until the mid-1980s the medals were named on the reverse.

Other: Until the early 1970s the silver Corps of Commissionaires Long Service Medal was struck in sterling silver by J.R. Gaunt of Montreal. Since that time the medals have been struck in base metal and been rhodium plated.

Number of Awards: unknown

Obsolete Bronze Commissionaires Long Service Medal, obverse

CHAPTER 25

Mention in Dispatches

The tradition of mentioning valuable services of a particular officer or man in dispatches to the King has a long history, dating back long before the advent of gallantry awards or meritorious service awards intended for people other than generals.

The present tradition of issuing mentions in dispatches originated in the Royal Navy as a mechanism for allowing flag officers to learn of the service and actions of naval officers serving at sea. Exemplary action would be noted and placed on an officer's record and was, in the long term, often crucial in securing promotions. As the British Empire expanded, it was no longer just the navy that saw action far away from the British Isles, but also the army. Thus the practice spread to the land forces, although it would not be until 1844 that it was extended to non-commissioned officers.

Mentions in dispatches became widely used during the Anglo-Boer War of 1899–1902, and a handful of Canadians were awarded them. Prior to the establishment of the broad range of British gallantry awards, there was no real intermediate award for bravery in the field that did not warrant either the Distinguished Conduct Medal, Distinguished Service Order or Victoria Cross, and the MID filled this gap.

During the First World War, mentions in dispatches were awarded to 5,467 Canadians. Because the British honours system quickly expanded in this period to include a variety of intermediate bravery awards, MIDs were not greatly used by the Canadian Expeditionary Force. Also because of the expansion, the MID lost its cachet as an award of much significance: soldiers would much rather receive a medal than a simple bronze oak leaf. Indeed, more Canadians received the Military Medal than were awarded MIDs.

Each recipient awarded an MID had his name listed in the *London Gazette*, and he received a certificate from Britain's secretary of state for war, along with a small oak leaf branch for wear on their Victory Medal. The certificate stated, "By the King's Order the name of _____ was published in the *London Gazette* on _____ as mentioned in Despatch for distinguished service. I am charged to record His Majesty's high appreciation." The certificate was signed by the secretary of state for war.

This practice continued when the Second World War commenced (Canadians were awarded 9,666), and again during the Korean War (Canadians received 279). By the time of the Second World War the names were also being listed in the *Canada Gazette.* MIDs continued to be awarded until 1967, when the practice went into abeyance following the establishment of the Canadian honours system.

The MID was reinstated in Canada "for the purpose of according recognition to members of the Canadian Armed Forces on active service, and other individuals working with or in conjunction with the Canadian Forces, for valiant conduct, devotion to duty or other distinguished services." While the MID had become a very junior award during the two world wars, its regained some of its prestige during the Korean War, when so few bravery awards such as the Military Cross and Military Medal were awarded. This situation prevails to this day: on most United Nations peacekeeping missions, relatively few — if any — bravery decorations are awarded, yet important service is rendered that warrants recognition and "mention." The Canadian MID regulations came into effect on 1 November 1990, although the actual letters patent were not signed until 13 May 1991.

Recommendations for the MIDs are forwarded by the chief of the defence staff to the governor general. The CDS receives the recommendations from field commanders. Like other bravery and valour awards, the MID can be awarded posthumously.

Mention in Dispatches insignia

Criteria: Awarded for valiant conduct, devotion to duty or other distinguished service that is recognized by mention in dispatches.

Insignia: The full-size insignia is a bronze oak leaf, 28 mm long, with prongs on the reverse for mounting. A 20 mm bronze oak leaf is worn on undress ribbons.

Wear: The insignia is worn on the designated ribbon (if the MID is awarded for service in a particular UN mission, the MID is worn on the ribbon of the UN medal awarded for that mission). If there is no designated ribbon, the insignia is worn on the left breast pocket. Prior to 1991, MIDs awarded without a designated ribbon were worn after medals or the undress ribbons.

Other: Recipients are also awarded an award certificate that summarizes the reason for award (a citation); the certificate is signed by the governor general.

Number Awarded: 93

CHAPTER 26

Canadian Forces Commendations

The Commander-in-Chief Unit Commendation and Canadian Forces Unit Commendation are roughly based on the Presidential Unit Citation awarded to units of the United States Army, Navy and Air Force. The Commander-in-Chief Unit Commendation is analogous to a junior battle honour. The American Presidential Unit Citation was created on 26 February 1942, and originally styled the "Distinguished Unit Citation," but this was changed to "Presidential Unit Citation" on 3 November 1966. The principal requirement for the Presidential Unit Citation is extraordinary heroism in the presence of the enemy.

The Chief of the Defence Staff Commendation and Command Commendation are similar in principal to the King's (later Queen's) Commendation for Brave Conduct, which was awarded to members of the Canadian Forces until 1966, and the King's (later Queen's) Commendation for Valuable Conduct in the Air, which was awarded to members of the Royal Canadian Air Force (and other Commonwealth air forces) during the Second World War. The commendations were awarded "in recognition of meritorious service ... or of gallantry not reaching the standard required for"[40] award of a gallantry medal. The Canadian Chief of the Defence Staff Commendation and Command Commendations differ from the King's Commendation for Brave Conduct in that, like the King's Commendation for Valuable Conduct in the Air, the CDS Commendation can be awarded for meritorious service as well as bravery. The Command Commendation is more akin to a junior Mention in Dispatch. Both the Chief of the Defence Staff Commendation and Unit Commendation rank below a Mention in Dispatch.

*Commander-in-Chief
Commendation Bar*

COMMANDER-IN-CHIEF COMMENDATION

Origins: The Commander-in-Chief Unit Commendation is roughly patterned after the Presidential Unit Citation used in the United States. It was established by the governor general on 7 November 2000, through a formal letter submitted to the chief of the defence staff. Recommendations are prepared and forwarded to the director of history and heritage at DND Headquarters through the senior Canadian officer in the active theatre of operations. Awards are decided by the Canadian Forces Decorations and Commendations Advisory Committee. The commendation is presented by the commander-in-chief.

Criteria: The commendation may be awarded to any unit or subunit of the Canadian Forces, or to any similar organization of a Commonwealth or foreign armed force working in conjunction with the Canadian Forces, that has performed an extraordinary deed or activity of a rare high standard in extremely hazardous circumstances. Commander-in-Chief Unit Commendations are restricted to war or warlike conditions in an active theatre of operations. Service that is considered beyond the demands of normal duty and which does not qualify for the Commander-in-Chief Unit Commendation may be considered for the Canadian Forces Unit Commendation.

Description: The commendation consists of a scroll, insignia and pennant.

Scroll: A framed, gold-embossed scroll inscribed with the name of the formation, unit or subunit being recognized. The scroll also bears the award citation and is signed by the commander-in-chief (the governor general).

Insignia: A gold bar bearing a viceregal lion in the centre (the lion is in full colour). The insignia is worn for life by members of the unit or those attached to said unit during the action being recognized. Persons posted to a specific unit that has been recognized, but who were not serving with the unit when the award was made, wear the insignia while serving with that particular unit and cease to wear it when they leave. This insignia is worn in the centre of the left breast pocket. Those who are only attached to the unit wear it on the flap of the right breast pocket.

Pennant: A rectangular flag, divided into three equal sections, coloured navy blue, red and sky blue (representing the three branches of the Canadian Forces) and defaced in the centre with the viceregal lion in full colour. The pennant is flown by the unit that has been recognized, and can also be flown from the yardarm of HMC ships. The flying of the pennant shall not displace a commissioning or distinguishing pennant or flag; it may be flown at sea for special occasions approved by the senior officer present (such as Canada Day or the Queen's birthday); it shall be flown in harbour from sunrise to sunset, and when entering or leaving harbour.

Number of Awards: Three, to the 1st Battalion of the Royal 22nd Regiment for its 1992 opening of the Sarajevo Airport; to the 2nd Battalion of the Princess Patricia's Canadian Light Infantry for its display of courage during the 1993 Medak Pocket operation in the Former Yugoslavia; and to the 3rd Battalion of the

Canadian Forces Unit Commendation obverse

Canadian Forces Unit Commendation reverse

Princess Patricia's Canadian Light Infantry for its service in Afghanistan in 2002.

CANADIAN FORCES UNIT COMMENDATION

Origins: A junior version of the Commander-in-Chief Unit Commendation, although the CF Unit Commendation predates the C-in-C Unit Commendation.

Criteria: Awarded to any formation, unit or subunit of the Canadian Forces, or to any similar organization of a Commonwealth or foreign armed force working with or in conjunction with the Canadian Forces, that has performed a deed or activity considered beyond the demands of normal duty. It may be awarded to winners of competitions only under very exceptional circumstances.

Description: A framed, gold-embossed scroll, inscribed with the name of the formation, unit or subunit concerned. The scroll bears an appropriate citation and is signed by the chief of the defence staff.

Medallion: A table medal not intended for wear, but meant to serve as a permanent symbol of the award. The medallion bears a modified version of the Canadian Forces badge representing the three services.

Flag: A rectangular flag, divided horizontally into three equal sections of navy blue, red and sky blue, and defaced in the centre with the symbols of the three services (an anchor, crossed swords and an eagle), with oak leaves at the base and surmounted by a Royal crown.

The flag is flown for only one year after the announcement of the award, then it is retained by the unit as a historical artifact.

CHIEF OF THE DEFENCE STAFF COMMENDATION

Chief of the Defence Staff Commendation Bar

Origins: Similar to the King's Commendation for Valuable Services in the Air. A junior award intended to recognize valuable service that falls short of meriting bestowal of a military valour decoration or meritorious service decoration.

Criteria: Awarded to a member of the Canadian Forces who has performed a deed or activity beyond the demands of normal duty. This award can also be presented to Commonwealth and foreign troops.

Insignia: A gold-coloured bar bearing three equally-spaced maple leaves. The bar is worn on the left breast pocket just below the pocket flap.

Other: Recipients of the CDS Commendation also receive a framed, gold-embossed scroll inscribed with the member's name and an appropriate citation and signed by the CDS.

COMMAND COMMENDATION

Command Commendation Bar

Origins: A junior version of the Chief of the Defence Staff's Commendation. Similar to a junior Mention in Dispatch.

Criteria: Awarded to a member of the Canadian Forces who has performed a deed or activity beyond the demands of normal duty. This award can also be presented to Commonwealth and foreign troops.

Insignia: A silver-coloured bar bearing three equally-spaced maple leaves. The bar is worn on the left breast pocket just below the pocket flap.

Other: Recipients also receive a scroll signed by an appropriate National Defence Headquarters group principal or chief of staff (sea, land or air).

MAXIMUM DISTRIBUTION CHART
(per 100 people under command over six months)

Conditions	Mention in Dispatches	CDS Commendation	Command Commendation
War	1	2	3
Hostilities	0	5	12
Field Operations	none	0	51
Peacetime	none	few	few

CHAPTER 27

Commendations

The two commendations that follow are roughly based on the various Canadian Forces commendations, although the Vice-Regal Commendation and the Minister of Veterans Affairs Commendations tend to be awarded primarily to civilians. Both of these awards come in the form of a small bar and a lapel pin, as it was seen as inappropriate to develop specific medals or decorations for each.

THE VICE-REGAL AND COMMISSIONERS' COMMENDATION

Origins: While Canadians are eligible to receive the Royal Victorian Order, many render important services to the lieutenant governors and territorial commissioners which — although significant — do not warrant appointment to the order. To remedy the need for a junior award to recognize these contributions, the Chancellery developed the Vice-Regal and Commissioners' Commendation.

In the early 1990s a proposal was developed to create a Vice-Regal Decoration — largely based on the Royal Victorian Order — to be awarded by lieutenant governors and territorial commissioners, but the plan was not approved because there was a general fear that such a decoration would not only complicate the Canadian honours system, but would prompt various federal and provincial departments to insist on creating their own decorations and medals.

Vice-Regal and Commissioners' Commendation

Vice-Regal and Commissioners'
Commendation

The Queen approved use of the Crown on the insignia in July 1998, and the Commendation was created in January 1999.

Criteria: Awarded to persons who, in the course of their duties as a paid or volunteer staff member, have performed one or more commendable acts that have benefited the office of a lieutenant governor or territorial commissioner. Nominations are submitted to the Chancellery by a lieutenant governor or territorial commissioner.

A maximum of two nominations (or, in the case of larger viceregal households, 10 per cent of the staff), may be submitted at per year. The Chancellery administers the program and maintains a register of recipients.

Insignia: A gold bar 35 mm wide and 10 mm high, enamelled in blue. In the centre is a circle containing three red maple leaves, surmounted by a Royal crown. This bar is worn below official orders and medals on formal occasions. The lapel pin is a 10 mm circular badge depicting three red maple leaves in the centre, the circle surmounted by a Royal crown. Recipients of the commendation also receive a certificate.

Other: The insignia was designed by the staff of the Canadian Heraldic Authority.

THE MINISTER OF VETERANS AFFAIRS COMMENDATION

Origins: Veterans' groups had long encouraged the minister of Veterans Affairs to develop some sort of award that could be used to recognize veterans as well as nonveterans who have devoted their lives, or a significant amount of time, to assisting those who have served in Canada's armed forces. Although requests for such an award can be traced back to the 1960s, it was not until late 2000 that the concept for this award was fully developed.

Criteria: Awarded to those who have contributed to the care and well-being of veterans, and/or those who have contributed to the remembrance of the contributions, sacrifices and achievements of veterans. The commendation is intended primarily for veterans, but on rare occasions it may be awarded to nonveterans.

There is no limit on the number of annual awards. Nominations are submitted to the minister of Veterans Affairs and reviewed by the ministry's Commendation Selection Committee. The Queen approved the use of the Royal crown on the insignia in April 2001, and the commendation was officially created on 4 March 2002.

Insignia: A gold bar 35 mm wide and 10 mm high; at the centre is a stylized red poppy, superimposed with a gold maple leaf, surmounted by a Royal crown. This bar is worn below official orders and medals on formal occasions. The lapel pin is a 10 mm badge in the shape of a stylized red poppy, edged in gold and superimposed with a gold maple leaf, surmounted by a Royal crown. Recipients of the commendation also receive a certificate.

Other: The insignia was designed by the staff at the Canadian Heraldic Authority.

Minister of Veterans Affairs
Commendation
Top: Lapel pin
Bottom: Award bar

CHAPTER 28

Commonwealth and Foreign Awards

The bestowal of Commonwealth and foreign awards upon Canadians has been a perennial topic of debate. The best-known case in this respect was that of Lord Black of Crossharbour. The British government asked the Canadian government if it could make Conrad Black a peer of the United Kingdom, thereby appointing him to the British House of Lords. Although Black was a dual citizen at the time, the Canadian government refused permission. After a lengthy court battle, Black decided to renounce his Canadian citizenship so that he could accept the peerage.

The practice of governments seeking permission from one another to bestow honours upon foreign nationals is neither new nor unique to Canada. Throughout the Commonwealth there have long been regulations requiring such assent. During the two world wars, the British government gave unrestricted license for British subjects to receive foreign awards from allied nations. But while one could receive a particular honour, special approval had to be received from the King to wear it. Unrestricted permission for wear was often given, with the foreign decorations being worn after all British medals and in order of the date of award.

During peacetime, the norm has been for more restricted permission to be granted; that is, the recipient may only wear the particular honour while in the country from which it was granted (or its embassy), or while the head of state of the particular country is on a visit.

In Canada, the same practice was followed during the First World War, but matters changed during the Second World War. Foreign awards had to be approved by the Awards Co-ordination Committee, although there are few instances of the committee refusing to allow a particular award to be granted — indeed, the honours were often conferred before the committee had even learned of them! Following the end of the Second World War, Canada reverted to a policy of not allowing its citizens to accept any foreign awards, although exceptions were made for Prime Minister William Lyon Mackenzie King, who was awarded four foreign honours: the Grand Cross of the Légion d'Honneur from France, the Grand Cross of the Order

John Diefenbaker, wearing the insignia of the Order of the Companion of Honour

of the Oak Crown from Luxembourg, the Grand Cross of the Order of Leopold I from Belgium, and the Grand Cross of the Order of the Netherlands Lion. It is ironic that, while King imposed the most stringent restrictions upon other Canadians accepting British and foreign awards, he remains to this day the most honoured prime minister in Canadian history!

By 1956 a new policy was in place, one that allowed Canadians to accept foreign honours only if they were awarded in connection with saving, or attempting to save, a life. Canadians were officially prohibited from receiving foreign awards for other reasons, although the rule was only sporadically enforced. A unique breach in this policy occurred when a former member of the Royal Canadian Air Force, Norman Robert Thompson (who would later become the leader of the Social Credit Party), was made a Grand Cross of the Order of the Star of Ethiopia, making him the only Canadian to

Second World War medals: 1939–45 Star, France and Germany Star, Canadian Volunteer Service Medal and clasp, 1939–45 War Medal with Mention in Dispatch, Efficience Medal, French Croix de Guerre

receive such an award. The honour had been bestowed upon him by the Emperor of Ethiopia without any consultation with the Canadian government. Thompson had been instrumental in developing the Ethiopian education system, and so it was decided to allow the award to stand. There was little else the Canadian government could do in such cases. An entirely new policy was devised in 1968, which was essentially the same as that which is in place today: decisions as to whether or not a Canadian can accept a Commonwealth or foreign honour are made by the Honours Policy Committee, a body composed of various deputy ministers, the secretary to the governor general, and the clerk of the Privy Council. Still, as the case of Conrad Black indicates, there remains a certain grey area in respect to the current policy: that of dual citizens.

The current policy, reprinted below, allows Canadians to accept Commonwealth and foreign honours provided that permission is first sought from the Canadian government and that the award is being made for specific services. Canada does not engage in the practice of reciprocal diplomatic awards; that is, when a foreign head of state visits, he or she is not automatically presented with the Order of Canada. Similarly, when the governor general travels abroad, he or she does not receive foreign honours merely for visiting.

Recipients of Commonwealth and foreign honours wear the particular honour after all of their Canadian orders, decorations and medals, in the order that they were awarded, in each category.

Canadian Forces regulations set out that "[i]f, despite tactful advice, a foreign government presents a member of the CF with an order, decoration or medal at an official function without gaining prior Canadian Government approval, the member diplomatically cannot refuse the award. The member shall not wear it thereafter," although he or she may apply for permission to wear it after a full explanation is made to National Defence Headquarters.

Policy Respecting the Awarding of an Order, Decoration or Medal by a Commonwealth or Foreign Government
Privy Council, January 1988

1. Any Commonwealth or foreign government desiring to award an order, decoration or medal to a Canadian citizen shall obtain prior approval from the Government of Canada.

2. Commonwealth and foreign governments desiring to award orders, decorations or medals to Canadian citizens shall submit their proposals to the Government of Canada through their diplomatic missions in Canada.

3. The Government of Canada will consider granting the approval referred to in section 1 for the awarding of an order, decoration or medal offered in recognition of:
   (a) an extraordinary service to mankind;
   (b) conspicuous bravery in saving or attempting to save a life;
   (c) any exceptional service rendered to the country desiring to make the award; or
   (d) any substantial act or acts contributing to better relations between Canada and the country desiring to make the award.

4. The Government of Canada *shall not* grant approval referred to in Section 1 for an award:
   (a) that is at variance with Canadian policy or the public interest;
   (b) that carries with it an honourary title or confers any precedence of privileges;
   (c) that is conferred otherwise than by a Head of State or a government recognized as such by Canada;
   (d) that is conferred in recognition of services by an individual in the employ of Her Majesty in Right of Canada or of a province in the normal performance of official duties; or
   (e) that is in respect of events occurring more than five years before the offer of the award.

5. The Honours Policy Committee may advise and recommend on the interpretation and application of this policy on the disposition of cases arising there from.

CHAPTER 29

Protocol

Although Canada has one of the most egalitarian honours systems in existence, it is nevertheless a system with its own hierarchy. To ensure that the appropriate respect is accorded to each award, they are to be worn in a specific order. This chapter sets out the various mounting styles, when to wear which medals, and how to care for your medals. Many of us have attended official functions only to be confronted with a sea of eminent Canadians, all wearing their orders, decorations and medals in a variety of "unofficial" ways. Unless you are the governor general or an official from the Chancellery, do not attempt to correct them. You will invariably be treated as an uncouth upstart. These matters are best left to those who deal with them on a daily basis.

METHODS OF MOUNTING

There are two methods of mounting used in this country, swing mounting and court mounting. Swing mounting quite literally allows the medals to swing around, as the ribbons are attached to a straight bar about 2 cm wide and as long as necessary to allow for all the medals to be worn. Court mounting is somewhat more complex: the medals are hung from their ribbons and then sewn onto a backing board to prevent them from flopping around. The board is concealed by the ribbons. About 3 cm of the medal hangs over the backing board. Swing mounting used to be more practical, as medals required regular polishing, but it has largely been replaced by court mounting. Court mounting also prevents the medals from hitting each other and becoming damaged. In Royal or vice-regal presence, court mounting is generally mandatory.

FULL-SIZE AND MINIATURE MEDALS

Example of swing-mounted medals

Full-size medals are those officially presented to a person by the government. These are worn during the daytime, while miniature medals are typically worn during the evening with formal dress. Miniature medals are small replicas of the full-size decoration and must be purchased privately — they are not provided by the government. The section below, entitled "Wearing Your Medals," discusses when full-size and miniature medals should be worn.

Example of miniature set, court mounted

Court-mounted full-sized medals

INVESTITURES

These happy occasions usually occur at Government House, Ottawa, or the Citadelle in Quebec City. Long before the event you will be sent an information package detailing the time and place. Investees are usually allowed one guest only.

WEARING YOUR MEDALS

Full Evening Dress

Men (White Tie)
The miniature insignia of all orders, decorations and medals should be worn suspended from a medal bar attached to the left lapel of the coat.

Only one full-size neck badge should be worn, suspended from a miniature-width ribbon. The ribbon is worn under the band of the tie so that the badge hangs 3 cm below the bow. A miniature of this badge should be included in those worn on the medal bar.

Up to four stars of orders may be worn on the left side of the coat.

Women (Long Evening Dress)
The miniature insignia of all orders, decorations and medals should be worn suspended from a medal bar attached to the left side of the dress. If in possession of only one such award, it may be worn on a bow.

Only one full-size badge, which would be worn at the neck by men, should be worn. This badge is worn on a bow and attached to the dress immediately above the miniatures. A miniature of this badge should also be included in those worn from the medal bar. Since 1998, women have been permitted to wear the full-size neck badge at the neck as men do.

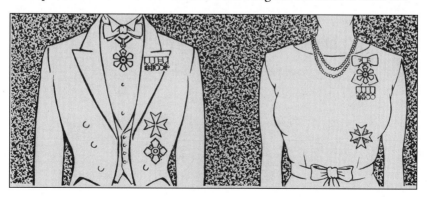

Up to four stars of orders may be worn on the left side of the dress. The Queen sometimes wears more than one order insignia on a bow, although this is largely due to her position as Sovereign.

Dinner Jacket

Men (Black Tie)
The miniature insignia of all orders, decorations and medals should be worn suspended from a medal bar attached to the left lapel of the coat.

Only one full-size neck badge should be worn, suspended from a miniature-width ribbon. The ribbon is worn under the shirt collar so that the badge hangs 3 cm below the bow. A miniature of this badge should be included in those worn on the medal bar.

Only one star of an order should be worn on the left side of the coat.

Women (Long Evening Dress)
The miniature insignia of all orders, decorations and medals should be worn suspended from a medal bar attached to the left side of the dress. If in possession of only one such award, it may be worn on a bow.

Only one full-size neck badge should be worn. This can be worn at the neck or on a bow above the medal bar on the left shoulder.

Only one star of an order should be worn on the left size of the dress. Both the Queen and governor general are permitted to wear more than one order insignia on a bow on the left shoulder.

Morning Dress

Men (Tailcoat or Director's Short Black Coat)
Those full-size orders, decorations and medals that are suspended from the medal bar are worn attached to the left side of the coat.

Only one full-size neck badge should be worn, suspended from a full-width ribbon. The ribbon is worn under the shirt collar so that the badge rests on the tie immediately below the knot.

Up to four stars of orders may be worn on the tailcoat, and only one star on the director's short black coat, attached to the left side below the insignia on the medal bar.

Women (Afternoon Dress)
Those full-size orders, decorations and medals that are suspended from a medal bar are worn attached to the left side of the dress. If in possession of only one such award, it may be worn on a bow.

Only one full-size neck badge should be worn. This can be worn at the neck or on a bow above the medal bar on the left shoulder.

Only one star of an order should be worn on the left side of the dress below all other insignia.

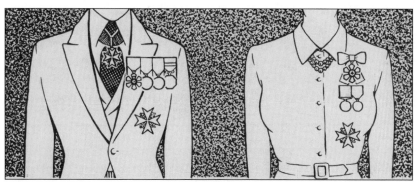

Lounge Suit

Men
Those full-size orders, decorations and medals that are suspended from a medal bar are worn attached to the left side of the coat.

Only one neck badge should be worn, suspended from a full-width ribbon. The ribbon is worn under the shirt collar so that the badge rests on the tie, immediately below the knot.

The stars of orders should not be worn with lounge suits.

Women

When attending a function where men are wearing lounge suits, women should, if the function is during the day, wear their full-size orders, decorations and medals that are worn from a medal bar. If the function is in the evening, the miniatures may be worn.

Only one full-size neck badge should be worn. This can be worn at the neck or on a bow on the left shoulder, above the medal bar.

The stars of orders should not be worn on these occasions.

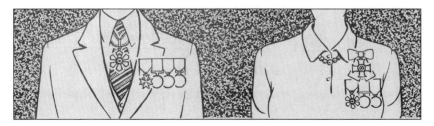

Uniforms

Members of uniformed organizations, such as the Canadian Forces, Police Forces, the St. John Ambulance Brigade, the Corps of Commissionaires, etc., should wear the insignia of their orders, decorations and medals as laid down in the dress regulations of the organization to which they belong.

Set out here are guidelines for those who wear their decorations with uniforms of military pattern and are not subject to other regulations.

Women, when wearing a coat of military pattern, wear all the insignia of their orders, decorations and medals in exactly the same manner as men.

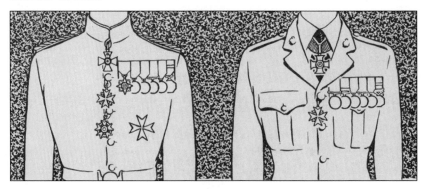

High-Neck Tunic

Full-size orders, decorations and medals mounted on a medal bar should be worn attached to the tunic over the left breast pocket.

Up to three neck badges may be worn. The senior badge should be suspended from its ribbon, which is worn inside the collar of the tunic in such a way that the badge hangs outside with about one inch of the ribbon emerging from the opening of the collar. The second and third badges are worn with the ribbons emerging from the second and third buttonholes.

Up to four stars of orders may be worn on the left side of the tunic.

Open-Neck Tunic

Full-size orders, decorations and medals mounted on a medal bar should be worn attached to the tunic over the left breast pocket.

Two neck badges may be worn. The senior badge is to be suspended from the full-width ribbon, which is worn under the collar of the shirt so that the badge rests on the tie immediately below the knot. The second badge is worn with its ribbon emerging from the top buttonhole. Naval officers wear two neck badges, one above the other, around the neck.

Up to four stars of orders may be worn on the left side of the tunic.

Formal Evening Dress

Those members of the uniformed organizations who wear a formal military pattern evening dress (mess kit) should wear their decorations in the same manner as for civilian evening dress (white tie).

Overcoats

Only those full-size orders, decorations and medals that are mounted on a medal bar should be worn on an overcoat at outdoor functions. Neither neck badges nor stars of orders should be worn (they may be worn underneath). Generally, orders, decorations and medals should *not* be worn on an overcoat as they are much more vulnerable to becoming wet and damaged.

Lapel Badges

Included in the insignia of some orders and decorations is a lapel badge or boutonniere. This badge may be worn on the left lapel of the coat with any order of dress at any time when full-size or miniature insignia or the undress ribbon is not being worn. Women may wear this badge in a similar position on the dress or jacket. Only one such device should be worn at any one time.

Care and Cleaning

Most modern Canadian operational service medals, exemplary service medals, UN/NATO service medals and the Canadian Forces Decoration are made of metals that do not require polishing. Indeed, they were designed to require no care other than proper handling. The Order of Canada, Order of Military Merit, Order of Merit of the Police Forces, Royal Victorian Order, Canadian bravery and valour decorations, meritorious service decorations and RCMP Long Service Medal are all made from silver or gilded silver. These should only be cleaned with a silver dip cleaner, not an actual polish.

In the case of those honours that are enamelled — the Cross of Valour, Order of Canada, Order of Military Merit, Order of Merit of the Police Forces and Royal Victorian Order — avoid using harsh cleaners and do not place them in an ultrasound cleaner (the type often used by jewellers to clean rings), as it may damage the enamel. Similarly, do not expose any enamelled insignia to extreme heat or cold; this, too, will crack the enamel. While quite beautiful and durable, these insignia should still be handled with care.

Postnominal Designations

Many Canadian orders and decorations are accompanied by postnominal designations or letters. These are sets of letters that recipients can place after their names to denote the fact that they have been honoured. These letters should always be placed ahead of academic degrees such as B.A., B.Eng., M.D., Ph.D., etc. The order in which these postnominals are placed after a person's name is the same as they appear in the Canadian Order of Precedence (seen below). Only the designation P.C., for Privy Councillor, takes precedence over all other honours except the Victoria Cross and Cross of Valour. Additional awards of the same honour are denoted by an asterisk (*) (this does not apply to bars awarded to the Canadian Forces Decoration). A person who had been awarded the Meritorious Service Cross and Bar would place M.S.C.* after his or her name.

ORDER OF PRECEDENCE FOR CANADIAN HONOURS

V.C.	Victoria Cross
C.V.	Cross of Valour
P.C.	Privy Councillor
C.C.	Companion of the Order of Canada
O.C.	Officer of the Order of Canada
C.M.	Member of the Order of Canada
C.M.M.	Commander of the Order of Military Merit
C.O.M.	Commander of the Order of Merit of the Police Forces
C.V.O.	Commander of the Royal Victorian Order
O.M.M.	Officer of the Order of Military Merit
O.O.M.	Officer of the Order of Merit of the Police Forces
L.V.O.	Lieutenant of the Royal Victorian Order
M.M.M.	Member of the Order of Military Merit
M.O.M.	Member of the Order of Merit of the Police Forces
M.V.O.	Member of the Royal Victorian Order
Order of St. John	All grades: letters only used within the order
G.O.Q./O.Q./C.Q.	All grades of the Ordre National du Québec
S.O.M.	Saskatchewan Order of Merit
O.Ont.	Order of Ontario
O.B.C.	Order of British Columbia
A.O.E.	Alberta Order of Excellence
O.P.E.I.	Order of Prince Edward Island
O.M.	Order of Manitoba
O.N.B.	Order of New Brunswick
O.N.S.	Order of Nova Scotia
O.N.L.	Order of Newfoundland and Labrador
S.M.V./E.V.M.	Star of Military Valour
S.C./E.C.	Star of Courage
M.S.C./C.S.M.	Meritorious Service Cross
M.V.M.	Medal of Military Valour
M.B.	Medal of Bravery
M.S.M.	Meritorious Service Medal
R.V.M.	Royal Victorian Medal
C.D.	Canadian Forces Decoration
O.M.C.	Ontario Medal for Good Citizenship
S.V.M.	Saskatchewan Volunteer Medal

Commonwealth orders or decorations that include postnominals follow here, if awarded after 1972. For example, General John de Chastelain was awarded the Order of the Companions of Honour by the British government in 1998; thus his postnominals are General John de Chastelain, O.C., C.M.M., C.D., C.H.

CHAPTER 30

Components of Canadian Orders, Decorations and Medals

COMMON ELEMENTS

With the exception of fewer than ten awards in the Canadian honours system, all were designed by Bruce Beatty. After serving in the Second World War, Beatty served in the art section of the RCAF and later the Office of the Governor General.

All of Canada's honours, decorations and medals have common elements incorporated into them. The maple leaf is used on almost every Canadian award, as is either the Royal cypher and crown or an effigy of the Queen. These represent the two principal Canadian symbols: the maple leaf, as used by the St. John the Baptist Society, dates back to the 1840s, and the crown or the image of the Sovereign has been a constant in Canada for the past five hundred years. The use of these symbols, and the fact that so many awards were designed by the same person, creates the sense that, although all Canadian awards extant were developed over a period of almost four decades, they are all part of a continuum. As a result, the Canadian honours system, with its diverse awards, enjoys a remarkable continuity.

The Sovereign's Badge

Her Majesty Queen Elizabeth II possesses two Canadian Sovereign's badges, one for the Order of Canada and one for the Order of Military Merit. These are both worn on bows on her left shoulder. Made of gold and encrusted with precious stones and enamelled, these badges symbolize her position as Sovereign of the various Canadian orders and Canada's head of state. It is expected that a Sovereign's badge for the Order of Merit of the Police Forces will also be manufactured and presented to the Queen.

Chancellor's Chain

The governor general serves as chancellor of the three main Canadian orders and as prior of the Order of St. John. For the Order of Canada, the Order of Military Merit and the Order of Merit of the Police Forces, the governor general possesses a Chancellor's Chain, which is usually worn only at investitures. These insignia incorporate the regular insignia of a Companion or Commander, along with various other elements of the particular order. In the case of the Order of Canada, the Chancellor's Chain is a chain composed of twelve plain snowflakes interchanged with ten circlets containing the motto of the order and a maple leaf; the chain is joined in the middle by the shield and crown of the Royal Arms of Canada, which is attached to the insignia of the Companion of the Order of Canada.

As each governor general ceases to be the Chancellor of the various Canadian orders when he or she leaves office, governors general do not retain the Chancellor's Chain.

Principal Commander's Chain

Both the Principal Commander of the Order of Military Merit (the chief of the defence staff) and the Principal Commander of the Order of Merit of the Police Forces (the commissioner of the RCMP) possess Principal Commander's Chains. These chains incorporate the various symbols that relate to Canada and the particular order in question. These chains are differentiated from the ones worn by the governor general only by the central device from which the Commander's insignia is hung.

Breast Badge

The only order in the Canadian honours system to be accompanied by a breast star is the Order of St. John (the top two levels: Bailiff/Dame Grand Cross and Knight/Dame of Justice or Grace). These insignia are worn on the lower left breast. Some early plans for the Order of Canada — never adopted — called for a breast badge or star to accompany the neck badge.

The Insignia

Insignia are the main parts of a particular order, decoration or medal. They come in various shapes and sizes, from snowflake or cross designs to decagonal or circular. Orders are generally enamelled, while decorations are in a shape (other than circular) such as a cross or decagon. On medals, the obverse usually depicts the Queen (who sanctions all awards), while the reverse bears some symbol or allegory associated with the purpose for the medal. The insignia of the various orders and valour or gallantry decorations are usually made of sterling silver, while other medals are made of bronze or rhodium-plated metal.

COMPONENTS OF THE INSIGNIA

The Suspender Bar

This is the piece that links the insignia to the ribbon. In the case of honours worn around the neck (CV, CC, OC, CMM and COM), the ribbon passes through a straight hanger which is connected to the insignia by a small ring. Other decorations have plain bars or stylized bars incorporating inverted fleurs-de-lys, a crown or a maple leaf.

RIBBON

SECOND SERVICE CLASP

SERVICE CLASP

SUSPENDER BAR

OBVERSE

The Suspender Ring

This is a small ring mounted on the top of a particular medal, through which the ribbon passes.

The Ribbon

The ribbon is the piece of material from which a particular insignia is suspended. Ribbons are often as symbolically rich as the actual medal or decoration. For instance, the ribbon for the Order of Canada is modelled on the Canadian flag, while the ribbon used on the Peacekeeping Service Medal symbolizes voluntarism (green), the colours of Canada (red and white) and the United Nations (symbolized by light blue).

Bars

For valour, bravery and meritorious service decorations as well as long service medals, bars are awarded for subsequent awards. These slide over the ribbon and are sewn into place.

Clasps

Often also referred to as "bars," clasps are awarded with the various operational service medals to denote service in a particular theatre or operation. Clasps are also awarded with the Queen's Medal for Champion Shot to denote the year in which the recipient won the competition.

MINIATURE ORDERS, DECORATIONS AND MEDALS

These are miniatures (usually half the size) of the full-size insignia, and are worn when the recipient is dressed in a mess kit or evening dress (gown, tuxedo or tails).

Lapel Badges

A special aspect of Canadian orders and certain decorations is that the recipients are also authorized to wear a special lapel badge, usually a one-sixth-scale version of the actual award. This idea was introduced in 1967, when plans for the Order of Canada were being developed, although it would not be until

1972 that the lapel badges were actually instituted. The idea of lapel badges has its roots in several traditions. France has a long history of allowing recipients of various orders to wear a small swatch or boutonniere of ribbon to represent the highest award held by an individual. In the 1940s the United States began allowing recipients of decorations to wear a small lapel insignia made of metal — usually a miniature of the ribbon of the decoration in question. Canada appears to be the first to have initiated the practice of making the lapel badge in the form of the order itself, and not the ribbon of the order.

Recipients of the Order of Canada wear a small pin in the shape of a snowflake. The various levels are differentiated by the colour of the maple leaf in the centre of the lapel badge: red for Companions, gold for Officers and silver for Members. Similarly, recipients of the Order of Military Merit and Order of Merit of the Police Forces also receive a small pin in the shape of the cross of the order. As with the Order of Canada, the various levels are differentiated by the colour of the maple leaf in the centre of the lapel badge: red for Commanders, gold for Officers and silver for Members. Recipients of all bravery and meritorious service decorations also receive lapel badges which are miniature versions of their insignia.

Undress Ribbon Bars

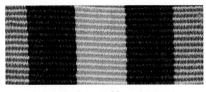

Undress Ribbon Bar

Undress ribbon bars are typically only worn by members of the Canadian Armed Forces, police and firefighters, although members of various government agencies who wear official uniforms often wear undress ribbon bars when full-sized medals are not worn. These are worn on the left breast, with the most senior award closest to the centre of the chest. The ribbons are worn in the order as set out in the order of precedence.

Undress Ribbon Bar Emblems

Undress Ribbon Bar emblems

Several Canadian honours are accompanied by ribbon bar devices. For the Victoria Cross, Cross of Valour, Order of Military Merit and Order of Merit of the Police Forces, a miniature version of the actual insignia is worn in the centre of the undress ribbon bar. Recipients of the Order of St. John, regardless of level, wear a silver Maltese cross in the centre of their undress ribbon. The Order of Canada is unique in that recipients do not wear a miniature version of the insignia on their undress ribbon bar, but rather a coloured maple leaf: red for Companions, gold for Officer and silver for Members.

Recipients of a bar of the Victoria Cross or Cross of Valour are authorized to wear two miniature versions of their particular decoration on their undress ribbons, signifying a second award. The addition of an insignia to denote a second award was originally the idea of King George V, who was concerned that recipients of multiple gallantry awards had no way to display their additional awards on their undress ribbons.[41] Thus a small silver rose (rosette) was developed to be worn. In the Canadian context, this principle is personified by both rosettes (worn on the CD ribbon for multiple awards) and a variety of maple leaf devices which are worn on other decorations and medals to denote multiple awards or bars.

 Red maple leaf. Worn on the undress ribbon of the Companion of the Order of Canada, and to denote a fourth bar to the Special Service Medal, General Campaign Star and General Campaign Medal.

 Gold maple leaf. Worn on the undress ribbon of the Officer of the Order of Canada, Medal of Military Valour, Star of Military Valour and Star of Courage. Second awards of the MMV and SMV are denoted by a second gold maple leaf. Worn on the undress ribbon by recipients of a bar to the Star of Courage. Also worn to denote a third bar to the Special Service Medal, General Campaign Star and General Service Medal.

 Silver maple leaf. Worn on the undress ribbon of the Member of the Order of Canada. Second awards of the MB are denoted by a silver maple leaf. Worn on the Special Service Medal, General Campaign Star and General Service Medal to denote the award of two bars. Worn on the Gulf and Kuwait Medal and South-West Asia Medal to denote award of a bar. Recipients of bars to the various exemplary service medals wear one silver maple leaf for each bar.

Rosette. Worn to denote the award of each additional bar to the Canadian Forces Decoration.

Oak leaf emblem. Worn to denote the award of a mention in dispatch.

Silver numerals. Worn on United Nations service medals and Multinational Observer Force Medal to denote multiple tours.

Bronze numerals. Worn on certain NATO service medals to denote multiple tours.

CHAPTER 31

Canadian Honours in Heraldry

Heraldry — that is, the granting of arms — is in itself a form of honour and should not be overlooked. When an individual or corporate body petitions for arms and is awarded a grant, it signifies that the Crown has deemed that person or body worthy of recognition.

The development of heraldry in Canada largely mirrors the development of our national honours system. At various times the French and British systems of heraldry have been used in Canada. While Canadians acquired their own system of national honours in 1967, the development of a distinctive Canadian heraldic granting agency did not come until 1988, with the founding of the Canadian Heraldic Authority. Prior to that date, Canadians could petition the College of Arms in London or the Court of the Lord Lyon in Scotland. To this day heraldic grants, like other honours, decorations and medals, emanate from the Crown. Some notable Canadians who have been granted arms include Bruce Beatty, Alan Beddoe, R.B. Bennett, Sir Frederick Loomis, John R. Matheson, Vincent Massey, Roland Michener and others.

The Royal Arms of France were the first armorial bearings to be used in Canada, and they were typically surrounded by the Collar of the Order of the Holy Spirit, France's highest honour of the pre-revolutionary period. Similarly the British Royal Arms were — and continue to be — surrounded by the "garter," the insignia of England's premier order, the Most Noble Order of the Garter, which contains the motto *Honi Soit Qui Mal y Pense.*

The practice of displaying the insignia of honours with coats of arms can be traced to the early fifteenth century, shortly after the establishment of the Order of the Garter. Knights of the Garter would often encircle the shields of their arms with the motto of the order, a practice that was commonplace by the time of the reign of Henry VII (1485–1509).

It was only in the early nineteenth century that it became common for the insignia of orders to be hung from the shield of a person's coat of arms.

In more recent times, it has been customary for the holders of the higher ranks of the British Orders of Chivalry (Knights and Dames, Companions and Commanders) to surround their shields with the circlet bearing the motto of the order to which they belong. Only the motto circlet of the most senior honour is used. Thus, a Knight of the Order of the British Empire who is also a Companion of the Order of the Bath surrounds his shield with the motto circlet of the Order of the British Empire, as a KBE takes precedence over a C.B., even though the Order of the Bath is more senior in terms of age.

In the British system, Officers and Members of the various orders are not permitted to place a motto circlet around their shields; however, in the Canadian system all holders of the three Canadian state orders (the Order of Canada, the Order of Military Merit and the Order of Merit of the Police Forces) may do so.

In Canada, the general rule related to the inclusion of the insignia of orders and decorations in heraldic grant is that such insignia must be an official honour from the Crown. In the case of foreign orders and decorations, the award must have been officially sanctioned by the Crown — that is, it must have been approved by the Government Decorations Committee, which acts on behalf of the governor general.

In 1994, the Queen approved the addition of an augmentation to the Canadian coat of arms: the "motto circlet" of the Order of Canada was added to it. This follows a tradition, common in many countries, of incorporating some part of the insignia of the senior national honour in the national coat of arms.

BASIC HERALDRY

Armorial bearings consist of many different elements, and there are rules governing their general structure and just what may be included. The central part of any coat of arms is the *shield*, sometimes called the *arms*. Below the shield is a *motto* on a scroll; the phrase or word placed here may be written in any language, although Latin, English and French tend to be the most common in Canada.

Above the coat of arms is the *helm* or *helmet*, and this is surrounded by the *mantling*. Above the helm is a *wreath*, upon which sits the *crest*. The crest was originally used as an identifying mark placed on the top of a knight's helmet at a tournament. The helmet was shielded from the sun by colourful cloth mantling, held in place by a wreath of twisted cloth.

The crest is usually in the form of an animal, bird or mythological beast. Madame Jeanne Sauvé chose a dove bearing an olive branch in its beak — the symbol of peace.

As noted above, recipients of such honours as the Order of Canada and Order of Military Merit are entitled to place a motto circlet around their shields. In the case of the Order of Canada and Order of Military Merit, the circlet contains the motto of the order, while that of the Order of Merit of the Police Forces simply contains the words *Canada — Merit — Mérite*.[42] Members of Canadian orders may also hang the insignia of their order(s) from the bottom of their shields. A maximum of three orders may be hung from the shield.

Senior state figures, such as lieutenant governors or Privy Councillors, or members at the highest level of the Order of Canada (Companions), the Order of Military Merit, the Order of Merit of the Police Forces and the

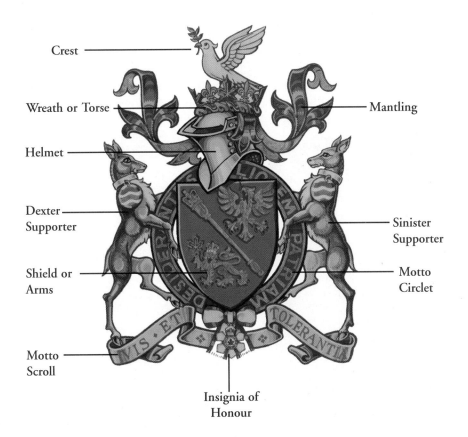

Crest

Wreath or Torse

Helmet

Dexter Supporter

Shield or Arms

Motto Scroll

Mantling

Sinister Supporter

Motto Circlet

Insignia of Honour

Royal Victorian Order (Commanders), can also be granted what are known as *supporters*. These are usually animals or mythological beasts, placed on either side of the shield.

In heraldry, the colouring of a coat of arms is done with *metals* and *colours*. The metals are known as *or* (gold) and *argent* (silver or white). The most common colours are *gules* (red), *azure* (blue), *sable* (black), *vert* (green) and *purpure* (purple). One of the principal rules of colouring in heraldry is that metals cannot be placed over metals, nor may colours be placed over colours.

For a comprehensive discussion of Canadian heraldry, please consult *A Canadian Heraldic Primer* (2001) by Dr. Kevin Greaves or *Beddoe's Canadian Heraldry* (1981) by Lieutenant Commander Alan Beddoe.

Pre-1987 Examples

Major General Sir Frederick Loomis, one of Canada's great First World War military leaders, petitioned for arms in 1915 and was awarded a grant later that year. Loomis's grant included three of the honours he had been awarded by King George V during the war: Knight Commander of the Order of the Bath (his shield is surrounded by the motto of the order), Companion of the Order of St. Michael and St. George, and Companion of the Distinguished Service Order.

Loomis Arms

Massey Arms

Vincent Massey petitioned the College of Arms while he was agent general to Washington. The grant came years before he was made either a Companion of Honour or governor general of Canada.[43] Massey's bookplate includes the insignia of the Order of the Companions of Honour and the Order of St. John. Although Massey was one of the first Canadians appointed to the Order of Canada, his demise only a few months after being appointed to the order prevented a further alteration to include the insignia of the order that he had played such an important role in creating.

Pre-1987, Including the Order of Canada

As the first recipient of the Order of Canada, Roland Michener became the first person to have the insignia of the order included in his grant of arms. This was done in 1968 by the College of Arms in London. The Companion's insignia was hung from his shield, although the motto circlet of the order was not included.

Neither Jules Léger nor Edward Schreyer petitioned for arms during their terms as governor general. After 1987, Léger's family applied for and received a posthumous grant from the Canada Heraldic Authority. Schreyer would go on to petition for arms after his term as governor general had expired.

Michener Arms

Jeanne Sauvé was the last governor general to receive arms from the College of Arms in London.

Post-1988

After the creation of the Canadian Heraldic Authority, several new developments occurred relating to the inclusion of insignia of Canadian orders, decorations with grants of arms.

Today, the most common insignia to be included in grants of arms are the Canadian Forces Decoration, the Order of St. John, the Order of Canada, the Order of Military Merit, the Royal Victorian Order and the various provincial orders.

With a grant, the Canadian Heraldic Authority will include the insignia of an order or decoration that has been officially sanctioned by the Canadian government. The only *medal* that it has included to date is the Royal Victorian Medal, which, since 1984, has been classified as a decoration. Similarly, recipients of the Canadian Forces Decoration have been allowed to include their insignia in grants. In the case of recipients of the Order of Canada, Order of Military Merit, Order of Merit of the Police Forces or Royal Victorian Order, there are specific guidelines for the display of insignia with coats of arms.

The holders of the top levels of these orders (Companion in the case of the Order of Canada, and Commander in the case of the Order of Military Merit, Order of Merit of the Police Forces and the Royal Victorian Order) are entitled to be granted supporters. This is also true of persons appointed to the top level of the Order of St. John of Jerusalem, a Bailiff or Dame Grand Cross.

Holders of any of the national orders — the Order of Canada, the Order of Military Merit and the Order of Merit of the Police Forces — are permitted to surround their shield with the motto circlet of the order in question. In general, when one possesses the Order of Canada and another order, the Order of Canada takes precedence. As with Companions and Commanders, the recipients of the lower levels of the various national orders are entitled to surround their arms with the motto circlet of the particular order that they have received.

The following section examines the inclusion of various insignia in grants of arms, and is divided by the order or decoration received by the individual in question.

Order of Canada

Dextraze Arms

Fedoruk Arms

Pelletier Arms

General Jacques Dextraze,
C.C., C.M.M., C.B.E., D.S.O., C.D.

General Dextraze served in the Second World War and later rose to become the chief of the defence staff. During the 1964 crisis in the Belgian Congo he was made a Commander of the Order of the British Empire in recognition of his bravery. His grant includes the insignia of a Commander of the Order of the British Empire, a Commander of the Order of Military Merit and a Companion of the Order of Canada.

Sylvia Olga Fedoruk,
O.C., S.O.M.

As lieutenant governor of Saskatchewan, Sylvia Fedoruk was entitled to supporters. Her grant includes the motto circlet of the Order of Canada, as well as the insignia of an Officer of the Order of Canada and that of the Saskatchewan Order of Merit, both on bows. The Maltese cross of the Order of St. John is depicted behind the arms.

Jean-Michel Pelletier, C.M.

Members of the Order of Canada are also entitled to use the motto of the order around their shield. Pelletier's grant of arms includes his Member's insignia.

349

Order of Military Merit

Lieutenant General James Cyrille Gervais, C.M.M., C.D.

General Gervais's grant of arms includes only the insignia of the Order of Military Merit and the motto circlet.

Owen William Lockyer, O.M.M., C.D.

William Lockyer's grant includes three insignia: those of an Officer of the Order of Military Merit, an Officer of the Order of St. John and the Canadian Forces Decoration.

Gervais Arms   *Lockyer Arms*

Royal Victorian Order and Royal Victorian Medal

Kevin Stewart MacLeod, L.V.O.

Kevin MacLeod's grant includes the insignia of a Lieutenant of the Royal Victorian Order. The difference between this insignia and the more junior grade of Member of the Royal Victorian Order is that it is enamelled in white and edged in gold, while the M.V.O. is of frosted silver. Similarly, the LVO can be distinguished from the insignia of a Commander of the Victorian Order because the CVO is worn around the neck and not on a straight ribbon, as the LVO and MVO are.

Yves Chevrier, C.M., R.V.M., C.D.

Yves Chevrier's grant is unique in that it is the only one granted by the Canadian Heraldic Authority that includes the Royal Victorian Medal. Chevrier is also a Member of the Order of Canada and a long-serving member of the staff at Government House.

MacLeod Arms

Chevrier Arms

Order of St. John of Jerusalem

Eric Lawrence Barry, G.St.J., C.D.

As Bailiff Grand Cross of the Order of St. John, Eric Barry's grant includes the sash insignia of that grade. His shield is superimposed upon a Maltese cross (symbol of the order), which is a further indication of his appointment to the most senior grade of the Order of St. John. Barry is also Lord Prior of the Order.

Barry Arms

Canadian Forces Decoration

Douglas Maxwell Fowler, C.D.

Douglas Fowler's grant includes the Canadian Forces Decoration hung from his shield.

Daniel Joseph Patrick Gleeson, C.D.

A former member of the Canadian Airborne Regiment, Daniel Gleeson displays his arms with the Canadian Forces Decoration with two clasps (each of which represents ten years of additional service).

Fowler Arms

Gleeson Arms

Provincial Orders

Joseph Segal, C.M., O.B.C.

As a member of both the Order of Canada and the Order of British Columbia, Segal's grant includes both insignia. Because the Order of Canada takes precedence over the Order of British Columbia, it is hung on the dexter side.

Segal Arms

Commonwealth Orders

The Right Honourable Pierre Trudeau, P.C., C.C., C.H.

Pierre Trudeau's grant includes the insignia of both the Order of Canada and the Order of the Companions of Honour. Trudeau is the only Canadian to have included the Order of the Companions of Honour in his grant.

Alfred Allison Rogers, O.B.E.

Although Canada ceased using the British honours system in 1967, Canadians who receive British and other Commonwealth honours approved of by the Canadian government are permitted to include the insignia of their award in their grant of arms. Alfred Rogers' grant includes the insignia of an Officer of the Order of the British Empire hanging from his shield.

Trudeau Arms

Rogers Arms

Foreign Orders

As with British and Commonwealth honours, when Canadians receive foreign awards they are permitted to include the insignia of their award in their grant of arms. Canadian orders are always given precedence over Commonwealth and foreign awards.

Donn Larsen, Order of the Dannebrog (Denmark)

Donn Larsen's grant includes the insignia of one of Denmark's prestigious honours, the Order of the Dannebrog. Note the inclusion of the unique

Larsen Arms

Mitchell Arms

Kerwin Arms

Danish-style ribbon, which is quite different from the Canadian and Commonwealth method of mounting medals.

John Donald Mitchell, United States Silver Star

As a Commander of the Order of St. John and a holder of the United States Silver Star (a gallantry award), John Mitchell's grant includes both insignia.

John Larkin Kerwin, Companion of the Order of Canada and Officer of the Legion of Honour (France)

The grant to John Larkin Kerwin includes both the insignia of a Companion of the Order of Canada and an Officer of the Legion of Honour (France).

With the relaxation of Canadian government policy towards the acceptance of Commonwealth and foreign honours, it is certain that the number of unusual honours included in Canadian grants will increase. Thus, a new and interesting field of study is certain to emerge in the years to come.

CHAPTER 32

Future Prospects

Since 1967, the Canadian honours system has grown to become a truly national institution. The Order of Canada is now widely accepted as the pre-eminent national honour, awarded for the most outstanding service at both the national and local level. Similarly, members of the Canadian Forces now receive a wide variety of bravery, meritorious service and operational service awards. This is a most significant change from pre-1967 Canada, where the most that new members of the Royal Canadian Navy, Canadian Army or Royal Canadian Air Force could expect to receive during their entire careers was a Canadian Forces Decoration and possibly a United Nations medal. Canada now has its own national honours system, one which blends elements from its past with contemporary symbols.

With the recent granting of official recognition to provincial awards and the creation of the Order of Merit of the Police Forces, the Canadian honours system is anything but a stagnant institution.

Since 1967 more than 4,000 Canadians have been recognized with the Order of Canada, and nearly 3,100 with the Order of Military Merit. The Meritorious Service Decorations are beginning to be more widely used as well.

This past growth does not preclude possible additions and changes. It is unfortunate, however, that some changes are made for the wrong reasons, often jeopardizing a fundamentally good system. The 1998 decision to place the three levels of the Order of Canada ahead of all other Canadian awards — save the Victoria Cross and Cross of Valour — flies in the face of common sense. That a Member of the Order of Canada who has rendered exemplary service of a primarily local, albeit important, nature should rank ahead of a former chief of the defence staff who was appointed a Commander of the Order of Military Merit for thirty-five years of service at the national and international levels is silly. One reason cited for this recent move was that it would ensure that all Canadians are aware of the Order of Canada's importance. Yet one would hardly expect that the average Canadian could explain the order of precedence for honours and decorations, and placing all three levels of the Order of Canada ahead of almost every other decoration will certainly not change this. Numerous members of the Order of Canada have expressed their dissatisfaction with this decision. The reason that the Order of Canada has different levels is to differentiate between the international, national or regional character of the recipients. It would seem that grouping all three together is an attempt to blur this important distinction. One member of the order demanded, "How can you rank my CM along the same lines of Gerhardt Herzberg's C.C.? He won the Nobel Prize, for heaven's sake; my service was much more specific and modest." Without question the Order of Canada should return to its pre-1998 position in the Canadian Order of Precedence.

Over the past two decades there has been a proliferation in long service awards, and most specifically the exemplary service medals. All of these additions were genuinely warranted and serve an excellent purpose: to recognize long and exemplary service. There remains, however, no reward for longtime members of the federal and provincial civil services. At best they receive a pressboard plaque bearing a sticker with the Royal Arms of Canada at the top and an engraved replica of the prime minister's signature. The government should consider the creation of a Canadian Order of the Legion of Service to recognize exemplary and meritorious service in the civil service. Prior to 1946, Canadians were eligible for the Imperial Service Order, and until 1952 civil servants often received the Imperial Service Medal for this type of service. Such an addition to the Canadian honours system has been too long in coming and is certainly needed. Canada is one of the few countries in the world that does not possess a mechanism to recognize the meritorious service of its civil servants. One possible method would be to have a Legion of Service, consisting of a three-levelled order and a Public Service Medal. While civil servants are eligible for the Order of Canada, it is rarely awarded to all but a very few of the most senior civil servants.

This sort of award could also serve the cause of national unity, in that civil servants across the country at both the federal and provincial levels would be recognized. A Public Service Medal could also be created and awarded to those who have served for twenty years in the federal or provincial civil service. While awards of such a medal would be automatic after the requisite amount of time — and the fulfillment of a "good conduct" requirement, as with the Canadian Forces Decoration and the exemplary service medals — appointments to the Legion of Service would be made on the advice of an advisory committee similar to those used by the Order of Canada, the Order of Military Merit and for meritorious service decorations.

Another necessary change would be to abolish the Order of Merit of the Police Forces and replace it with a civil division of a new Order of Merit — which would essentially divide the existing Order of Military Merit into military and civil divisions. Establishing this sort of institution would be much more practical than allowing the fire services, correctional services and emergency medical services to create their own orders along the lines of the Order of Merit of the Police Forces. Indeed, the Order of Merit of the Police Forces has set a precedent for such "occupational awards," and many other groups have as much right to such an order as do the police.

Over the past decade, a number of official awards have been established that reward service not normally recognized by awards contained in the Canadian honours system — most specifically, the Governor General's Caring Canadian Award and the Vice-Regal Commendations. These awards are accompanied by a certificate and lapel pin. The proliferation of awards that are mere five-dollar lapel pins is worrisome. The service rendered by the recipients of these awards is akin to that required for the Meritorious Service Medal, thus the awarding of such a humble token is inappropriate and inadequate. Perhaps the MSM could be awarded to these people — as was intended when it was created — or actual medals, such as a good citizenship or volunteer medal, could be developed. The lapel pin could be retained and worn on a daily basis, while the medal would be saved for special occasions. These days it seems as though everyone is wearing a lapel pin of some sort, and the significance of such an award is reduced by this fact. The symbolism of a medal is that much stronger.

A significant problem that has afflicted the Canadian honours system is the quality of the awards themselves. In particular, the service medals issued to Canadians have been, until recently, of a scandalously low quality. Often poorly struck and issued with chrome-like finishes, most are devoid of the high level of craftsmanship that was once common. The absence of naming on medals is another problem. Naming costs relatively little (about two to five dollars per medal), but it imbues each medal awarded with significance to the recipient, as it becomes a personal token of recognition. One must question why countries such as Britain, Australia, Kenya and Zimbabwe all issue well-struck, named medals, yet Canada is unable to do the same. The practice of offering contracts to produce honours to the lowest bidder, regardless of quality, must cease. Hopefully, with time, Canada will return to issuing high-quality, named, service medals. The recent issue of the General Campaign Star and General Service Medal offers some hope for those keen to return to awards worthy of the service rendered in their receipt.

Now that all ten provinces have created their own orders, further province-specific awards, such as bravery awards, long service medals and commemorative medals, should not be recognized at the federal level. If each province is permitted to continue adding medals to the broader Canadian Order of Precedence, we will quickly end up with not only the largest, but also the most confusing and "balkanized" honours system in the world. Surely we do not wish to end up with a system similar to that which existed in Imperial Germany, where every state had a complex system of honours and awards to accompany an equally complex imperial system. The federal government has shown great reluctance to dissuade the provinces from creating new awards. Many officials have quietly admitted that this is more a result of the desire to smooth over rocky federal-provincial relations than because Ottawa actually approves of the awards.

We should avoid creating a myriad of departmental awards similar to those developed in South Africa during the apartheid period. Unfortunately, the establishment of the Order of Merit of the Police Forces seems to be a step in this direction. From the late 1870s to the early 1960s, France created multilevelled honours for every government department, from the ministry of Tourism to the postal service. More than fifteen separate orders were created. This system was so complicated that it was replaced by the Order of National Merit in 1963.

In Canada, the creation of new awards has not been limited to the provinces. Many police departments have also created their own awards for long service and bravery, and even the Canadian Senate has its own set of long service awards. Because these awards do not emanate from the Crown, they are "unofficial," and wearing them with official awards is tantamount to wearing sporting medals with a Golden Jubilee Medal. Without question the nation needs a more uniform adherence to the Canadian Order of Precedence for wearing orders, decorations and medals.

Individual institutions should continue to be allowed to create their own internal awards, but they should come in the form of plaques, award cups, certificates and large table medals — not in the form of medals that might be worn alongside official awards, that can be mistaken for official awards, and which, in some cases, can be linked to a desire, rooted in vanity, to have more medals and ribbons on one's chest. Such quasi-official awards diminish the significance of real orders, decorations and medals.

The future for the Canadian honours system is secure, provided that the calibre and quality of those recognized by it remains high. If there is a further proliferation of awards and an ever-increasing number of people appointed to the various national orders, the system's integrity will certainly be compromised. Future additions and expansions must be examined and weighed much more carefully than in the past. There is no longer an "honours vacuum" in Canada, and future additions might even appear frivolous to an ever-fickle public. Similarly, a formal education campaign should be initiated to familiarize Canadians, young and old, with the Canadian honours system and how it strives to recognize people from all walks of life who have devoted their lives to the welfare of humankind. There is a desperate need to highlight and show the heritage of Canada's honours system through a museum. This, too, would serve to maintain the prestige and honour of the Canadian honours system.

1927 Diamond Jubilee Medal obverse   *1927 Diamond Jubilee Medal reverse*

APPENDIX 1

The Canadian Order of Precedence of Orders, Decorations and Medals

CANADIAN ORDERS, DECORATIONS AND MEDALS DIRECTIVE, 1998

P.C. 1998-591, 2 April, 1998

His Excellency the Governor General in Council, on the recommendation of the Prime Minister, hereby makes the annexed Canadian Orders, Decorations and Medals Directive, 1998.

ORDER OF PRECEDENCE

1. The sequence for wearing the insignia of Canadian orders, decorations and medals, and the post-nominal letters associated with the orders, decorations and medals, are the following:

Victoria Cross (V.C.)
Cross of Valour (C.V.)

NATIONAL ORDERS
Companion of the Order of Canada (C.C.)
Officer of the Order of Canada (O.C.)
Member of the Order of Canada (C.M.)
Commander of the Order of Military Merit (C.M.M.)
Commander of the Order of Merit of the Police Forces (C.O.M.)*
Commander of the Royal Victorian Order (C.V.O.)
Officer of the Order of Military Merit (O.M.M.)
Officer of the Order of Merit of the Police Forces (O.O.M.)*
Lieutenant of the Royal Victorian Order (L.V.O.)
Member of the Order of Military Merit (M.M.M.)
Member of the Order of Merit of the Police Forces (M.O.M.)*
Member of the Royal Victorian Order (M.V.O.)
The Most Venerable Order of St. John of Jerusalem (all grades) (postnominal
    letters only for internal use by the Order of St. John)

PROVINCIAL ORDERS
Ordre national du Québec (G.O.Q., O.Q., C.Q.)

The Saskatchewan Order of Merit (S.O.M.)
The Order of Ontario (O.Ont.)
The Order of British Columbia (O.B.C.)
The Alberta Order of Excellence (A.O.E.)
The Order of Prince Edward Island (O.P.E.I.)
The Order of Manitoba (O.M)*
The Order of New Brunswick (O.N.B.)*
The Order of Nova Scotia (O.N.S.)*
The Order of Newfoundland and Labrador (O.N.L.)*

DECORATIONS
Star of Military Valour (S.M.V.)
Star of Courage (S.C.)
Meritorious Service Cross (M.S.C.)
Medal of Military Valour (M.M.V.)
Medal of Bravery (M.B.)
Meritorious Service Medal (M.S.M.)
Royal Victorian Medal (R.V.M.)

WAR AND OPERATIONAL SERVICE MEDALS
(See section 5 for complete list.)
Korea Medal
Canadian Volunteer Service Medal for Korea
Gulf and Kuwait Medal
Somalia Medal
South West Asia Service Medal*
General Campaign Star*
General Service Medal*

SPECIAL SERVICE MEDAL WITH BARS
Pakistan 1989–90
Alert
Humanitas
NATO/OTAN
Peace/Paix
Ranger*

PEACEKEEPING MEDAL
Canadian Peacekeeping Service Medal

UNITED NATIONS MEDALS
Service (Korea)
Emergency Force
Truce Supervision Organization in Palestine and Observer Group in Lebanon
Military Observation Group in India and Pakistan

Organization in Congo
Temporary Executive Authority in West New Guinea
Yemen Observation Mission
Force in Cyprus
India/Pakistan Observation Mission
Emergency Force Middle East
Disengagement Observation Force Golan Heights
Interim Force in Lebanon
Military Observation Group in Iran/Iraq
Transition Assistance Group (Namibia)
Observer Group in Central America
Iraq/Kuwait Observer Mission
Angola Verification Mission
Mission for the Referendum in Western Sahara
Observer Mission in El Salvador
Protection Force (Yugoslavia)
Advance Mission in Cambodia
Transitional Authority in Cambodia
Operation in Somalia
Operation in Mozambique
Observation Mission in Uganda/Rwanda
Assistance Mission in Rwanda
Mission in Haiti
Verification of Human Rights and Compliance with the Comprehensive
    Agreement on Human Rights in Guatemala
Assistance Mission for Rwanda*
Confidence Restoration Operation in Croatia*
Preventive Deployment Force, Former Yugoslavia*
Mission in the Central African Republic*
Preventive Deployment Force (Macedonia)*
Military Observer Mission in Prevlaka (Croatia)*
Interim Administration Mission in Kosovo*
Observer Mission in Sierra Leone/UN Mission In Sierra Leone*
Assistance Mission East Timor/Transitional Authority East Timor*
Mission in the Democratic Republic of the Congo*
Mission in Ethiopia and Eritrea*
Special Service Medal*
Headquarters Medal*

NATO MEDALS
NATO Medal with a "Former Yugoslavia" Bar
NATO Medal with a "Kosovo" Bar
Article 5 Medal for Operation Eagle Assist
Article 5 Medal for Operation Active Endeavour
Non-Article 5 Medal for Operations in the Balkans

INTERNATIONAL COMMISSION AND ORGANIZATION MEDALS
International Commission for Supervision and Control (Indo- China)
International Commission of Control and Supervision (Vietnam)
Multinational Force and Observers (Sinai)
European Community Monitor Mission (Yugoslavia)
INTERFET*
European Union Defence Policy Medal*

COMMEMORATIVE MEDALS
Canadian Centennial Medal (1967)
Queen Elizabeth II's Silver Jubilee Medal (1977)
125th Anniversary of the Confederation of Canada Medal (1992)
Queen Elizabeth II Golden Jubilee Medal (2002)*

LONG SERVICE AND GOOD CONDUCT MEDALS
R.C.M.P. Long Service Medal
Canadian Forces Decoration (C.D.)

EXEMPLARY SERVICE MEDALS
Police Exemplary Service Medal
Corrections Exemplary Service Medal
Fire Services Exemplary Service Medal
Canadian Coast Guard Exemplary Service Medal
Emergency Medical Services Exemplary Service Medal*
Peace Officer Exemplary Service Medal*

SPECIAL MEDAL
Queen's Medal for Champion Shot

OTHER MEDALS
Ontario Medal for Good Citizenship (O.M.C.)
Ontario Medal for Police Bravery
Ontario Medal for Firefighters Bravery
Saskatchewan Volunteer Medal (S.V.M.)
Ontario Provincial Police Long Service and Good Conduct Medal
Service Medal of the Most Venerable Order of St. John of Jerusalem
Commissionaire Long Service Medal

2. The Bar to the Special Service Medal is worn centred on the ribbon. If there is more than one Bar, they are spaced evenly on the ribbon with the most recent uppermost.

3. Commonwealth orders, decorations and medals the award of which is approved by the Government of Canada are worn after the Canadian orders,

decorations and medals listed in Section 1, precedence in each category being set by date of appointment or award.

4. Foreign orders, decorations and medals the award of which is approved by the Government of Canada are worn after the orders, decorations and medals referred to in sections 1 and 3, precedence in each category being set by date of appointment or award.

5. Notwithstanding sections 1, 3 and 4, a person who, prior to June 1, 1972, was a member of a British order or the recipient of a British decoration or medal referred to in this section, may wear the insignia of the decoration or medal together with the insignia of any Canadian order, decoration or medal that the person is entitled to wear, the proper sequence being the following:

Victoria Cross (V.C.)
George Cross (G.C.)
Cross of Valour (C.V.)
Order of Merit (O.M.)
Order of the Companions of Honour (C.H.)
Companion of the Order of Canada (C.C.)
Officer of the Order of Canada (O.C.)
Member of the Order of Canada (C.M.)
Commander of the Order of Military Merit (C.M.M.)
Companion of the Order of the Bath (C.B.)
Companion of the Order of St. Michael and St. George (C.M.G.)
Commander of the Royal Victorian Order (C.V.O.)
Commander of the Order of the British Empire (C.B.E.)
Distinguished Service Order (D.S.O.)
Officer of the Order of Military Merit (O.M.M.)
Lieutenant of the Royal Victorian Order (L.V.O.)
Officer of the Order of the British Empire (O.B.E.)
Imperial Service Order (I.S.O.)
Member of the Order of Military Merit (M.M.M.)
Member of the Royal Victorian Order (M.V.O.)
Member of the Order of the British Empire (M.B.E.)
Member of the Royal Red Cross (R.R.C.)
Distinguished Service Cross (D.S.C.)
Military Cross (M.C.)
Distinguished Flying Cross (D.F.C.)
Air Force Cross (A.F.C.)
Star of Military Valour (S.M.V.)
Star of Courage (S.C.)
Meritorious Service Cross (M.S.C.)
Medal of Military Valour (M.M.V.)

Medal of Bravery (M.B.)
Meritorious Service Medal (M.S.M.)
Associate of the Royal Red Cross (A.R.R.C.)
The Most Venerable Order of St. John of Jerusalem (all grades) (postnominal
    letters only for internal use by the Order of St. John of Jerusalem)
Provincial Orders (order of precedence as set out in Section 1)
Distinguished Conduct Medal (D.C.M.)
Conspicuous Gallantry Medal (C.G.M.)
George Medal (G.M.)
Distinguished Service Medal (D.S.M.)
Military Medal (M.M.)
Distinguished Flying Medal (D.F.M.)
Air Force Medal (A.F.M.)
Queen's Gallantry Medal (Q.G.M.)
Royal Victorian Medal (R.V.M.)
British Empire Medal (B.E.M.)

WAR AND OPERATIONAL SERVICE MEDALS
Africa General Service Medal (1902–1956)
India General Service Medal (1908–1935)
Naval General Service Medal (1915–1962)
India General Service Medal (1936–1939)
General Service Medal — Army and Air Force (1918–1962)
General Service Medal (1962–)
1914 Star
1914–1915 Star
British War Medal (1914–1918)
Mercantile Marine War Medal (1914–1918)
Victory Medal (1914–1918)
Territorial Force War Medal (1914–1919)
1939–1945 Star
Atlantic Star
Air Crew Europe Star
Africa Star
Pacific Star
Burma Star
Italy Star
France and Germany Star
Defence Medal
Canadian Volunteer Service Medal
Newfoundland Second World War Volunteer Service Medal (see section 6)
War Medal (1939–1945)
Korea Medal
Canadian Volunteer Service Medal for Korea
Gulf and Kuwait Medal

Somalia Medal
South West Asia Service Medal
General Campaign Star
General Service Medal

SPECIAL SERVICE MEDAL
(The order of precedence is as set out for the Special Service Medal with Bars
in Section 1.)

UNITED NATIONS MEDALS
(The order of precedence is as set out for the United Nations Medals in
Section 1.)

INTERNATIONAL COMMISSION MEDALS
(The order of precedence is as set out for International Commission and
Organization Medals in Section 1.)

POLAR MEDALS
(The order of precedence is by order of date awarded.)

COMMEMORATIVE MEDALS
King George V's Silver Jubilee Medal (1935)
King George VI's Coronation Medal (1937)
Queen Elizabeth II's Coronation Medal (1953)
Canadian Centennial Medal (1967)
Queen Elizabeth II's Silver Jubilee Medal (1977)
125th Anniversary of the Confederation of Canada Medal (1992)
Queen Elizabeth II Golden Jubilee Medal (2002)

LONG SERVICE AND GOOD CONDUCT MEDALS
Army Long Service and Good Conduct Medal
Naval Long Service and Good Conduct Medal
Air Force Long Service and Good Conduct Medal
R.C.M.P. Long Service Medal
Volunteer Officer's Decoration (V.D.)
Volunteer Long Service Medal
Colonial Auxiliary Forces Officer's Decoration (V.D.)
Colonial Auxiliary Forces Long Service Medal
Efficiency Decoration (E.D.)
Efficiency Medal
Naval Volunteer Reserve Decoration (V.R.D.)
Naval Volunteer Reserve Long Service and Good Conduct Medal
Air Efficiency Award
Canadian Forces Decoration (C.D.)

EXEMPLARY SERVICE MEDALS
(The order of precedence is as set out for Exemplary Service Medals in Section 1.)

SPECIAL MEDAL
Queen's Medal for Champion Shot

OTHER MEDALS
(The order of precedence is as set out for Other Medals in Section 1.)

6. The Newfoundland Volunteer War Service Medal has the same precedence as the Canadian Volunteer Service Medal.

7. The insignia of orders, decorations and medals not listed in this Directive, as well as foreign awards the award of which has not been approved by the Government of Canada, shall not be mounted or worn in conjunction with the orders, decorations and medals listed in this Directive.

8. The insignia of orders, decorations and medals shall not be worn by anyone other than the recipient of the orders, decorations or medals.

REPEAL
9. The Canadian Orders, Decorations and Medals Directive 1 is repealed.

* Asterisk denotes an award added to the Order of Precedence after passage of the 1998 order-in-council.

APPENDIX 2

Establishment and Amendments to Canadian Orders, Decorations and Medals

This is the first comprehensive list of approval and order-in-council dates compiled for the Canadian honours system. The process for approving medals for wear by Canadians was not standardized until the late 1970s, and thus, some information is not complete. This is especially true with respect to the first twelve United Nations Service Medals issued to Canadians.

ORDER OF CANADA

Order-in-Council Number	Date of Registration	Change(s)
1967-389	March 2, 1967	Establishment of the Order of Canada
1972-809	March 1, 1972	Restructuring of the order to CC, OC, CM (abolition of Medal of Service and Medal of Courage)
1983-750	March 17, 1983	Enlargement of the Order of Canada (OC and CM levels)
1994-2026	December 6, 1994	Increase in number of annual awards OC and CM
1995-694	April 25, 1995	Increase in number of annual awards of the CC
1997-552	April 15, 1997	Change in honorary appointment policy
1998-1373	August 24, 1998	Increase in number of annual awards OC and CM. Also change in honorary appointment policy.
1999-1743	October 1, 1999	Increase in number of annual awards OC and CM
2001-303	March 1, 2001	Increase in size of the advisory council

ORDER OF MILITARY MERIT

Order-in-Council Number	Date of Registration	Change(s)
1972-810	March 1, 1972	Establishment of the order
1972-1798	August 24, 1972	Modification of number of annual appointments
1977-2841	October 6, 1977	Modification of sections relating to honorary appointments

ORDER OF MERIT OF THE POLICE FORCES

Order-in-Council Number	Date of Registration	Change(s)
2000-1390	August 24, 2000	Establishment of the order

BRAVERY DECORATIONS

Order-in-Council Number	Date of Registration	Change(s)
1972-811	May 1, 1972	Establishment of the CV, SC and MB
1997-123	January 28, 1997	Updating the membership of the Canadian Decorations Advisory Committee (expansion)

MILITARY VALOUR DECORATIONS

Order-in-Council Number	Date of Registration	Change(s)
1992-2577	December 10, 1992	Establishment of the VC, SMV and MMV

MERITORIOUS SERVICE DECORATIONS

Order-in-Council Number	Date of Registration	Change(s)
1984-1831	May 29, 1984	Establishment of the MSC
1991-1060	June 6, 1991	Establishment of the civil division of the MSC and both civil and military divisions of the MSM
1999-135	February 4, 1999	Expansion of the civil advisory committee

OPERATIONAL SERVICE MEDALS

Order-in-Council Number	Date of Registration	Change(s)
1984-1832	May 29,1984	Establishment of the Special Service Medal
1991-860	May 13, 1991	Establishment of the Gulf and Kuwait Medal
1991-1061	June 6, 1991	Pakistan 1989–90 Bar
1991-1177	June 20, 1991	Establishment of the Korea Voluntary Service Medal
1992-2294	November 12, 1992	Re-establishment of the Special Service Medal
1992-2435	November 26, 1992	Alert Bar
1992-2436	November 26, 1992	NATO + OTAN Bar
1992-2437	November 26, 1992	Peace—Paix Bar
1993-449	March 9, 1993	Humanitas Bar
1993-449	March 9, 1993	Jugoslavija Bar
1993-450	March 9, 1993	Cancellation of Jugoslavija Bar
1995-2003	November 28, 1995	Amendments to the criteria for the Alert Bar
1995-2004	November 28, 1995	Amendment to the criteria for the Peace—Paix Bar
1995-2005	November 28, 1995	Amendment to the criteria for the NATO+OTAN Bar
1996-1982	December 19, 1991	Establishment of the Somalia Medal
1997-124	January 28, 1997	Amendment to the criteria for the Humanitas Bar
Act of Parliament 1997, ch. 31	April 25, 1997	Establishment of the Peacekeeping Service Medal

Order-in-Council Number	Date of Registration	Change(s)
1999-1741	October 1, 1999	Regulations relating to approval of Bars for the SSM
1999-1742	October 1, 1999	Establishment of the Ranger Bar
1999-1858	October 21, 1999	Regulations for the Peacekeeping Service Medal
2002-1254	July 17, 2002	Establishment of the South West Asia Medal
2004-0287	March 24, 2004	Establishment of the Campaign Service Star and the General Service Medal
2004-0753	June 17, 2004	Establishment of the Allied Force Bar for the General Campaign Star
2004-0754	June 17, 2004	Establishment of the Allied Force Bar for the General Service Medal
2004-0755	June 17, 2004	Establishment of the ISAF Bar for the General Campaign Star
2004-0756	June 17, 2004	Establishment of the ISAF Bar for the General Service Medal

THE UNITED NATIONS SERVICE MEDALS[44]

Order-in-Council Number	Date of Registration	Change(s)
*	**	UNEF I (First UN Emergency Force)
*	**	UNTSO (Truce Supervision Organization)
*	**	UNOGIL (UN Observer Group in Lebanon)
*	**	UNMOGIP (Observer Group in India and Pakistan)
*	**	ONUC (Operations des Nations Unies au Congo)
*	**	UNTEA (UN Temporary Executive Authority W. New Guinea)
*	**	UNYOM (UN Yemen Observer Mission)
*	**	UNFICYP (UN Peacekeeping Force in Cyprus)

Order-in-Council Number	Date of Registration	Change(s)
*	**	UNIPOM (UN India-Pakistan Observer Mission)
*	**	UNEF II (Second UN Emergency Force)
*	**	UNDOF (UN Disengagement Observer Force)
*	**	UNIFIL (UN Interim Force in Lebanon)
1989-1159	June 15, 1989	UNIIMOG (UN Iran-Iraq Military Observer Group)
1990-1370	June 28, 1990	UNTAG (UN Transition Assistance Group Namibia)
1990-1636	July 27, 1990	ONUCA (UN Observer Group in Central America)
1992-234	February 6, 1992	UNIKOM (UN Iraq-Kuwait Observer Mission)
1992-247-01	March 27, 1992	MINURSO (UN Mission for the Referendum in Western Sahara)
1992-260-01	March 27, 1992	ONUSAL (UN Observer Mission in El Salvador)
1992-1736	July 28, 1992	UNPROFOR (UN Protection Force in Former Yugoslavia)
1993-1350	June 16, 1993	Extension of UNPROFOR Medal to Canadian Police
1993-1351	June 16, 1993	UNAMIC (UN Advance Mission in Cambodia)
1992-1737	July 28, 1992	UNTAC (UN Transitional Authority in Cambodia)
1993-1352	June 16, 1993	Extension of UNTAC Medal to Canadian Police
1994-631	April 21, 1994	UNOSOM (United Nations Operation in Somalia)
1994-1152	July 4, 1994	ONUMOZ (UN Operation in Mozambique)
1995-1482	August 30, 1995	UNOMUR (UN Observer Mission in Uganda-Rwanda)
1995-1483	August 30, 1995	UNMIH (UN Mission in Haiti)
1998-53	January 26, 1998	MINUGUA (UN Mission for Verification of Human Rights in Guatemala)

Order-in-Council Number	Date of Registration	Change(s)
1994-1153	July 4, 1994	UNAMIR (UN Assistance Mission for Rwanda)
*	**	UNCRO (UN Confidence Restoration Operation in Croatia)
2000-278	March 2, 2000	UNPREDEP (UN Preventative Deployment Force, Former Yugoslavia)
1999-1859	October 21, 1999	MINURCA (UN Mission in the Central African Republic)
2000-278	March 2, 2000	UN Preventative Deployment Force (Macedonia)
2001-279	March 2, 2000	UNMIBH (UN Mission in Bosnia and Herzegovina)
2001-280	March 2, 2000	UNMOP (UN Mission of Observers in Prevlaka, Croatia)
2001-281	March 2, 2000	UNMK (UN Mission in Kosovo)
2001-298	March 1, 2001	UNAMSIL (UN Mission in Sierra Leone)
2001-299	March 1, 2001	UNAMET/UNTAET (UN Mission in East Timor and UN Transitional Administration in East Timor)
2001-300	March 1, 2001	MONUC (UN Organization Mission in the Democratic Republic of the Congo)
2001-1405	August 1, 2001	UNMEE (UN Organization Mission in Ethiopia and Eritrea)
1999-2132	December 1, 1999	UNHQ (United Nations Headquarters Service)
1997-1216	August 28, 1997	UNSSM (United Nations Special Service)

NATO MEDALS

Order-in-Council Number	Date of Registration	Change(s)
1995-1484	August 30, 1995	NATO Medal, Former Yugoslavia Bar
2000-282	March 2, 2000	NATO Medal, Kosovo Bar
2003-1296	August 22, 2003	NATO Non–Article 5 Operations in the Balkans Medal
2003-1297	August 22, 2003	NATO Article 5 Operation Active Endeavour Medal
2003-1298	August 22, 2003	NATO Article 5 Operation Eagle Assist Medal

INTERNATIONAL ORGANIZATIONAL MEDALS

Order-in-Council Number	Date of Registration	Change(s)
*	**	International Commission for Supervision and Control Service
1973-2241	July 27, 1973	International Commission of Control and Supervision, Vietnam 1973
1986-1854	August 13, 1986	Multinational Force and Observer's Medal
1994-629	April 21, 1994	European Community Monitor Mission Medal
2001-301	March 14, 2001	International Force East Timor Medal
		European Union Defence Security Policy Medal, and subsequent bars

CANADIAN FORCES DECORATION

Order-in-Council Number	Date of Registration	Change(s)
1949-6335	December 15, 1949	Establishment of the CD
*	**	Change of Effigy
1981-2310	August 19, 1981	Modernization Amendment

ROYAL CANADIAN MOUNTED POLICE LONG SERVICE MEDAL

Order-in-Council Number	Date of Registration	Change(s)
1928-2169	December 6, 1928	Establishment of the RCMP Officer's Decoration and the RCMP Long Service Medal
1933-29	January 14, 1934	Cancellation of the RCMP Officer's Decoration and establishment of the RCMP Long Service Medal (for all ranks)
1945-1981	March 16, 1945	Allowance for service in the Armed Forces during the Second World War to count towards the Long Service Medal
1947-4877	November 28, 1947	Change of King George VI title to remove *Ind Imp*, and change to *Georgivs VI Dei Gratia Rex*
1951-4333	August 15, 1951	Amendments to medal regulations
1954-218	February 12, 1954	Establishment of the bronze, silver and gold Long Service Bars/Clasps
1954-415	March 18, 1954	Rewording of order-in-council 1954-218
Ministerial Order	2004	Establishment of the Silver and Gold Bar for forty years' service

EXEMPLARY SERVICE MEDALS

Order-in-Council Number	Date of Registration	Change(s)
1983-2130	July 14, 1983	Establishment of the Police Exemplary Service Medal
1984-1830	May 29, 1984	Establishment of the Corrections Exemplary Service Medal
1985-2564	August 13, 1985	Establishment of the Fire Service Exemplary Service Medal
1990-2308	October 25, 1990	Establishment of the Canadian Coast Guard Exemplary Service Medal

Order-in-Council Number	Date of Registration	Change(s)
1994-632	April 21, 1994	Establishment of the Emergency Medical Forces Exemplary Service Medal
1995-784	May 16, 1995	Amendments to the Corrections Exemplary Service Medal, broadening definition of correction service officer
2004-652	May 11, 2004	Establishment of the Peace Officer Exemplary Service Medal

COMMEMORATIVE MEDALS

Order-in-Council Number	Date of Registration	Change(s)
The Queen	June 27, 1966	Establishment of the Centennial Medal
The Queen	May 18, 1977	Establishment of the Queen Elizabeth II Silver Jubilee Medal
1992-962	May 7, 1992	Establishment of the Canada 125 Medal
2002-195	February 15, 2002	Establishment of the Queen Elizabeth II Golden Jubilee Medal

THE QUEEN'S MEDAL FOR CHAMPION SHOT

Order-in-Council Number	Date of Registration	Change(s)
1991-1282	July 10, 1991	Establishment of the Queen's Medal for Champion Shot

MENTIONS IN DISPATCHES

Order-in-Council Number	Date of Registration	Change(s)
1991-861	May 13, 1991	Establishment of the MID regulations

CANADIAN MEMORIAL CROSS

Order-in-Council Number	Date of Registration	Change(s)
1919-2374	December 1, 1919	Establishment of the Memorial Cross
1940-4210	August 27, 1940	Revision of criteria for issue of the Memorial Cross to include airmen, merchant seamen and firefighters
1950-5812	December 5, 1950	Criteria expanded to include those involved in UN missions and NATO operations
1976-1715	November 4, 1976	Revision of criteria for issue of the Memorial Cross

CANADIAN FORCES COMMENDATIONS

Order-in-Council Number	Date of Registration	Change(s)
Established by the Governor General	November 7, 2000	Establishment of the Commander-in-Chief Unit Commendation
Established by the CDS	November 1980	Establishment of the Canadian Forces Unit Commendation
Established by the CDS	April 1974	Establishment of the Chief of the Defence Staff Commendation
Established by the CDS	July 1995	Establishment of the Command Commendation

ORGANIZATIONAL SERVICE MEDALS

Order-in-Council Number	Date of Registration	Change(s)
Established by the Corps of Commissionaires	August 20, 1948	Establishment of the Canadian Corps of Commissionaires Long Service Medal
1998-301	February 26, 1998	Official recognition of the Canadian Corps of Commissionaires Medal

Notes

* No known order-in-council was issued to approve this medal; rather, it was internally approved by the Department of National Defence and subsequently included in the Canadian Order of Precedence.

** Date of authorization is unknown.

Equalizaton Chart, Pre-1967
Canadian/British Honours and the
Modern Canadian Honours System

Current Canadian Honour Award	Pre-1967 British/or Canadian Honour Award
Victoria Cross	Victoria Cross
Cross of Valour	George Cross
Companion of the Order of Canada	Knight of the Garter, Knight of the Thistle, Knight Grand Cross of the Order of the Bath (Civil Division), Knight Grand Cross of the Order of St. Michael and St. George, Knight Grand Cross of the Order of the British Empire (Civil Division)
Order of Merit	Order of Merit
Order of the Companion of Honour	Order of the Companion of Honour
Officer of the Order of Canada	Knight Commander of the Order of the Bath, Knight Commander of the Order of St. Michael and St. George, Knight Commander of the Order of the British Empire
Member of the Order of Canada	Companion of the Order of the Bath, Companion of the Order of St. Michael and St. George, Commander of the Order of the British Empire
Commander of the Order of Military Merit	Knight Grand Cross of the Order of the Bath (Military Division), Knight Grand Cross of the Order of St. Michael and St. George, Knight Grand Cross of the Order of the British Empire (Military Division)
Commander of the Order of Merit of the Police	Knight Grand Cross of the Order of the Bath (Civil Division), Knight Grand Cross of the Order of St. Michael and St. George, Knight

	Grand Cross of the Order of the British Empire (Civil Division), Knight of the Order of the British Empire (Civil Division)
Commander of the Royal Victorian Order	Commander of the Royal Victorian Order
Officer of the Order of Military Merit	Companion of the Order of the Bath (Military Division), Commander of the Order of the British Empire (Military Division)
Officer of the Order of Merit of the Police	Companion of the Order of the Bath (Civil Division), Commander of the Order of the British Empire (Civil Division)
Lieutenant of the Royal Victorian Order	Lieutenant of the Royal Victorian Order
Member of the Order of Military Merit	Officer of the Order of the British Empire (Military Division), Member of the Order of the British Empire (Military Division)
Member of the Order of Merit of the Police	Officer of the Order of the British Empire (Civil Division), Member of the Order of the British Empire (Civil Division)
Member of the Royal Victorian Order	Member of the Royal Victorian Order
The Order of St. John (all levels)	The Order of St. John (all levels)
Star of Military Valour	Military Cross, Distinguished Service Cross, Distinguished Flying Cross, Distinguished Conduct Medal, Conspicuous Gallantry Medal (Naval and Air)
Star of Courage	George Medal, Empire Gallantry Medal
Meritorious Service Cross (Military)	Distinguished Service Order, Air Force Cross
Meritorious Service Cross (Civil)	Commander of the Order of the British Empire (Civil Division)
Medal of Military Valour	Military Medal, Distinguished Service Medal, Distinguished Flying Medal
Medal of Bravery	Order of the British Empire for Gallantry, Queen's Gallantry Medal,* Queen's Commendation for Brave Conduct

Meritorious Service Medal (Military)	Officer of the Order of the British Empire (Military Division), Member of the Order of the British Empire (Military Division), Air Force Medal
Meritorious Service Medal (Civil)	Officer of the Order of the British Empire (Civil Division), Member of the Order of the British Empire (Civil Division)
Royal Victorian Medal	Royal Victorian Medal

* The Queen's Gallantry Medal was not established until 1974, and is partially based on the Canadian Star of Courage.

APPENDIX 4

Research and Values

The information listed in this appendix contains a number of Web addresses and other information that invariably changes with time. Thus, to ensure that you have the most accurate and up-to-date information you can, visit **http://www.dominionofcanada.com**, where I will update information as it changes. Information about new medals and developments in the Canadian honours system will also be included on this page.

RESEARCHING CANADIAN MEDAL GROUPS AND RECIPIENTS

For those interested in researching the recipients of Canadian medals from the War of 1812, the Fenian Raids, the Red River Rebellion (1870), the North West Rebellion (1885), the Nile Expedition, the Anglo-Boer War and the First World War, service records — or, at the very least, confirmation of medal entitlement — can be obtained from:

> Library and Archives of Canada
> 395 Wellington St.
> Ottawa, ON K1A 0N4
> http://www.collectionscanada.ca

Researching Second World War, Korean War and modern medal groups is more difficult, as access-to-information rules prohibit the release of information of anyone who has been dead for less than twenty years. Direct descendants (family members) are not subject to this rule. In either case, you *must* be able to provide proof of death. A wide variety of military publications issued by the Canadian Army, Royal Canadian Navy and Royal Canadian Air Force can often provide confirmation of the award of the Canadian Forces Decoration and, in the case of officers, promotions and postings.

Information on recipients of the Order of Canada, Meritorious Service Decorations, Bravery Awards and even the 2002 Golden Jubilee Medal can be found on the governor general's website or be confirmed by writing to the Chancellery.

Office of the Governor General
Chancellery
1 Sussex Dr.
Ottawa, ON K1A 0A1
http://www.gg.ca

The Department of National Defence's Directorate of History and Heritage also has an interesting website that offers information about honours and awards. Visit **http://www.forces.gc.ca/hr/dhh/.**

SOCIETIES AND CLUBS

There are a number of organizations that bring together those interested in researching and collecting Canadian orders, decorations and medals. All of these organizations publish journals or magazines, and most have local branches and hold annual conventions. These conventions bring together collectors from all across Canada and the world, and they provide a unique venue to meet with others who share an interest in this fascinating hobby.

The Military Collectors' Club of Canada
Secretary Treasurer
PO Box 64009
RPO Morse Place
Winnipeg, MB R2K 4K2
http://www.marway-militaria.com/mcc_club_page.htm

The Orders and Medals Research Society
General Secretary, OMRS
PO Box 1904
Southam CV47 2ZX
United Kingdom
http://www.omrs.org.uk (email: generalsecretary@omrs.org.uk)

The Canadian Society of Military Medal and Insignia
Secretary
17 Friars Court
St. Catharines ON L2N 6B4
http://www3.sympatico.ca/bkeevil/CSMMI (email: frothy@vaxxine.com)

The Orders and Medals Society of America
Secretary
PO Box 198
San Ramon, CA 94583
U.S.A.
http://www.omsa.org (email: dpeck9696@aol.com)

VALUE OF ORDERS, DECORATIONS AND MEDALS

It is difficult, at best, to place fixed values upon many Canadian orders, decorations and medals. Such honours as the Cross of Valour and Commander of the Order of Military Merit have never come onto the open market. I have not addressed the values of each medal in this publication because they fluctuate and because they are subject to dispute even amongst the most reputable dealers. Nevertheless, in an effort to provide this sort of information, I have posted a chart of approximate values under "Current Values" at **http://www.dominionofcanada.com.**

I have listed approximate ranges that reflect the prices realized in major auctions containing Canadian material, as well as prices reflected in militaria lists and at militaria shows.

Because many medal groups on the market also include awards from the pre- and post-1967 Canadian honours system, the website includes values for many honours bestowed upon Canadians dating back to the Fenian Raids. Again, as opposed to a set price, I have listed a rough price range.

APPENDIX 5

Ribbon Chart

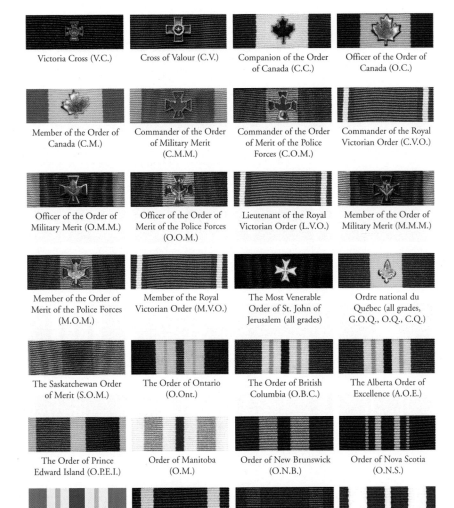

Victoria Cross (V.C.)

Cross of Valour (C.V.)

Companion of the Order of Canada (C.C.)

Officer of the Order of Canada (O.C.)

Member of the Order of Canada (C.M.)

Commander of the Order of Military Merit (C.M.M.)

Commander of the Order of Merit of the Police Forces (C.O.M.)

Commander of the Royal Victorian Order (C.V.O.)

Officer of the Order of Military Merit (O.M.M.)

Officer of the Order of Merit of the Police Forces (O.O.M.)

Lieutenant of the Royal Victorian Order (L.V.O.)

Member of the Order of Military Merit (M.M.M.)

Member of the Order of Merit of the Police Forces (M.O.M.)

Member of the Royal Victorian Order (M.V.O.)

The Most Venerable Order of St. John of Jerusalem (all grades)

Ordre national du Québec (all grades, G.O.Q., O.Q., C.Q.)

The Saskatchewan Order of Merit (S.O.M.)

The Order of Ontario (O.Ont.)

The Order of British Columbia (O.B.C.)

The Alberta Order of Excellence (A.O.E.)

The Order of Prince Edward Island (O.P.E.I.)

Order of Manitoba (O.M.)

Order of New Brunswick (O.N.B.)

Order of Nova Scotia (O.N.S.)

Order of Newfoundland (O.N.L.)

Star of Military Valour (S.M.V.)

Star of Courage (S.C.)

Meritorious Service Cross (M.S.C.) (Civil)

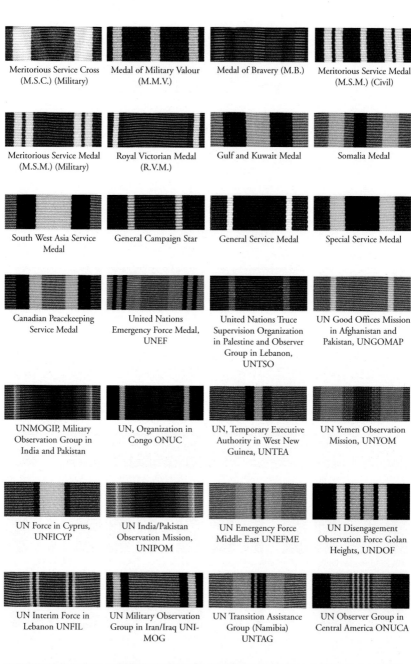

Meritorious Service Cross (M.S.C.) (Military)

Medal of Military Valour (M.M.V.)

Medal of Bravery (M.B.)

Meritorious Service Medal (M.S.M.) (Civil)

Meritorious Service Medal (M.S.M.) (Military)

Royal Victorian Medal (R.V.M.)

Gulf and Kuwait Medal

Somalia Medal

South West Asia Service Medal

General Campaign Star

General Service Medal

Special Service Medal

Canadian Peacekeeping Service Medal

United Nations Emergency Force Medal, UNEF

United Nations Truce Supervision Organization in Palestine and Observer Group in Lebanon, UNTSO

UN Good Offices Mission in Afghanistan and Pakistan, UNGOMAP

UNMOGIP, Military Observation Group in India and Pakistan

UN, Organization in Congo ONUC

UN, Temporary Executive Authority in West New Guinea, UNTEA

UN Yemen Observation Mission, UNYOM

UN Force in Cyprus, UNFICYP

UN India/Pakistan Observation Mission, UNIPOM

UN Emergency Force Middle East UNEFME

UN Disengagement Observation Force Golan Heights, UNDOF

UN Interim Force in Lebanon UNFIL

UN Military Observation Group in Iran/Iraq UNI-MOG

UN Transition Assistance Group (Namibia) UNTAG

UN Observer Group in Central America ONUCA

UN Iraq/Kuwait Observer Mission UNIKOM

UN Angola Verification Mission UNAVEM

UN Mission for the Referendum in Western Sahara MINURSO

UN Observer Mission in El Salvador, ONUSAL

UN Protection Force
(Yugoslavia)
UNPROFOR

UN Advance Mission in
Cambodia UNAMIC

UN Transitional Authority
in Cambodia, UNTAC

UN Operation in Somalia
UNSOM

UN Operation in
Mozambique, ONUMOZ

UN Observation Mission
in Uganda/Rwanda
UNAMUR

UN Assistance Mission in
Rwanda UNAMIR

UN Mission in Haiti
UNMIH

UN Verification of Human
Rights and Compliance
with the Comprehensive
Agreement on Human
Rights in Guatemala
MINUGUA

MINURCA, UN Mission
Central African Republic

UNPREDEP, UN
Preventative Deployment
Force (Macedonia)

UNMIBH, UN Mission
in Bosnia Herzegovina

UNMOP, UN Military
Observer Mission in
Prevlaka (Croatia)

UNMIK, UN Interim
Administration Mission in
Kosovo

UNOMSIL/
UNAMSIL, UN Observer
Mission in Sierra Leon,
UN Mission in Sierra Leon

UNAMET/UNTAET, UN
Assistance Mission East
Timor/UN Transitional
Authority East Timor

MONUC, UN Mission in
the Democratic Republic
of Congo

UNMEE, UN Mission in
Ethiopia and Eritrea

UN Special Service
UNSSM

UN Headquarters Service
UNHQ

NATO Former Yugoslaiva

NATO Kosovo

NATO Former Yugoslav
Republic of Macedonia

NATO Article 5,
Operation Eagle Assist

NATO Article 5,
Operation Active
Endeavour

NATO Non-Article 5,
Balkans

ICSC, International
Commission for
Supervision and Control
Indo China

ICCS, International
Commission of Control
and Supervision Vietnam

MFO, Multinational
Force Observer Medal

ECMMY, European
Community Monitor
Mission Yugoslaiva

INTERFET, International
Force East Timor

ESDP, European Security
and Defence Policy
Service Medal

Canada Centennial
Medal, 1967

Queen Elizabeth II Silver
Jubilee Medal, 1977

Canada 125ᵗʰ Anniversary
of Confederation Medal

Queen Elizabeth II Golden
Jubilee Medal, 2002

Royal Canadian Mounted
Police Long Service Medal

Canadian Forces
Decoration (C.D.)

Police Exemplary Service
Medal

Correctional Service
Exemplary Service Medal

Fire Services Exemplary
Service Medal

Coast Guard Exemplary
Service Medal

Emergency Medical Service
Exemplary Service Medal

Peace Officer Exemplary
Service Medal

Queen's Medal for
Champion Shot Medal

Order of St. John Long
Service Medal

Canadian Corps of
Commissionaires Long
Service Medal

NOTES

1   House of Commons, *Debates*, 18 April 1967, p. 14968 (Pearson).
2   See Ivan De La Bere, *The Queen's Order of Chivalry* (London: William Kimber, 1961), p. 99.
3   The idea of a civilian and military division had been proposed by Vincent Massey in March 1966.
4   NAC, R 5769, Vol. 11, Lochnan Papers, Report of the Decorations Committee, 9 January 1970.
5   NAC, R 5769, Vol. 11, Lochnan Papers, Report of the Decorations Committee , 9 January 1970.
6   Harold Gillingham, *French Orders and Decorations* (New York: The American Numismatic Society, 1922), p. 20.
7   In all, 177 have been awarded since the order was instituted in 1902. Other recipients include Florence Nightingale, Jan Smuts, Sir Winston Churchill and Baroness Margaret Thatcher.
8   A total of 315 have been awarded since the order was created in 1917. In addition to the eight Canadian recipients, Lord Tweedsmuir — Canada's governor general from 1935–1940 — was a recipient. Other prominent holders of the order include more than fifteen Commonwealth prime ministers, as well as Eric Hobsbawn, Stephen Hawking, Sir Alec Guinness, Field Marshal Jan Smuts and Amatyr Kumar Sen.
9   For a history of the St. John Ambulance in Canada consult Strome Galloway's *The White Cross in Canada, 1883–1983* (Ottawa: St. John Priory of Canada, 1983).
10 Aside from the Prior and Vice-Priors, the Priory in Canada has a number of officers: Chancellor, Vice Chancellor, Immediate Past Chancellor, National Commissioner, Treasurer, Chief Executive Officer and Hospitaller. There are also eleven provincial and territorial councils: British Columbia/Yukon, Alberta, North West Territories, Saskatchewan, Manitoba, Ontario, Federal District, Quebec, New Brunswick, Nova Scotia/Prince Edward Island and Newfoundland.
11 Revised Statutes of Quebec, Vol. 1, 1888, Chapter 7, 1601–7.
12 The first joint award occurred in 2004.
13 These were awarded to Doreen Ashburnham-Ruffer (converted from an Albert Medal), Gordon Bastian (converted from an Albert Medal), Ernest Frost (con-

verted from an Empire Gallantry Medal), Karl Gravell, Roderick Gray, James Hendry, John Patton, John Rennie, Arthur Ross, and Kenneth Spooner.

14 NAC, MG 26 N4, Pearson Papers, Vol. 1, 003-4, Memorandum for the prime minister, John Hodgson to Lester Pearson, 19 March 1968.

15 COCS, C135, "Canadian Attitudes to Imperial Honours, 1943–1967," Esmond Butler to Sir Michael Adeane, 20 April 1972.

16 In particular, Colonel N.A. Buckingham and Commissioner Stevenson of the RCMP felt that there should be separate awards that were not necessarily incorporated in the Order of Canada. Carl Lochnan at the Department of the Secretary of State seems to have been one of the first to suggest the creation of three separate awards.

17 NAC, R5769 Vol. 11, Lochnan Papers, Carl Lochnan to G.G.E. Steele, 26 October 1968.

18 This proposal was first devised on 28 October 1968, at the meeting of the subcommittee of the Government Decorations Committee.

19 Canada, House of Commons. *Debates*, 30 December 1971, (Ottawa: Queen's Printer, 1972), p. 10,859.

20 NAC, RG 2, Vol. 6318, Cabinet Minutes, 29 July 1971.

21 Royal Warrant constituting the Victoria Cross (amended), 1920.

22 M.J. Crook, *The Evolution of the Victoria Cross* (London: Midas Books, 1975), p. 30.

23 QUA, Matheson Papers, File 296, DND proposal, 27 October 1966, Memorandum to the Defence Council, Awards for the Canadian Forces.

24 NAC, RG 2, Vol. 9, File H-5. Order-in-Council 1943-7964, 14 October 1943, Arrangements for the creation of the Canada Medal, Section 7 (a)–(c).

25 RG 2, Vol. 377, Minutes of the ACC, 15 October 1943 (for Canada Medal as Canadian Meritorious Award), and DHH, 75/601 File 25, Memorandum from Major General H.F.G. Letson to the minister of National Defence (Army), 29 March 1944.

26 QUA, Matheson Papers, Series 1, File 296, Proposal for the establishment of the Forces Meritorious Decoration and Forces Meritorious Medal, 27 October 1966.

27 Canadian Forces Honours Policy, 15 September 1982.

28 Order-in-council 1991-1060, 6 June 1991.

29 For an excellent discussion of the origins and development of the North West Canada Medal, consult Barbara Wilson's *The Military General Service, 1793-1814, Egypt 1882-89, North West Canada 1885 Medal Roll*, London: Spink and Son, 1975.

30 NAC, RG 7 G 21, Vol 113, number 205, vol 1.

31 NAC RG 24, File 5916, File HQ 51-4-64.

32 It is worth noting that every Canadian who served in Korea volunteered, and in some ways the Canadian Queen's Korea Medal could be considered the Voluntary Service Medal. Nevertheless, pressure was brought to bear and the KVSM was created.

33 Lawrence Borts, *United Nations Medals and Missions* (Greenville: Keys Printing, 1998), p. 36.

34 Despite the fact that the order-in-council requires the medal to be made from tombac, issues have been found in a variety of materials. Since the Royal Canadian Mint ceased manufacturing the medals in the late 1980s there have been a myriad of varieties and problems with the production.

35 Nicholas Dirks, *The Hollow Crown: Ethnohistory of an Indian Kingdom* (Cambridge: Cambridge University Press, 1987), p. 129.

36 NAC, R 5769, Vol 12, File 16, Lochnan Papers.

37 NAC, R 5769, Vol 12, File 16, Lochnan Papers, Centennial Commissioner to Lamontage, 10 March 1964.

38 NAC, RG 2, Cabinet Submission From Paul Hellyer and Maurice Lamontage, 11 May 1965.

39 NAC, R 5769, Vol 12, File 16, Lochnan Papers., O.G. Stoner (Privy Council Office Staff) to Jean Miquelon (Chairman of the Decorations Committee), 30 September 1965.

40 J.M.A. Tamplin and P.E. Abbott, *British Gallantry Awards* (London: Doubleday Press, 1972), p. 343.

41 M.J. Crook. *The Evolution of the Victoria Cross* (London: Midas Books, 1975), p. 268.

42 Prior to 2005 grants that included the motto circlet of the Order of Military Merit contained the words "CANADA MERIT MÉRITE."

43 Following his retirement as governor general, Massey was awarded, by Royal Warrant, special recognition: a "Canton Azure containing the Royal Crest for Canada."

44 Listed in the order that the medals are worn (in Canada) and not by the date the medal was added to the Canadian honours system. Not all UN medals are listed here, as there are a number of missions that Canada has not participated in.

BIBLIOGRAPHY

Abbott, P.E., and J.M.A. Tamplin. *British Gallantry Awards.* London: Nimrod Dix, 1981.

Alexander, E.G.M. *South African Orders, Decorations and Medals.* Cape Town: Human & Rousseau, 1986.

Barber, Richard. *The Knight and Chivalry.* London: Longman, 1970.

Blatherwick, John F. *Canadian Orders, Decorations and Medals.* Toronto: Unitrade Press, 2003.

Blondel, Jacques. *Guide Pratique des Décorations.* Paris: Lavauzelle, 1986.

Coddington, Deborah, and Alister Taylor. *Honoured by the Queen: New Zealand.* Auckland: Maxwell Printing, 1994.

Crook, M.J. *The Evolution of the Victoria Cross.* London: Midas Books, 1975.

Cullen, Tom. *Maundy Gregory: Purveyor of Honours.* London: Quality Book Club, 1975.

Daizell, Mick and Paul Riches. *Mentioned in Despatches, 1948–1968.* London: Privately published, 1999.

de la Bere, Sir Ivan. *The Queen's Orders of Chivalry.* London: William Kimber and Company, 1961.

De-la-Noy, Michael. *The Honours System.* London: Allison & Busby, 1985.

Dorling, H. Taprell. *Ribbons and Medals.* London: George Phillip & Son, 1963.

Fauteux, Aegidius. *Les Chevaliers de Saint-Louis en Canada.* Montreal: Éditions des Dix, 1940.

Ford, Frank. "Titles of Honour in Canada." *Queen's Quarterly,* 1902. Vol. X, No. 1.

Gardam, John. *The Canadian Peacekeeper.* Burnstown, Ont.: General Store Publishing House, 1992.

Gaffen, Fred. *In the Eye of the Storm: A History of Canadian Peacekeeping.* Toronto: Deneau & Wayne, 1987.

Galloway, Peter. *The Order of the British Empire.* London: Austin and Son, 1996.

———. *The Order of Saint Patrick.* Chichester: Phillmore & Company, 1983.

———. *The Order of St. Michael and St. George.* London: Third Millennium Publishing, 2000.

———. *The Order of the Companions of Honour.* London: Third Millennium Publishing, 2002.

Galloway, Peter, et al. *Royal Service: The Royal Victorian Order.* London: Victorian Publishing, 1996.

Galloway, Strome. *The White Cross in Canada, 1883–1983*. Ottawa: St. John Priory of Canada, 1983.

Gillingham, Harold. *French Orders and Decorations*. New York: The American Numismatic Society, 1922.

Gordon, Lawrence. *British Battles and Medals*. Aldershot: Gale and Polden, 1947.

Heywood, Valentine. *British Titles*. London: Adam & Charles Black, 1951.

Joslin, Edward Charles. *The Standard Catalogue of British Orders, Decorations and Medals*. London: Spink & Son, 1976.

Joslin, Edward Charles, A.R. Litherland and B.T. Simpkin. *British Battles and Medals*. London: Spink & Son, 1988.

Lochnan, Carl. *History of Honours in Canada*. Unpublished manuscript, 1976.

Mackenzie, Sir Edward. "The Baronets of Nova Scotia: Their Country and Cognizance," *Proceedings and Transactions of the Royal Society of Canada*, Second Series Vol. VII, May, 1901.

Macmillan, Gerald. *Honours for Sale: The Strange Story of Maundy Gregory*. London: The Richards Press, 1954.

Maton, Michael. *The National Honours and Awards of Australia*. Kenthurst, New South Wales: Kangaroo Press, 1995.

McCreery, Christopher. "Questions of Honour: Canadian Government Policy Towards British Titular Honours, 1867–1935." Master's thesis, Queen's University, 1999.

———. *Honour, Nation and Citizenship in a Multicultural Polity: Federal Public Honours in Canada, 1917–1997*. Doctoral thesis, Queen's University, 2003.

McMillan, James. *The Honours Game*. London: Frewin Press, 1969.

O'Shea, Phillip. *Honours, Titles, Styles and Precedence in New Zealand*. Wellington: Government Printer, 1977.

Patterson, Stephen. *Royal Insignia: British and Foreign Orders of Chivalry from the Royal Collection*. London: Merrell Holberton, 1998.

Risk, James C. *The History of the Order of the Bath and Its Insignia*. London: Spink & Son, 1972.

Shell, Donald. *The House of Lords*. New York: Harvester Press, 1992.

Stone, Lawrence. "The Inflation of Honours." *Past and Present*, No. 3 (1958).

Stacey, C.P. "Lord Monck and the Canadian Nation." *Dalhousie Review*, No. 13 (1935).

Thomas, Wendy. *The Register of Canadian Honours*. Toronto: T.H. Best Printing Company, 1991.

Thomson, Donald Walter. "The Fate of Titles in Canada." *Canadian Historical Review* (1929).

Tozer, Charles. *The Insignia and Medals of the Grand Priory of the Most Venerable Order of the Hospital of St. John of Jerusalem*. London: Hayward & Son, 1975.

Vickers, Hugo. *Royal Orders: The Honours and the Honoured*. London: Broadwall, 1996.

Walker, John. *The Queen Has Been Pleased: The British Honours System at Work*. London: Secker & Warburg, 1986.

Werlich, Robert. *Orders and Decorations of All Nations.* 2nd ed. Washington: Quaker Press, 1974.

Wigney, Edward H. *Mentioned in Despatches of the CEF.* Nepean, Ont.: Self-published, 2000.

Wilson, Sir Arnold, and J.H.F. McEwen. *Gallantry: Its Public Recognition and Reward in Peace and in War at Home and Abroad.* London: Oxford University Press, 1939.

Journals of the Orders and Medals Research Society, 1942–2004.

PHOTO CREDITS

AC: Author's Collection, Christopher McCreery
CHA: Photo courtesy of the Canadian Heraldic Authority
DND: Photo courtesy of the Department of National Defence, Directorate of History and Heritage
DNW: Photo courtesy of Dix Noonan Webb Auction House, London (UK)
NAC:Photo courtesy of the National Archives of Canada
RCMP: Photo courtesy of the Royal Canadian Mounted Police

	PHOTO OF	PAGE	CREDIT
	Queen Elizabeth II	6	Department of National Heritage
Chapter 1	Waterloo Medal	16	DNW
	Navy Long Service Medal	17	DNW
	Naval General Service Medal	18	DNW
Chapter 2	Order of St. Louis	22	Major Claude Villeneuve Collection
	Knight Commander of the Bath	25	Vicken Koundakjian Collection, photo by Sgt. Eric Jolin
	Baronet of Nova Scotia	25	DNW
	GCMG	27	NAC
	British Empire Medal	28	DND
	Order of the British Empire	28	DND
	First World War Trio	30	AC, photo by Sgt. Eric Jolin
	Imperial Service Order Group	32	AC, photo by Sgt. Eric Jolin
	Indian Chief Medal	32	NAC
Chapter 3	Bronze Confederation Medal	34	AC, photo by Sgt. Eric Jolin
	Mackenzie King in Uniform	35	NAC
	Picture of W.F. Nickle	37	Queen's University Archives
Chapter 4	Royal Order of Canada	47	NAC, artwork by Dr. Charles Comfort
	Canadian Award and Decoration of Honour	47	NAC, artwork by Lt. Cdr. Alan Beddoe
	The Canada Medal	48	Office of the Governor General, photo by Sgt. Eric Jolin
	The Canadian Medal of Honour	49	NAC, unknown artist
	The Order of Military Merit 1966	50	NAC, unknown artist
	Turpin/Massey design of Order of Canada	50	University of Toronto, Massey Papers
	Multi Leveled Order of Military Merit Picture of Sash and Breast Star	51	Photo by author, artwork by Bruce Beatty
Chapter 5	Original Order of Canada with 4 dots	54	NAC, photo by John Evans
	Award Certificate of the O.C.	59	Joyce Bryant Collection, photo by Sgt. Eric Jolin
	Sovereigns Insignia of the O.C.	60	NAC, photo by John Evans
	Principal Companion of O.C.	61	NAC, photo by John Evans
	Companion O.C.	61	NAC, photo by John Evans
	Case for the Chancellors Chain of the Order of Canada	62	Office of the Governor General, photo by Sgt. Eric Jolin

	PHOTO OF	PAGE	CREDIT
	Officer O.St.J.	119	DND
	Serving Member O.St.J.	119	DND
	Serving Member Lapel Pin	120	DND
Chapter 10	Quebec Agricultural Medal	121	AC, photo by Sgt. Eric Jolin
	Early Small Quebec Agriculture Medal	121	AC, photo by Sgt. Eric Jolin
	Order of Agricultural Merit	122	AC, photo by Sgt. Eric Jolin
	Ordre National du Quebec, Grand	126	Office of the Lieutenant Governor of Quebec
	Ordre National du Quebec, Officer	126	Office of the Lieutenant Governor of Quebec
	Ordre National du Quebec, Knight	126	Office of the Lieutenant Governor of Quebec
	The Saskatchewan Order of Merit	127	DND
	The Saskatchewan Order of Merit Augmented	128	Office of the Lieutenant Governor of Saskatchewan
	The Order of Ontario	129	DND
	The Order of British Columbia	131	DND
	The Alberta Order of Excellence	132	DND
	The Order of Prince Edward Island	133	DND
	The Order of Manitoba	134	DND
	The Order of New Brunswick	136	DND
	The Order of Nova Scotia	137	DND
	The Order of Newfoundland and Labrador	139	Office of the Lieutenant Governor of Newfoundland
Chapter 11	Canadian Humane Society Medal	142	AC, photo by Sgt. Eric Jolin
	Cross of Valour	146	DND
	Cross of Valour	147	DND
	Cross of Valour Prototype	147	Photo by author, artwork by Bruce Beatty
	Cross of Valour Lapel Pin	147	DND
	Bar for C.V.	147	Vicken Koundakjian Collection, photo by author
	Star of Courage	148	DND
	Star of Courage Lapel Pin	148	DND
	Bar for S.C.	148	Vicken Koundakjian Collection, photo by author
	Medal of Bravery	149	DND
	Medal of Bravery Lapel Pin	149	DND
	Bar for M.B.	149	Vicken Koundakjian Collection, photo by author
Chapter 12	Victoria Cross	152	NAC
	Victoria Cross Canada	155	DND
	Bar for the Victoria Cross Canada	156	DND
	Star of Military Valour	156	DND
	Medal of Military Valour	157	DND
	Medal of Military Valour Lapel Pin	158	DND
	Bar for MMV	158	DND
Chapter 13	Prototype M.S.C.	160	Photo by author, artwork by Bruce Beatty
	Prototype M.S.D.	160	Photo by author, artwork by Bruce Beatty
	Prototype M.S.M.	160	Photo by author, artwork by Bruce Beatty
	Meritorious Service Cross	162	DND
	MSC Lapel Pin	162	DND
	M.S.C. ribbon Civil	163	DND
	Meritorious Service Medal	163	DND
	M.S.M. civilian ribbon	164	DND

PHOTO OF	PAGE	CREDIT
UNPREDEP	217	DND
UNBIH	218	DND
UNMOP	219	DND
UNMIK	220	DND
UNOMSIL	221	DND
UNAMET	222	DND
MONUC	222	DND
UNMEE	222	DND
UNSSM	223	DND
UNHQ	224	DND

Chapter 16	NATO Certificate	225	Captain Carl Gauthier Collection, photo by author
	Nato Medal Yugoslavia Ribbon	226	DND
	Kosovo Ribbon	228	DND
	FYROM	230	DND
	Eagle Assist Ribbon	232	DND
	Active Endeavour Ribbon	233	DND
	Balkans Ribbon	234	DND

Chapter 17	ICSC Medal	238	DND
	ICCS Certificate	240	Captain Carl Gauthier Collection, photo by author
	ICCS Medal	240	DND
	ICCS Medal Canadian	240	DND
	MFO Medal	242	DND
	ECMMY Medal	243	DND
	INTERFET Medal	244	DND
	Euro Security Medal	247	DND

Chapter 18	George VI C.D.	252	DND
	Efficiency Decoration	252	DND
	Efficiency Medal	252	DND
	Army LSGC	252	DND
	RNR Decoration	252	DND
	RCN LSGC	252	DND
	RCAF Air Efficiency Award	253	DND
	RCAF LSGC	253	DND
	George VI C.D. in silver	255	DND
	Elizabeth C.D. Specimen	255	DND
	Elizabeth C.D. Current	256	DND
	Old Issue CD Bar	257	Lou Grimshaw Collection, photo by author
	Slide on CD Bar	257	AC, photo by author
	CD Bar	258	DND

Chapter 19	Old RCMP Medal Transmittal Box	260	Graham Neale Collection, photo by Dr. Neale
	RCMP Certificate	260	Arnold Kay Collection, photo by author
	RCMP English Current Certificate	261	Captain Carl Gauthier Collection, photo by author
	RCMP French Current Certificate	261	Captain Carl Gauthier Collection, photo by author
	RCMP English	261	RCMP
	RCMP French	262	RCMP
	RCMP George V	263	RCMP
	RCMP George VI Second Type	263	RCMP
	RCMP George VI First Type	263	Graham Neale Collection, photo by Dr. Neale
	RCMP Old Reverse	263	RCMP
	RCMP One Star Bar	263	RCMP

PHOTO OF	PAGE	CREDIT
Court Mounted Minis	328	Medals of Joyce Bryant, photo by Sgt. Eric Jolin
4 Wearing Medals Diagrams	329-332	Office of the Governor General

Chapter 30

Undress Ribbon Bar with 9 ribbons	341	AC, Photo by author
Undress Ribbon	341	DND
Silver Maple Leaf	342	DND
Gold Maple Leaf	342	DND
Red Maple Leaf	342	DND

Chapter 31

Basic Heraldry Diagram	345	Canadian Heraldic Authority, diagram by Jennifer Scott
Loomis Arms	346	Canadian Heraldic Authority
Massey Arms	346	AC, photo by author
Michener Arms	347	CHA
Dextraze Arms	349	CHA
Fedoruk Arms	349	CHA
Pelletier Arms	349	CHA
Gervais Arms	350	CHA
Lockyer Arms	350	CHA
MacLeod Arms	351	CHA
Chevrier Arms	351	CHA
Barry Arms	351	CHA
Fowler Arms	352	CHA
Gleeson Arms	352	CHA
Segal Arms	352	CHA
Trudeau Arms	353	CHA
Rogers Arms	353	CHA
Larsen Arms	354	CHA
Mitchell Arms	354	CHA
Kerwin Arms	354	CHA

INDEX